"ONE OF THE MOST IMPORTANT BOOKS ON UFOLOGY EVER PUBLISHED"

"It is clear that UFO phenomena are world-wide. Can this mass of evidence be explained by hoaxes or terrestrial causes? Most unlikely, I believe. There is a good deal of evidence that 'flying saucers' do exist and even that they may be extraterrestrial in origin.

"*British UFO Research Association* is to be congratulated for putting together the evidence of those who believe and those who disbelieve. This is one of the most important books on ufology ever published."

From the Foreword by
Major Sir Patrick Wall, MC VRD RM (Retd.)

D0802662

PHENOMENON
FORTY YEARS OF FLYING SAUCERS

Edited by

John Spencer and Hilary Evans

AVON BOOKS ◆ NEW YORK

Published in Great Britain as *Phenomenon: From Flying Saucers to UFOs—Forty Years of Facts and Research*

AVON BOOKS
A division of
The Hearst Corporation
105 Madison Avenue
New York, New York 10016

First Avon Books Printing: January 1989

CONTENTS

FOREWORD

UFOs – are they fiction, fact, myth, or reality? At this point in time, 'flying saucers' cannot be proved or disproved. For a number of years, there has been an unofficial committee in the House of Lords, which I have often attended, that has been shown what is purported to be proof not only that 'flying saucers' exist, but that alien beings have landed amongst us. Evidence has been given in the forms of both actual experiences and of photographs.

Undoubtedly, as explained in this book, there have been official cover-ups, both in the USA and in Britain. Over the past thirty-three years, I myself have asked a number of questions in the House of Commons on this matter.

Do I believe? I keep an open mind. Many sightings have been made by unimpeachable witnesses. Much of this evidence, and the further evidence of actual landings, are recorded in this book.

Are there UFOs and, if so, where do they come from? Leaving aside the distant past, let us concentrate on the post-war period. Undoubtedly the phenomena has increased since the start of the nuclear age, a fact that led US authorities to set up official investigations such as Project Blue Book and the Condon Report. Both reported that a large proportion of UFO sightings could be attributed to natural origins, but some remained unexplained – and remain so today.

It is clear that UFO phenomena are world-wide. Can this mass of evidence be explained by hoaxes or terrestrial causes? Most unlikely, I believe. There is a good deal of evidence that 'flying saucers' do exist and even that they may be extraterrestrial in origin. If so, then the anti-mass field theory described in this book to account for their capabilities is one scientific explanation that merits serious consideration.

There has always been a confusion in the minds of many people between serious ufologists involved in the scientific analysis of evidence and the followers of fringe religious and cultist groups who fervently believe in extraterrestrial life. This book makes clear the distinction between them, a distinction that must be appreciated if a real understanding of the phenomena is ever to be realized.

BUFORA is to be congratulated for putting together the evidence of those who believe and those who disbelieve. This is one of the most important books on ufology ever published, and it should command a wide public.

Remember that landings on the moon would have been unthinkable to our grandparents. Who knows but that continued research and scientific study might not unlock an even greater mystery that today remains inexplicable.

Major Sir Patrick Wall, MC VRD RM (*Retd*)

ABOUT BUFORA AND ICUR

The British Unidentified Flying Object Research Association (BUFORA) is dedicated to the scientific investigation of UFO phenomena, and stresses the importance of an objective approach. It has two interlinked roles: research and investigation, as well as activities of an educational nature.

Aims:
1 To encourage, promote and conduct unbiased scientific research of unidentified flying object (UFO) phenomena throughout the United Kingdom.
2 To collect and disseminate evidence and data relating to unidentified flying objects (UFOs).
3 To co-ordinate UFO research throughout the United Kingdom and to co-operate with others engaged in such research throughout the world.

BUFORA does not advocate any particular theory and recognizes that there are a number of explanatory hypotheses. The Association does not hold or express corporate views.

BUFORA is run entirely by volunteers, relying solely on its members to fund and carry out its investigation, research and educational activities.

BUFORA publishes a bimonthly journal covering

current developments, research activities, noteworthy investigations and discussions of broader issues. In addition BUFORA publishes case histories, science papers and pamphlets on several specific subjects.

Lectures are normally held on the first Saturday evening of the month apart from a break during the summer. They provide an open forum for new ideas and viewpoints, attracting people from many parts of the country as well as overseas visitors.

Over the years BUFORA has sponsored a number of highly successful National and International conferences. The first London International UFO Congress, in 1979, attracted 400 people from twenty-one countries. The Fourth International Congress, the most recent, was in July 1987.

International co-operation: At the 1979 BUFORA International Congress researchers from many countries set up an International Committee for UFO Research (ICUR) to examine and agree international standards in UFO research, covering such matters as definitions, terminology, classification and compatible systems of data processing and exchange.

BUFORA is currently 'host' to ICUR: Robert Digby (a former chairman of BUFORA) is Chairman; Steven Gamble (BUFORA's Director of Research) is Secretary and John Spencer (BUFORA director and editor of this book) is Treasurer.

Membership of BUFORA is open to any person with a genuine and non-cultist interest in UFO research and who supports the general aims of the Association. Application forms and details of publications are available from:

Arnold West (Chairman)
BUFORA Ltd
16 Southway
Burgess Hill
Sussex, RH15 9ST

INTRODUCTION

UFO research is a worldwide activity, and this book reflects that fact. Its contributors are from many countries of the globe. We would have liked to include contributions from yet other countries but this was unfortunately not possible. Big as it is, this book could have been much bigger if space had not been limited: we are unhappily conscious that some aspects of our subject have received less attention than they deserve.

Deciding who to invite was a delicate and difficult matter. Obviously they had to be persons who are seriously involved, and who have demonstrated their ability to make a lasting contribution to our understanding of the subject. But we had to exclude many whose work has been chiefly as investigators, for though their practical work in the field is essential, it does not form part of the purpose of this book, which is essentially one of standing back and assessing the sum of our knowledge. Sometimes, as well, we had to choose between more than one person specialising in the same field, and some declined our invitation because of other commitments. Some promised papers never made the final deadline, and some important thinkers and investigators are, sadly, no longer with us.

For these reasons, we would like to take the

opportunity to pay tribute to those not represented here, but whose contribution to UFO research should not pass unacknowledged: Walt Andrus; V J Ballester Olmos; Keith Basterfield; Ted Bloecher; Michel Bougard; Charles Bowen; Michel Carrouges; Jerome Clark, Gordon Creighton; Joaquim Fernandes, Michel Figuet; Salvador Freixedo; Robert Girard; Irene Granchi; Loren Gross; Pierre Guerin; Richard Haines; Richard Hall; Leif Havik; Allan Hendry; Milton Hourcade; Carl Jung; Philip Klass; Fernand Lagarde; Alvin Lawson; Coral and Jim Lorenzen; Bruce Maccabee; James MacDonald; Claude Maugé; Bertrand Meheust; Aime Michel; John Michell; Michel Monnerie; Jim Moseley; Michael Persinger; Thierry Pinvidic; Gosta Rehn; Sebastian Robiou-Lamarche; Scott Rogo; Harley Rutledge; Margaret Sachs; Frank Salisbury; Ivan Sanderson; Berthold Schwarz; Jacques Scornaux; Jean Sider; Leo Sprinkle; Ronald Story; Leonard Stringfield; Jacques Vallee; Renato Vesco; Enrique Vicente; Pierre Vieroudy; David Webb; Jennie Ziedman — and Kenneth Arnold himself. To those named in this very subjective list, and to scores of others not named, UFO research owes as much as it does to our contributors.

There is one other name, which recurs frequently in these pages, and which deserves special mention; it is, of course, that of the late J Allen Hynek. Many of us knew him personally, as a friend as well as a researcher; but even those who knew him only from his writings and public appearances knew that he embodied all that is best in UFO research — the persistence, but also the lack of dogmatism; the confident belief in the importance of his cause, but also the willingness to listen to the ideas of others. Almost single-handed he showed how UFO research, though it might not constitute a science in its own right, could and should be conducted on scientific principles. We were fortunate, and privileged, to have such a man among us at such a time.

The views expressed in these pieces are those of the individual authors: there has been no censorship and only such direction as was needed to make a reasonably balanced book. For this reason you may find one text contradicting another, some personal opinions which you may find unacceptable, viewpoints ranging from the sceptical to the fantastic. Nevertheless, each of our contributors is a serious researcher, whose opinions were not arrived at lightly; all deserve a hearing. BUFORA takes no responsibility for what are presented as facts (though we have done a reasonable amount of checking); even less is it responsible for the ideas expressed.

Further, please bear in mind that many of the contributions are condensed from the original work, usually by the authors themselves, sometimes by the editors. This has been necessary to produce a well-balanced review of the subject; those interested in further details of any of the articles included are welcome, indeed encouraged, to contact BUFORA, who are in communication with the authors.

Copyright in the book as a whole is BUFORA's: copyright in individual text remains with the authors. We also should point out that copyright in UFO photographs and sketches is notoriously vague. If we have unwittingly infringed any copyrights, we hereby apologise.

Finally, on behalf not only of BUFORA but of the worldwide ufological community, the editors thank those who have worked so hard and so enthusiastically to make this book possible. That busy men and women, many of them able to command fees as writers and lecturers, have been willing to give their time and trouble for little financial reward, is a magnificent tribute to the unselfish pursuit of truth which makes UFO research one of the greatest quests for knowledge in the history of scientific research.

Let us now hand over to Lionel Beer to 'set the scene' for a review of what must be the most exciting and enigmatic phenomenon the human race has yet faced ...

J.S. H.E.

PART I
REPORTING UFOs

THE COMING OF THE SAUCERS

Lionel Beer, FRAS

Aerial phenomena have been reported for centuries, described by witnesses of the time in familiar terms; coloured globes, flying shields, etc. The ancient Sanscrit epics the *Ramayana* and the *Mahahbarata* describe 'vimanas', aerial chariots, and give descriptions of battles that sound like modern nuclear or laser warfare: 'flowing flashes which sped from a circled bow'. Even the *Old Testament* contains ambiguous but evocative descriptions such as the 'pillar of fire' in *Exodus* and the 'flying scroll' in Zechariah.

Authors such as Lord Clancarty (Brinsley Le Poer Trench), Desmond Leslie, Raymond Drake and Erich von Daniken have proposed evidence to support the notion that the earth has been visited by extraterrestrials from the dawn of history. Some of these authors have gone even further and suggested that *homo sapiens* are the product of genetic engineering and that man is part of a breeding experiment on a planetary scale. Recent books dealing with hypnotic regression cases have added fuel to this fire. Are we – as Charles Fort suggested – someone's property?

HISTORICAL PERSPECTIVE

Since Roman times writers have delighted in listing 'prodigia', such as the bow-shaped object seen in the clear sky over the Temple of Saturn in Rome in BC 173. Pierre Della Francesca (1402-92) of Arezzo, Italy, painted a number of religious frescoes that include lenticular clouds looking remarkably saucer-shaped. The sixteenth and seventeenth centuries saw much religious and political upheaval in Europe and it was normal to interpret aerial phenomena as divine warnings. Well-known to ufologists are the Basel and Nurembourg broadsheet woodcuts, of 1566 and 1561 respectively, which include features such as globes and flying crosses that would not be out of place in modern sighting accounts.

A collection of unusual items was published by T. Forcet, in London in 1646. A particular item is entitled 'Strange Signs From Heaven.' It tells how, on 20 May, 'strange sights and unwanted sounds were seen and heard by divers, honest, sober and civil persons and men of good credit.' They saw men in the air, striving, struggling and tugging together, one holding a drawn sword. Later, 'betwixt Newmarket and Thetford, there was observed a pillar of cloud to ascend to the earth, with bright hilts of a sword towards the bottom of it.' The phenomena lasted for about an hour and a half.

In later years numerous accounts were abstracted from the annals of learned journals. From the French journal *L'Astronomie*, of 1885, there is what has been billed as the first photograph of a UFO, taken on 12 August 1883 at the Zacatecas Observatory in Mexico by Jose Bonnila. He was observing sun-spots at the time and saw over 300 objects crossing the solar disc, of which, with the aid of wet plates at 1/100th of a second, he was able to take several pictures. (There has since been reasonable speculation that Bonilla had witnessed high flying geese.)

In 1878 there is what appears to be the first mention of the term 'saucer'. Farmer John Martin, of Dallas, described his experience to his local paper, reprinted the following day by the *Denison Daily News* of Denison, Texas, on 25 January. He had seen a large orange 'object' in the sky, which was moving very fast, while out hunting. 'When directly overhead it was the size of a large saucer and evidently at great height.'

MAN'S OWN FIRST AERIAL VOYAGES

One hundred years earlier, on 21 November 1773, following successful experiments by Joseph and Etienne Montgolfier the previous year, the first authenticated manned aerial ascent took place. The Montgolfier brothers' superior quality wallpaper-and-linen hot-air balloon was piloted by Jean Pilatre de Rozier and Francoise Laurent, the Marquis d'Arlandes. Measuring 78,000 cubic feet, it lifted off from a garden in the Bois de Boulogne, Paris, on a flight lasting twenty six minutes and covering some seven and a half miles. It was man's first three-dimensional perspective of his environment and significant also because from that time on strange sights in the sky *could* have been man-made. Ten days later, on 1 December, Messieurs J.A.C. Charles and Marie-Noel Robert made the first manned flight suspended from a hydrogen balloon.

Possibly the earliest partially successful *manned* airship flight was made by Henri Giffard in Paris in 1852 in a steam(!)-powered dirigible. An internal gas-combustion engine was fitted to an airship in Vienna in 1872. In 1884 Arthur Krebs flew in the electrically-powered 'La France' airship. By the end of the 19th century, airship technology was coming into its own. Thus a manned airship was probably responsible for the great airship flap (an intense wave of sightings) over the central United States in 1896 and 1897. The late Dr Geoffrey Doel, a past president of BUFORA, made out a convincing case for this: Entrepreneur Edward Joel Pennington started a company called The Mount Carmel Aerial Navigation Company in about 1890, and he filed patents for a four-cylinder radial engine for the propulsion of an aerial vessel. In 1891 he exhibited a thirty-foot airship, powered through its tethering cable by an electrically turned airscrew. In 1895 Pennington deposited patents with the American Patents Office for a full-sized airship, having earlier announced his intention to open a passenger service between Chicago and New York. Two photographs of the mystery airship taken by Walter McCanna in 1897 showed a distant object closely resembling the Pennington design.

What is not known for sure is why Pennington did not continue the development. Most likely he was shrewd enough to realize that aeronautical designers in France and Germany were well ahead of him and that the Zeppelins would not be long in coming.

Further sightings of what may have been airships occurred; on Caerphilly Mountain, Wales; over Peterborough; in East Anglia and even in New Zealand in 1909. [Nigel Watson takes up the story of the airships in 'The Great Airship Scare' in this book – Ed.]

FACT AND FICTION INTERMINGLE

The 1920s, 30s and 40s were the age of the 'dime' novel and science fiction 'pulp' magazines, which offered a diet of SF, sexual titillation and some practical electrical and mechanical advice.

Doubtless these 'pulp' books were influenced by the French author Jules Verne (1828–1905), whose books included *Clipper of the Clouds* (trans. 1887) and *From Earth to the Moon* (trans. 1873) and anticipated air and space travel. He in turn would have influenced H G Wells (1866–1946), whose *War of the Worlds* saw publication in 1898. Tarzan author, Edgar Rice Burroughs (1875–1950), also left his mark in the SF field with *A Princess of Mars* (1912), first in his Martian series, *Lost on Venus, Llana of Gathol*, etc.

In 1929, Hugo Gernsback created a pulp magazine called *Amazing Stories*, but by 1938 its circulation had dwindled to some 25,000 copies and it was then bought up by the Ziff-Davis Publishing Company of Chicago. Ziff appointed Ray Palmer, then twenty-eight, as editor. Palmer had been a science fiction fan since childhood. He had a vivid imagination and was not averse to creating controversy by writing under assorted pseudonyms, even in his own magazines.

In the early forties, *Amazing Stories* received a long letter, purporting to be genuine, from Richard Shaver on demonic troglodytes called 'deros', upon whose heads a host of human misfortunes could be laid. By about 1946, the 'Shaver Mystery' had boosted sales of *Amazing Stories* to 250,000 copies, and Palmer had clearly found his market. Palmer careered down the well-worn path of bug-eyed monsters, and when readers wrote in with personal 'sightings', Palmer had drawings made and published them. It was not unusual for the odd circular craft to decorate the cover.

Possibly no one was the more surprised by Kenneth Arnold's 1947 story, regarded as the UFO sighting that triggered off the 'modern era' and certainly gave the phenomenon it's first popular name – flying saucers – than Ray Palmer. Palmer's fiction had become reality! Viewed with hindsight, Arnold's sighting came in the middle of a UFO-flap in the United States that lasted into July.

Not long after Arnold's encounter, the Technical Intelligence Centre of the United States Air Force's (USAF) Air Material Command (later ATIC) began monitoring UFOs. The USAF used the code-name Project Sign, also known by the nick-name Project Saucer. Later investigations followed, using the names Grudge, Twinkle, and the more well-known Project Blue Book, finally closed down in 1969. Palmer's proprietor was apparently 'leaned on' by two Air Force officials with the aim of discouraging publication of further flying saucer stories.

Palmer, however, was so impressed by all that was

going on that he put out his own magazine in 1948. Thus *Fate* magazine was born, with Curtis Fuller as editor, and it has carried UFO stories ever since. The first issue ran Arnold's sighting of the previous year, its cover emblazoned with an exaggerated picture of one of the saucers. The story was published in book form as *The Coming of the Saucers* (1952), jointly written by Arnold and Palmer, though the first popular UFO book was probably Major Donald Keyhoe's *Flying Saucers Are Real*, (1950).

George Adamski, a Polish-American, became a saucer-celebrity when his 'true story', *Flying Saucers Have Landed*, was published in the autumn of 1953. It rapidly became an international bestseller, and has probably sold more copies than any other UFO title. Its cover displayed the archetypal Venusian scout-craft, which Adamski allegedly encountered at Desert Centre, California, on 20 November 1952. Adamski claimed he met a tanned Venusian man with long-blond hair. However, tanned Venusians with long blond hair had already appeared in the UK in 1950, in '*Dan Dare — Pilot of the Future*', a highly successful strip-cartoon in the *Eagle* comic, and Ray Palmer said more than once that he had seen the Adamski story in the late forties, when it was offered to *Amazing Stories*.

Flying Saucers Have Landed was part of a shoal of books that appeared in the early to mid-fifties. Many of these books were about contactees who claimed to have met and talked to aliens. In an era when both Russia and the USA were in a deadly race to develop nuclear weapons, it is significant that a number of the contact messages carried a ban-the-bomb theme. Whereas SF writers promoted bug-eyed monsters, witness reports almost unfailingly claimed that the beings were humanoid. Such reports continue to this day. Whether or not you believe that UFOs are extraterrestrial vehicles (the ET hypothesis) or you lean to one or more of the other main half-dozen theories, the ET hypothesis was the overriding belief in the late forties and early fifties, and one that infused popular culture.

CONCLUSION

Flying saucers were not a sudden invention in 1947. Humans had been seeing things in the sky for thousands of years, and in modern times the psychological groundwork had been laid by writers such as Verne, Wells, Burroughs, Fort, Palmer and many others. All it needed was an anonymous journalist in 1947 to give the phenomenon a name.

'IT SEEMS IMPOSSIBLE, BUT THERE IT IS'

Pierre Lagrange

HOW A NARRATIVE BECOMES, THROUGH A CHANGE OF COURSE, SOMETHING DIFFERENT:

On Tuesday 24 June 1947, Kenneth Arnold – a business and private pilot – took advantage of a trip in his own plane between Chehalis and Yakima (in Washington State) to spend some time in the region around Mount Rainier looking for a lost airplane. Earlier in the afternoon, while installing fire-fighting equipment for the Chehalis Central Air Service, he had talked with 'chief pilot' Herb Critzer 'among other things, about the possible location of a lost C-46 Marine transport which had gone down in the mountains.' A reward of $5000 had been offered by the victims' families for discovery of the wreck.

The sky was clear, it was three o'clock in the afternoon. Arnold had set his course for Yakima, and '[I] simply sat in my plane observing the sky and the terrain ... when a bright flash reflected on my plane.' The astonished Arnold believed that he must be too close to another plane. 'I looked every place in the sky and couldn't find where the reflection had come from until I looked to the left and the north of Mount Rainier where I observed a chain of nine peculiar aircraft flying from north to south at approximately

9500 foot elevation and going, seemingly, in a definite direction of about 170 degrees.' His first idea was that they were jet aircraft. The reflection came from them, for 'two or three of them every few seconds would dip or change their course slightly, just enough for the sun to strike them at an angle that reflected on my plane.' The craft were at some distance and it was hard to make them out clearly. But, when they passed in front of snow-covered Mount Rainier, Kenneth Arnold could clearly see their outlines. He was amazed: 'I thought it was very peculiar that I couldn't find their tails but assumed they were some type of jet planes.' What is more, he had never seen a plane flying so close to mountain peaks. And, to top it off, 'when the sun reflected from one or two or three of those units, they appeared to be completely round'. He reckoned that the objects were about twenty to twenty-five miles away. Thus they had to be fairly large in order to be visible. Using a bonnet-fastener, he compared them in size to a DC-4 to his left. The unidentified craft appeared to him to be smaller: '... their span would have been as wide as the furthest engines on each side of the fuselage of the DC-4'. He decided to calculate their speed by timing their passage between Mount Rainier and Mount Adams. 'As the last unit of this formation passed the southernmost high snow-covered crest of Mount Adams, I looked at my sweep second hand and it showed that they had travelled the distance in one minute and forty-two seconds. Even at the time this timing did not upset me as I felt confident that after I would land there would be some explanation of what I saw.' The whole observations took some two and a half to three minutes.

Turning the narrative over to other people in an attempt to find an explanation: Kenneth Arnold continued his search for the C-46 for fifteen or twenty minutes, but 'while searching for this marine plane, what I had just observed kept going through my mind.

I became more disturbed, so after taking a last look at Tieton Reservoir I headed for Yakima.' The $5000 reward suddenly seemed a lot less important to him. The pilots at Yakima airport, he thought, would be able to explain his observation. 'Around airports pilots are continually arguing about how fast our Army and Navy jets and missiles really can go.'

At about four o'clock, Kenneth Arnold finally arrived at Yakima. He went straight away to see Al Baxter, 'General Manager of Central Aircraft', to whom he told his story in private. His impression of this interview a few days later was that Baxter had not really believed him. Furthermore, one of the pilots that Al Baxter called in to hear the story had remarked that the craft were bound to have been Moses Lake guided missiles. 'I felt satisfied,' said Arnold, 'that that's probably what they were. However, I had never heard of a missile base at Moses Lake, Washington.'

Who take it up and alter its course themselves: Having filled up his plane he headed back to Pendleton. On landing, Arnold learned that his story had arrived ahead of him. The people he talked with at Yakima had telephoned Pendleton in order to notify them of Arnold's arrival and had spoken of his adventure. By the time Arnold landed at the large Pendleton airfield, there was already a sizeable group there to greet him. Arnold recounted 'No one said anything. They just stood around and looked at me ... [But] before very long it seemed everybody around the airfield was listening to the story of my experience.'

During the discussion, Arnold mentioned the speed he had calculated for the craft, and demonstrated on maps the actions of his mysterious craft. Those gathered around recalculated the speed with him. 'When it kept coming out in excess of 1700 miles per hour I thought, "Holy smoke, we're taking the measurement of distance far too high up on both Mount Rainier and Mount Adams." So we took a measurement of the very base, as closely as it could be determined, and which I knew from the map was far below the snow line. The distance was thirty-nine point eight miles.' Despite this, 'we still had a speed of over 1300 miles per hour'. On this basis Arnold concluded that the craft were 'guided missiles, robotly controlled' – in any case they were not manned for, 'The human body simply could not stand [such speeds], particularly considering the flipping, erratic movements of these strange crafts,' Arnold said.

Arnold then 'armed' himself with his maps and calculations and repaired to the local FBI office. 'I thought it was my duty to report these things ... I kind of felt I ought to tell the FBI because I knew that during the war we were flying aircraft over the pole to Russia, and I thought these things could possibly be from Russia.' He found the office shut.

Turning to the journalists: Having had no luck with the FBI, Arnold decided to look up the journalists from the *East Oregonian*. At the offices of the *East Oregonian* he met Nolan Skiff, editor of the 'End of the Week' column, and told him about his adventure. The latter, sceptical to start with, was rapidly convinced of Arnold's honesty.

Who take up the narrative, translate it, and change its course themselves: Another journalist who was present, Bill Becquette, thought the story had national interest, and decided to send off an Associated Press despatch. Here is the text of this despatch, which was to have many repercussions:

PENDLETON, Ore, June 25 (AP) – Nine bright saucer-like objects flying at 'incredible speed' at 10,000 feet altitude were reported here today by Kenneth Arnold, Boise, Idaho, pilot who said he could not hazard a guess as to what they were.

Arnold, a United States Forest Service employee engaged in searching for a missing plane, said he sighted the mysterious objects yesterday at three pm. They were flying between Mount Rainier and Mount Adams, in Washington State, he said, and appeared to weave in and out of formation. Arnold said that he clocked and estimated their speed at 1200 miles an hour.

Enquiries at Yakima last night brought only blank stares, he said, but he added he talked today with an unidentified man from Utah, south of here, who said he had seen similar objects over the mountains near Ukiah yesterday.

'It seems impossible,' Arnold said, 'but there it is.'

It seems that it is largely as a result of this despatch that the story was to be so taken up by the press. From this moment on Kenneth Arnold was dispossessed of his story, which now followed other paths and came back to him through journals or in the form of other reporters who wanted more information. In the same way that those who had heard his story from the Yakima pilots had gathered round waiting for his plane's touch down, Arnold found himself under siege from reporters who, without ever having heard his story in full would, he claimed, extract a few details from him that were rushed immediately into print. 'Of course many of these stories were distorted and inaccurate, and I didn't share the general excitement. I can't begin to estimate the number of people, letters, telegrams, and phone calls I tried to answer. After three days of this hubbub I came to the conclusion that I was the only sane one in the bunch.'

The multiplication of saucers: As soon as Arnold's story was known, 'flying disc' sightings proliferated. As we have seen, the first AP despatch was dated 25 June (towards the end of the morning). The north-west regional evening papers of the 25th already contained some reports of the news. On 26 June, the *Chicago Tribune* reported, as well as Arnold's story, another sighting made on 24 June by a Pendleton couple. On the same day, the *Phoenix Arizona Republic* and the *Baltimore Sun* drew on an AP despatch of 25 June (?) about a sighting by F Johnson, a prospector from Portland, who claimed to have seen five or six discs in the region around the Cascade Mountains on the morning of 24 June. Again on 26 June, the *Oklahoma City Times* reported an observation by a Byron Savage dating from 17 or 18 May while the *Kansas City Star* reported another sighting from West Davenport. There were many other reported sightings, and even more newspaper articles, over the next few days.

Commenting on this avalanche of reports, Arnold remarks ironically: 'From then on, if I was to go by the number of reports that came in of other sightings, of which I kept a close track, I thought it wouldn't be long before there would be one of these things in every garage. In order to stop what I thought was a lot of foolishness, and since I couldn't get any work done, I went out to the airport, cranked up my plane, and flew home to Boise.'

The *New York Times* and the saucers: A few articles from the *New York Times* give an overall idea of the debate sparked off by these phenomena.

There were no reports of saucers before 4 July and the paper made no reference to them between 25 June and 3 July, although numerous reports of sightings had emanated from the press agencies in the form of AP or UP despatches. On 4 July, the first article on the saucers in *The Times* deals with the Army's position on the question; quoting an Army Air Forces spokesperson in Washington that the sightings reported to date had 'not produced enough facts to warrant further investigation'. The same spokesperson went on 'we don't have a thing that would give any realism [to the] report made last week by a flying Boise (Idaho) businessman ... Air Forces people are inclined to believe either that the observers just imagined they saw something, or that there is some meteorological explanation for the phenomenon.' A Langley Field meteorologist said, the *Times* reported, 'solar reflections on low-hanging clouds produced spectral "flashes" which might have appeared like moving objects ... a small meteor might have broken up ... and icy conditions in high clouds produced "large hailstones" which might have flattened out and glided a bit.'

The *New York Times* of 6 July reported sightings by 'such reliable men as Captain E J Smith of United Airlines [and] co-pilot Ralph Stevens, another by some picnickers, and also mentions the first photo of a flying saucer, taken by coastguard Frank Ryman on 4 July. Military and civilian meteorologists were said to have 'shrugged their shoulders when first asked for an explanation'. Four-fifths of the article is taken up with explanations of the sightings in terms of natural phenomena. Thus the reporter cites an observation of 'dozens of the missiles over the city [Augusta, Maine] travelling northerly', and also includes a tentative explanation by Gordon A Atwater, curator of astronomy of the Hayden Planetarium, who believed the first reports to be 'entirely authentic', but the later ones he said were a 'mild case of meteorological jitters' with some 'mass hypnosis' thrown in.

The Planetarium had received numerous requests for explanations, its astronomer suggesting to a reporter that 'ice crystals, formed by nature high in the sky, could be as good an explanation as any.' Natural crystals, much larger than those obtained in the laboratory, 'could reflect the sun's rays like a small mirror and make the phenomena visible', while 'some have suggested that the flying saucers might be meteorites, but we are inclined to believe they are neither meteorological or astronomical in origin. ... No meteorites are disc-shaped, and they vary from a pinhead in size to one weighing thirty-six tons.'

The *New York Times* reporter also gathered several other opinions. The astronomer Dr Jan Schilt, a professor at Columbia, said 'the true answer would be

found from some phenomena seen during the two last
wars, when speeding airplanes churned up the
atmosphere and caused distortions of light rays' and
then went on to suggest that this effect might be largely
electrical in nature, due to the turmoil of the propeller
and wings causing something like "smoke-rings".'
Unless, perhaps, birds had caused the phenomenon;
or even the reflection of headlights on clouds.

Another series of sightings, made in states as distant
as Oregon, Michigan, Louisiana and Pennsylvania,
caused a researcher from the US Weather Bureau's
Division of Synoptic Reports and Forecasts to register
his scepticism: 'I'll have to see one before I make a
guess what they are.' And a representative of the
National Bureau of Standards in Washington said, 'It
is like one of these Loch Ness Monster stories. Once
the reports get about, everyone thinks they see it.'

The *New York Times* journalist specifies that an object
found near an Ohio farmhouse and of unknown origin
was 'declared by the Army Air Forces to be a
radiosonde', part of an observational balloon. Illustrat-
ing the feeling of the debate by the press itself, the
article finishes with two AP despatches. The first from
Los Angeles, refers to the opinion of an unidentified
'scientist in nuclear physics' claiming to be at the
California Institute of Technology, that the saucers
'might be the result of "transmutation of atomic
energy" experiments'. The second AP despatch, from
Denver, refuted this. David Lilienthal, Chairman of
the Atomic Energy Commission, swore that the
phenomenon was in no way linked to atomic tests,
though he added 'of course, I can't prevent anyone
from saying foolish things.'

A second article on the saucers in the same edition of
the *New York Times*, referred to the photograph taken
by the coastguard, which shows 'bright little specks in
perfect formation': '... the only trouble with the
photograph is that it was taken at five thirty pm on July
Fourth. Bright little specks are apt to appear in the sky

almost any time on the Glorious Fourth … we have no disposition, however, to laugh this phenomenon off. A lot of people have seen the discs, and one and all dismiss the thought that they were sun-spots – not the whirling spots on the sun itself but the after images of light on the human eye. The flying saucer could be real.' The reporter enumerates the different hypotheses put forward to date, including the extraterrestrial hypothesis. 'They may be visitants from another planet launched from spaceships anchored above the stratosphere,' he speculated.

The edition of 7 July publishes an AP report from San Francisco. Armed with cameras and associated photographic equipment, military planes had gone looking for saucers in Oregon and California as well as other places, but it was a fruitless search, according to the despatch. The Air Force had also decided to take an interest. According to Captain Tom Brown, public relations representative, the Army Air Force did not know what the saucers were, but they didn't believe that 'anyone in this country, or outside this country, has developed a guided missile that will go 1200 miles an hour as some reports have indicated.'

On 8 July, the readers of the *New York Times* learned that saucers were gaining ground. 'The Associated Press said that thirty-nine states, plus the District of Columbia and a part of Canada were playing host to the heavenly discs … Despite the humorous scepticism of scientists and military experts, the latest flock of rumours showed increasing imagination. No longer, for example, were the discs just white. In some cases they were in technicolour, with orange the predominant hue.' And in the same article, a professor of physiology from Sydney is credited with an experiment aiming to show 'how simple it was to see the "flying saucers" play tag among the stars'. He asked 450 students to 'stare fixedly at a point in the sky about a mile distant' with the result that 'within ten minutes twenty-two students were back with findings. They even drew pictures to prove that they had seen "flying discs".' The physiologist concluded: 'It was all due to the effect of red corpuscles of blood passing in front of the retina. This is well recognized and anybody interested can draw his own conclusions.' As soon as this explanation was published, the reporter notes, other explanations were proposed. One saucer which had collided with a plane turned out to have been a small publicity balloon. An object that fell noisily into a courtyard in Chicago 'turned out to be a circular saw'. Its discoverer notified the FBI. The Army claimed ignorance of other sightings, but said that enquiries were under way. The next day, 9 July, a saucer that had been brought in as having crashed near to an atomic test site turned out to be a balloon-probe.

The newspaper debate continued, although what the readers themselves believed we do not know. However, a Gallup Poll of 19 August 1947 revealed that though only one out of two Americans had heard of the Marshall Plan, nine out of ten had heard about the saucers.

Fleeing the journalists who come charging back: As the press debate was hotting up, Arnold returned home, where Dave Johnson, aviation editor of the *Idaho Statesman*, whom Arnold already knew as a 'man of respected ability and intelligence in matters related to military and civilian aviation', immediately turned up. As it turned out, Dave Johnson had no information that these craft were to do with the American forces, and Arnold, surprised at this, then 'really began to wonder'. Furthermore, Johnson told him that the Wright Field base wanted the complete story of what had happened. Nor was it the only one – press agencies and reporters were also interested; so much so that they laid siege to Arnold's home. The Pendletonian crush had been transported to Doris and Kenneth Arnold's Boise homestead. 'We began to feel like we were living in Grand Central Station,' commented Arnold.

All the better to come back to the saucers: Arnold was so upset by all the publicity that he decided to flee the reporters by going on a fishing trip with his friend, Colonel Paul Wieland, who had just returned from Europe.

During the flight to Sekiu, Arnold and Wieland talked about human capabilities for distinguishing distant craft that are moving fast (some of the arguments put forward against Arnold's sighting mentioned the fact that craft flying at some 1200 mph should have been, given their size, undetectable to the naked eye). Wieland told Arnold that artillery shells – considerably smaller than a plane – could definitely be seen quite easily travelling at six or seven hundred miles an hour if you were in the right position. Arnold took this as confirmation that his calculations and timing 'were not nearly as inaccurate as some newspaper experts were leading people to believe.'

On 5 July, Arnold and Wieland went from Sekiu to Seattle, where they learned that a United airlines team had sighted some flying discs the night before, after taking off from Boise airport. Arnold went off to buy a newspaper, to find out what was going on, and found himself staring at a photograph taken by Frank Ryman, a coastguard – the first photograph of a flying saucer ever taken. Paul Wieland totally forgotten, Arnold rushed to the International News Service offices to see the blow-ups of the picture. Having identified himself, Arnold was taken to a nearby room where Captain Smith and Ralph Stevens, the two United pilots who had made the sighting the day before, were conferring. At a local coffee shop, Smith retold the story of their sighting. Just before taking off, he said, someone had asked him if he believed in flying saucers and he had replied that he would believe in them the day that he saw one. Eight minutes later, going over Emmet in Idaho, he and his crew managed to see not one, but nine. First a group of five, then a second group of four. The objects were circular, with a flat underbelly, were *rough* on top and seemed about as big as the DC-3 they were flying. Arnold, hearing this story, was staggered. 'When Big Smith got through telling me this, and in spite of my own experience, I kept repeating to myself, "It's just amazing – simply amazing! Positively amazing!" Big Smithy's sighting somehow made mine small and insignificant.'

Arnold spent the next week going through the abundant correspondence that had sprung up following the news of his sighting. 'Not one letter that I recall, and I have most of them still in my files,' he wrote in 1952 'had even a note of criticism. This, to me, was rather surprising, since most of the newspapers were having a terrifically good time trying to make the public believe we were crazy, seeing visions, or recording corpuscles on the retinas of our eyeballs.'

Also, on 7 July, Arnold and Johnson flew over the sites of the sighting of 24 June. James L Brown, general manager of the *Statesman* Newspapers had asked Dave Johnson to try to catch sight of and photograph one of these saucers. The trip was unsuccessful.

The military enquiry: One of Kenneth Arnold's first actions on making his sighting had been to try to report it to the FBI. Wright Field base's request for a report gave him the opportunity to pursue this course. In a written report for them Arnold went beyond a simple biographical account – he gave the feelings about his sighting expressed by his fellow pilots, with whom he'd served in World War II, who had assured him that he had not been seeing things. They themselves had been warned that they might see such craft during their missions. Arnold also cited another veteran military pilot who assured him that the flying discs were experimental craft being tested by the American government, or some other country. Moreover, Arnold made clear that he did not as others had done, take what he saw lightly. He did not go looking for the publicity that came his way. According to him 'I reported something that I know any pilot would have reported'. Indeed, he said that he was rather surprised that the Army or the FBI – 'these two important protective forces of our country' – had not yet seen fit to hold an enquiry. He even said that he was prepared to sit a mental and physical examination 'for any determination they [the military] might wish to make as to the capabilities of my five senses'.

The work of the military enquiry: seeking out the witnesses: A few days later, Arnold received a visit from two members of the military enquiry who came from Hamilton Field in California. 'I was very happy to see them, I couldn't figure out why such an efficient body as Military Intelligence hadn't called on me before'. The two enquirers, Lieutenant Frank M Brown and Captain William Davidson, invited Arnold and his wife to dinner. Kenneth learned that they did not know any more about the flying saucers than he did. 'They said, frankly and openly, they didn't know what the flying saucers were. They had never seen one, they told us, but ever since my first report they were practically bug-eyed from watching the sky themselves.' After dinner, Arnold suggested to the two enquirers that they should meet E J Smith, the United Airlines pilot, who could give his testimony about the sighting of 4 July, an invitation they were delighted to accept, Smith being on their list of people to question. The party then adjourned to the Boise Municipal Airport to meet E J Smith.

Arnold was surprised to run into Dave Johnson of the *Idaho Statesman* there. 'I wondered how he knew,' he remarked. Brown and Davidson had wanted to meet Johnson as well, as he had made a sighting of some saucers on 9 July. After the discussion, during which, said Arnold, 'Everybody was talking at the same time ... [and] none of us found out much,' he and his wife invited Davidson and Brown to their home where they could talk without distraction. Arnold answered all the enquirer's questions. 'I stuck absolutely to the facts. I didn't consider my opinion important. I drew pictures for them and recounted my original observation as accurately as I could.'

Before leaving, the two military men looked over the mail that Arnold had received. They looked particularly closely, Arnold noted, at letters from the various groups who had asked for a copy of his written report of the sighting. 'I was happy they did go through my mail' he says 'as I didn't feel capable of evaluating much of the contents of the letters I had received.' And, as Arnold was taking the soldiers back to their hotel, they told him that he could contact them if anything strange should turn up. They advised him not to talk too much about his sighting.

To bring in reports of sighting … (which land up on the desks of scientific advisors): Brown and Davidsons' aim was to bring back an account from and an opinion about the observer they had observed. Before meeting Arnold, they had questioned Dave Johnson over the telephone, who had told them 'that as far as he was concerned anything Mr Arnold said could be taken very seriously and that he, Mr Johnson, actually believed that Mr Arnold had seen the aforementioned flying discs.' After they had, in turn, met Arnold, their opinion was the same as Johnson's.

Arnold's report landed on J A Hynek's desk. Hynek was the astronomer the Air Force had asked to study the reports so as to avoid any possible confusion with astronomical phenomena. Hynek quickly concluded that there didn't appear to be any 'astronomical explanation for this classic incident, which is the prototype of many of the later flying saucer stories.' He couldn't explain the phenomenon, he said, but he did pick up some incoherencies in Arnold's report. 'Arnold made drawings of objects showing definite shape and stated that objects seemed about twenty times as long as wide, estimating them as forty-five to fifty feet long. He also estimated the distance as twenty to twenty-five miles and clocked them as going forty-seven miles in 102 seconds, (1700 mph). If the distance was correct, then in order for details to be seen, objects must have been closer than six miles to have shown the detail indicated by Arnold. At this distance, angular speed observed corresponds to a maximum speed of 400 mph. In all probability therefore, objects were much closer than thought and moving at definitely "sub-sonic" speeds.'

Hynek's conclusion was that what Arnold had seen was some aircraft.

Amazing Stories but true: Towards 15 July 1947 Arnold received a letter from thirty-seven-year-old Raymond A Palmer. Palmer had, from an early age, read science fiction magazines and had been an active member of science fiction 'fandom' from 1930 onwards. He was in at the foundation of one of the very first groups of SF enthusiasts, the *Science Correspondence Club*, and launched *The Comet* – the first SF 'fanzine' (fan magazine) – which was edited by the club. His first SF short story in a professional review was published in June 1930. In 1938, he became editor-in-chief of *Amazing Stories*, which was moribund at the time but later attained its highest circulation under Palmer's editorship. From 1945 on, Palmer published, after some reworking, numerous texts by Richard Sharpe Shaver, who claimed to have visited the Earth's subterranean kingdoms in which dwelt the Deros and the Teros, two warring races. Presented in the same setting as SF stories, but as documents that reflected real experiences, these texts stirred a controversy as to their authenticity that reached to the heart of fandom. The *Amazing Stories* issue of June 1947 was entirely given over to Shaver's narratives, and when the first flying saucer stories appeared Palmer saw them as confirmation of Shaver's stories.

Shaver had claimed it should be possible to see the craft of these subterranean races flying in the heavens, as well as spaceships coming from other planets colonized by descendants of the people of Atlantis (who had emigrated at the time of the destruction of Atlantis some 12,000 years before). In the October 1947 issue, Palmer, in an editorial that was probably (taking production and printing delays into account) written during the summer, wrote, 'A part of the now world-famous Shaver Mystery has now been proved! On 25 June (and subsequent confirmation included earlier dates) mysterious supersonic vessels, either space ships or ships from the caves, were sighted in this country! A summation of facts proves that these ships were not, nor can be, attributed to any civilization now on the face of the Earth.'

Actors who were ready for the saucers: An interesting observation can be made here. As L Gross and J Keel have remarked, the arrival of the saucers did not surprise everyone: the readers of *Amazing Stories* had already had the chance to read accounts of sightings of strange vessels in the sky. Palmer had in his time introduced them to the European series of 'ghost rocket' sightings in 1946. And the June 1947 issue, to take but one example, contains, on top of an editorial by Palmer full of references to Charles Fort (the pioneer in the area of meteorological and UFO connected phenomena, which became known as 'Fortean Phenomena') and to unusual aerial phenomena 'such as the mysterious "air raid" suffered by Los Angeles during the war, and which the Army now reveals has never been explained, except that it was no private or military plane of our own, and none of the Japs or any foreign power, but was certainly tracked by radar, and observed by many people to "appear to be rocket ships" from three to five in number, on top of all this then, the number contained an article by Vincent Gaddis entitled 'Visitors from the Void', a collection of accounts of sightings of 'strange aeronefs' during the 1930s and 1940s.

Furthermore, groups already existed that compiled lists of unusual phenomena, from spiritualist and metapsychological occurrences to phantom planes. The 'Borderland Science Research Associates' kept their readers informed of these through their bulletin *Round Robin*. But the nerve-centre was above all occupied by the Fortean Society, a society dedicated to the memory of Charles Fort and presided over by Tiffany Thayer. This society's bulletin, *Doubt* had for a long time given over a large space to celestial manifestations. It is not surprising to find that the nineteenth issue, the one following the summer of 1947, was almost entirely devoted to the 'flying disks'.

Attempts to enroll Arnold: On 15 July, then, Kenneth Arnold received a first letter from Ray Palmer. Recalling the event, Arnold wrote in 1952: 'At the time, had I known who he was, I probably wouldn't have answered his letter. It wouldn't have been because he wasn't a sincere or a good man, but later I found he was connected with the type of publications that I not only never read but had always thought a gross waste of time for anyone to read.'

When he got the first letter, Arnold found that 'far from being anything sensational, ... it had a tone of softness and sincere interest that appealed to me'. In the end, he replied to Palmer's letter. Palmer asked Arnold if he would, for a fee, put his account down in writing. Arnold had already refused several offers to do so, but as Palmer seemed to him to be genuinely interested, he sent him a carbon copy of his report for Wright Field. In his next letter, Palmer referred to a sighting of some saucers in the port of Tacoma. According to Palmer, the two witnesses not only saw the saucers, but had some fragments from them in their possession. Palmer, intrigued by the affair, proposed to Arnold that, for a fee, he should go and make enquiries about the case during one of his trips in the area. And in particular he should try to bring back some of the fragments for him to see. Arnold could not decide: 'I just let the letter sit for a few days to think it over'.

Ray Palmer had sent him $200, to convince him to make the enquiry, and, feeling bound thereby to bring back an account, Arnold went to Tacoma. There, he persuaded one of the witnesses, Harold Dahl to give him the following account.

On 21 June, at about two in the afternoon, Dahl was sailing in the bay area east of Maury Island, a practically uninhabited region of Puget Sound. Then he and his companions noticed six 'doughnut' shaped craft. One of these craft was immobile, the five others were revolving on their own axes. Everybody on board the boat kept their eyes fixed on the spectacle. Dahl, fearing a crash, took the boat away from the area, but had the foresight to take several photographs even as he was moving away. Suddenly an explosion occurred inside the immobile saucer, its lower part shattering into thousands of metal fragments that fell into the sea. A few fell on the boat and damaged it, hurting Dahl's son and killing his dog. After this, the six craft disappeared into the sky.

Dahl also told Arnold afterwards that he had not breathed a word to anyone about the affair, but had nonetheless received a visit the next day from a man who had advised him not to tell anyone what he had seen.

Arnold was not convinced by this account, nor by the fragments that Dahl showed him a little later: 'Why, Harold, that's only a piece of lava rock!' he exclaimed. It was only when he read in the press of a similar case of material falling after the passage of some saucers that Arnold got interested in Dahl's story, (which had between times been confirmed by Crisman, who owned the boat with Dahl). 'Right there and then I became inwardly excited about the fragments I had seen the night before. I wanted some immediately and even though our meetings had been entirely in the talking stage I put a great more credence in Dahl's and Crisman's stories of their experiences. I seemed all of a sudden to wake up and wanted to get to doing things. I told Dahl I would like to see the photographs he had taken, even if they were bad, and asked Crisman for some of the white metal as well as other fragments he had stored in his garage.' In order to get to the bottom of the story, he decided to appeal to his allies for help. First of all he called on Captain Smith, who had become a friend. Arnold turned to Smith because he thought he was more qualified to determine the authenticity of Dahl's and Crisman's stories than he was. Smith agreed to come to Tacoma. Once he had interrogated the witnesses and generally gone over the same ground as Arnold, he decided to stay until the end of the enquiry. The press had, despite Smith and Arnold's discretion, got wind of their presence in Tacoma (apparently through anonymous calls, which continued all through their stay and which led Smith and Arnold to think that they were under some sort of surveillance).

Smith and Arnold then appealed to Brown and Davidson, the military investigators, who had advised Arnold to contact them if he heard anything interesting. 'We thought if there was any hoax in these stories the prospects of being interrogated by Military Intelligence would cause Crisman and Dahl to show their hand,' said Arnold. Brown and Davidson came to Tacoma, but after they had listened to Crisman's account (Dahl having refused to see them) they decided to return home. 'All of a sudden, Brown and Davidson lost all their enthusiasm ... Captain Smith and I invited them to stay the rest of the night with us ... [but] They would have none of it. They were flying back at once.'

Arnold was left with the impression that 'they thought Smith and I were the victims of some silly hoax.' A tragic footnote to the episode happened when the plane carrying Brown and Davidson home crashed after leaving Tacoma. The enquiry then went from bad to worse. As the press began to take up the story, one of the two witnesses disappeared and the other swore that it had all been nothing more than a gag. The Army published this denial. Despite all this, Arnold, though he had lost his initial enthusiasm by the end of the drama, later threw himself into other enquiries, his original scepticism replaced with an active curiosity. In 1950, a journalist reported that Kenneth Arnold, 'determined to prove he saw what he said he saw that June day in 1947', spent his spare time disc-hunting in his plane, accompanied by a high-speed movie camera equipped with a telescopic lens. Considering his pioneering investigative work and his many articles, it can certainly be said that Kenneth Arnold was one of the very first 'ufologists' – even though the term had yet to be coined.

THE GREAT AIRSHIP SCARE

Nigel Watson

One night in 1897, as farmworker John Halley was travelling along Jefferson Street, three miles west of Springfield, Illinois, his attention was caught by a large light high in the sky. It was about nine pm when this light, which he at first thought was a big balloon, appeared in the west and started flying in his direction. After a few minutes the owner of a nearby vineyard, Adolf Wenke, came over and joined him. At that moment the light started to descend. With abject fear, the two men heard the object emit a hissing sound and watched it land only a few hundred feet away from them. When they finally realized that the craft, which they regarded as a 'fangled thing', presented no threat to them they walked towards it to find out what it was. Almost immediately they met the pilot of the vehicle, a gentleman with a long beard, who readily answered their questions. In turn, he asked where he had landed and was surprised to learn he was near Springfield since he had left Quincy, 100 miles to the west, only thirty minutes earlier.

The aerial craft carried another man and the scientist's wife. They preferred to travel at night, said the bearded man, because the huge wings of his ship tended to attract too much attention during the day time. Although he wanted to keep the propulsion mechanism of the ship secret he did say that its carriage had an aluminium frame covered with canvas. On the side of his carriage was painted the letter 'M', which the man indicated when he was asked his name. For the purpose of navigation, the crew used an ordinary locomotive headlamp to light their way, and numerous other electrical gadgets were used to fly it. Before taking off again, the pilot implied that his craft would be used in Cuba, as soon as the United States 'Congress recognized Cuban belligerency.' Then he jumped into the carriage, pressed a button, the ship rose from the ground and was soon lost from sight.

Halley and Wenke had this strange encounter on the night of 14 April, 1897, at a time when the best airships in Europe could only manage speeds of between twelve and fourteen mph, and those in America were lucky to get near to those speeds for a short period of time. In 1897, nothing on Earth could fly as fast as the airship the men said they saw. Indeed, it is doubtful that anything like the craft described by them could ever be a viable flying machine.

It would be easy to assume, therefore, that the two farmers were merely jokers who thought it was a great jest to tell their story to credulous newspaper reporters. They certainly got the publicity any joker would be pleased with. If theirs had been the only story of this type we could have laughed with them at the expense of the city-slickers. However, from November 1896 until the middle of 1897 thousands of people throughout the USA reported that they had seen the lights of an airship in the sky. Speculation was rife that an inventor had created this marvellous new flying machine and was making long experimental flights at night in order to preserve his secrets until he patented them and sold them to the highest bidder. When the doyen of all inventors, Thomas Edison, was asked for his opinion, he said:

'I have no doubt that airships will be successfully constructed in the near future, but there has been too much talk about this supposed airship out west. I have always found that there is much talk before these ships are tried and very little afterward.

It is absolutely absurd to imagine that a man would construct a successful airship and keep the matter secret. When I was young we used to construct big coloured paper balloons, inflate them with gas, and they would float about for days. I guess someone has been up to the same game out West.

When an airship is made it will not be in the form of a balloon. It will be a mechanical contrivance, which must be of very light weight. At present no one has discovered such a motor, but we never know what will happen. We may wake up tomorrow morning and hear of some invention which sets us all eagerly to work within a few hours, as was the case with the Roentgen rays. This success may come.'

Many of the sightings were explained when hoaxers admitted that they had sent up balloons or kites with lights attached, and professor Hough of Northwestern University, Evanstown, Illinois, even suggested that airship witnesses had only seen the bright star Betelgeuse in the Orion constellation,

Yet, despite all this, stories about inventors were given considerable credence. For example, two farmers, Jerimah Collier and William York, claimed that they found the airship resting on Wood Patch Hill, Brown County, Indiana, during April 1897. The craft had been damaged and so the crew had picked that spot to carry out the repairs. According to them the airship belonged to E J Pennington. When he was tracked down to Martinsville on the morning of 19 April he made the following statement:

'I have an airship over in Brown County under-going some repairs. I selected that place to get away from crowds that the machine would naturally attract. I am going east and will not be back before Saturday [24 April] when I expect the machine to be repaired and here in town to meet me. We will start at once for Cuba, where we will join the patriots in their struggle for liberty ... The newspaper reports have been somewhat confusing because we have three machines in the air, and just now they are in central states. One of them will be at the Tennessee exposition. The report that the machine exploded the other night was the most natural thing in the world. Owing to the roof of our machine springing a leak one of our electrical circuits became grounded and the dynamo burned out. The display was something wonderful, but, fortunately, we have two sets of propelling machinery, and it did not bother us to keep going, but our lights were out for several hours. This is partly the damage we are to repair here.

About twenty years ago, UFO researchers became interested in 'The American Airship Scare' because the behaviour of those aerial objects and their occupants seemed to be very similar to that of reported 'flying saucers'. In 1971, Dr Geoffrey Doel, who was then President of the British UFO Research Association, supported the notion that Edward Pennington had secretly invented the airship responsible for the American sightings. This idea was dismissed by another authority, Peter Rogerson, who thought that, 'If Doel is correct he should write Pennington's biography and get the film rights.' In any case, there were plenty of other contenders for the title of 'The Inventor'.

One person, who called himself only S G, claimed that he and his brother, Zeb, after years of experimentation on a small farm in Adams County, Nebraska, finally took to the air one evening in April 1897:

... took our first aerial trip in our wonderful, yet simple, aero-motor. With a red light at the one end of our ship, and a green light at the other, and our ingenious searchlight easily accessible, we travelled about, and sometimes high above the clouds, sometimes so near to the Earth that we could understand the words of amazement and awe which were uttered with bated breath by the few fortunate mortals who happened to be below and thus got a glimpse of our great and wonderful invention. Since then we have roved about this country almost nightly, now in the north, now south, now east, now west, everywhere causing amazement, if not consternation.

Perhaps it was S G and Zeb who were seen at Harrison, Nebraska, on the night of 13 April when, for thirty minutes, a huge airship was seen by jurors, lawyers, judges and witnesses who had gathered there for the proceedings of the district court. They said they saw a bright white light and a variety of coloured lights shine from it as it went in a south-easterly direction. A J Habbiger thought he heard voices come from the black whale-shaped object, and was positive that something was moving on board that ship. E W Daily confidently asserted that the vessel was oval-shaped with a box-like structure hanging from it. At the stern there was a propeller and inside the oval object there appeared to be two men who were working hard on some machinery.

When the first few stories were collected from dusty old newspaper files it seemed clear that the airship reports represented sightings of a phenomenon that with chameleon-like finesse adapted itself to the assumptions of the people at the time. Thus, the mysterious force that made people see the airships was considered to be the same one that makes us see flying saucers today. However, increasing research has shown that what were at first thought to be the most convincing cases were nothing more than journalists' hoaxes designed to attract publicity and increase newspaper sales.

When looking through the massive collections of material on the American phantom airship it is not difficult to find weird and fantastic stories that are obviously meant to titillate newspaper readers. One such case involved an alleged 135,472 witnesses at St Paul, Minnesota, on 13 April 1897. It was 9.05 am when a cigar-shaped object with huge wings landed on the court-house square. After a wait of three minutes, the crowd of curious onlookers saw a hidden door open on the silver-coated craft and from it three beings stepped on to the bow.

> They were fashioned for the most part like ordinary men, save that there was no line of demarcation between the nose and the mouth, and they were furnished with immense gills on the sides of their heads, which resembled the fan-shaped ear of the elephant, and moved in and out with the regular respiration of the owners. The mouth was immense and stretched from gill to gill, while sticking out from their backs was something resembling a huge fin. Their feet were as pointed as tacks, and every time they stepped their feet stuck in the ship. These feet were made in this fashion they said in order to prevent them from slipping off the planet on which they lived. If they started to slip they stuck their feet in the planet several feet, and they stood no more show than a telegraph pole of slipping off into space. Concerning the fin they said it was used to guide them to where they wanted to go in case they did slip off. Their eyes looked like boiled eggs, and their hands were simply claws. This was essential, because in some places the air got so heavy that it was hard to dig their way out with the aid of ordinary figures. So they had claws instead.

From the UFO researcher's point of view, we have to consider if this panic was nothing more than an assortment of silly stories and misidentifications of man-made or natural objects. If we accept such an assumption we must ask why America was swept by rumours of this nature at that particular time, and then must go on to question whether or not today's UFO sightings are just as insubstantial in the cold light of objective reality.

Charles Fort, who never seriously believed that science had gained – or would ever gain – all the answers to the mysteries of our universe, guessed that the phantom airship sightings would be treated with scepticism. In New Lands, published in 1923, he prophetically said:

> Against such an alliance as this, between the jokers and the astronomers, I see a small chance for our data. The chance is in the future. If, in April, 1897, extra-mundane voyagers did visit this earth, likely enough they will visit again, and then the alliance against the data may be guarded against.

Unfortunately, the question still remains: Have 'they' or are 'they' visiting us?

[America was not alone in 'airship scares'. Britain, and indeed the whole of Europe, underwent similar experiences in 1909 and 1913, but against the background of the impending Great War the significance differed in emphasis. Ed]

GHOST ROCKETS AND
PHANTOM AIRCRAFT

Anders Liljegren and Clas Svahn

The saga of the ghost fliers began in the wilderness of the Swedish County of Västerbotten, near the border with Norway just below the Arctic Circle. In late November and early December 1933 the local population began to see strange distant lights that paced the valleys leading to Norway.

Behaving like airplane lights, it was theorized that a liquor smuggler was at work. The air force had no planes in the area, and the ambulance plane was grounded for repairs. Customs and the police were the first authorities to take action, searching for smugglers.

As reports of strange moving lights, aerial searchlights and engine sounds continued, and spread inland towards the Baltic coast in late December and early January 1934, the phenomenon became the subject of debate between competing newspapers. The conservative *Umebladet* triumphantly published the first close sighting of the plane:

'Mr Olov Hedlund was making an inventory of his kiosk in Sorsele in the early hours of 31 December 1933, when he heard the sound of an airplane. By moonlight he saw a large grey, unmarked machine on pontoons, or skis. The plane circled the railway station

at an altitude of some 400 metres before following the
railway towards the north.'[1]

Sightings that had proceeded at a rate of three to five
each day during December rose to ten to twenty-five
each day in January, after the newspaper report.
Indeed, 8 and 9 January had over forty reports each.[2]

The Swedish, Finnish and Norwegian air forces
made several attempts to come to grips with the
uninvited visitors, and exchanged data. Each significant Swedish case was investigated by local police
officers and carefully recorded. The resultant mass of
data at the Swedish northern regional staff is still
available for study and the extensive official Swedish
archives probably house even more data.

The Swedish air force organized repeated aerial
sweeps in the northern provinces together with radio
surveillance. The mystery is not yet solved, but in the
light of now declassified files in many European
countries the chances of some tentative conclusions are
probably greater today.

A seventeen-page secret memorandum from General Pontus Reuterswärd, who commanded the north
Swedish military area, to the Secretary of War, stated:
'The collected and analyzed data … has given me the
impression that unauthorized air traffic has occurred.'[3]

A Swedish historian, writing a treatise on Swedish
radio reconnaissance since World War 1, discovered an
analysis (by the General Staff in Stockholm) of 487
Scandinavian cases from the winter of 1933-4. Two
hundred and thirty four cases came from Norway, 96
from Sweden and 157 from Finland. They had been
sorted into four categories: 46 were 'credible', 64
'probably credible', 273 'others' and 104 'unbelievable'.

The Finnish General Staff published its own study of
the 1933-4 wave, in 1937. Of 111 reports, ten optical
sightings and five sounds were unexplained. The
Finns tried to find a pattern behind the sightings. They
stated: 'The mysterious phenomena were usually

observed for only a short time and never from two places at the same time. Thus one has never found an airplane moving from one point to another'.[4] The same 'localized' pattern has been theorized for UFO reports.[5]

Of course, solutions for the phantom aircraft should primarily be sought among known sources. Misinterpretations of stars, planets and other ordinary lights and sounds provided the bulk of the reports, especially during the 'psychosis periods' in the 1933-4 and 1936-7 winters when there was an abnormally high number of reports. Many sightings were identified as lawful civilian or military aircraft.

Two foreign nations remain prime suspects; Russia and Germany. Both had strong motives for sending airplanes on missions over northern Scandinavia. The north Swedish iron ore played a very important role and could have been a reason for interference from either nation. Germany might have wanted to secure its own future import of ore and might have wanted the training experience of flying and maintaining aircraft in polar areas during the winter.

Russia, on the other hand, might have wanted to study future ways to stop Germany and other European countries from receiving Swedish ore. Russia was a suspect, by the conservative press, as early as January 1934 and some military staff thought they could identify observed planes as Russian.

Valentin Sjöberg, a commentator writing for the conservative *Aftonbladet*, claimed there were no less than forty-three Russian airbases near the Russian-Finnish border, from Leningrad to the Kola peninsular.[6] Russian aircraft were regularly observed on the Finnish-Russian border and in the Arctic Sea to the north of Norway.

The problem of where the 'ghost fliers' had their base is crucial. Rumours told of land bases in Finland and Norway. The military staff believed instead that the aircraft were based at sea as mysterious ships had been seen off Norway's western and northern coasts during 'aircraft flaps'.

Sweden's first aircraft carrier was delivered in 1936. It carried six reconnaissance aircraft, which were 'thrown' into the air by a large German-built catapult. Germany also had such ships, with larger catapults.[7] It is highly probable that Russia, too, tested this technique for research and military purposes in their Arctic zone.

Aircraft violations continued in 1938 and during the war years, but now they were more clearly identified as Russian, German, British or American aircraft. From 1940-5 Swedish defence recorded 16,000 such violations and true 'ghost fliers' might be part of the 5890 of these that were unidentified.[8]

In 1939 the first known case of a rocket-like object was published in a north Swedish newspaper. A few such cases (aside from German V-1s and V-2s) are known from the war years. Some high-altitude phenomena over south Sweden in October 1944 and January 1945 remains unidentified. The Defence Staff thought they were new V-weapon constructions, but history tells us differently.

Literally hundreds of strange objects haunted the skies of Sweden throughout the whole of 1946. Every Swedish newspaper from that year contains stories of mysterious 'rockets'. In many cases the objects were mere lights in the dark but as the year ended the Swedish Staff of Defence had received over 200 reports of cigar-shaped objects – sometimes with wings – seen in broad daylight. These soon became known as the 'ghost rockets'.

Nine hundred and ninety seven reports came to the attention of the Defence Staff. To handle these a special group was formed by order of the Supreme Commander, chaired by Air Commodore Bengt Jacobsson.

The committee's first meeting was held at the Royal Air Administration on July 15, 1946.[9] The conference was the first of twelve held that year.

Besides Bengt Jacobsson, the committee's central persons were Air Director Henry Kjellson, Air Engineer Eric Malmberg, the FRA Executive Officer Olof Kempe, Air Director Karl Gustav Norén, Major Nils Ahlgren (head of the Air Defence section of the Defence Staff), the Head of FOA's telecommunications division, Martin Fehrm, and the Head of the material division at the Air Administrative, Karl-Arvid Norlin. All of these people attended more than half of the committee's meetings. In all thirty-eight persons were involved.

Out of almost 1000 reports received, a handful were investigated thoroughly. On at least twenty-eight occasions representatives of the Defence forces were sent to make a field investigation.

In a draft memorandum dated 3 December, 1946, Karl-Arvid Norlin established that 'nearly one hundred impacts have been reported and thirty pieces of debris have been received and examined by FOA'.[10]

Norlin also stressed that out of the 973 reports that had been brought to the Defence Staff's attention up to 29 November, 225 originated from 'observations of real physical objects', every one of these refers to objects seen in *broad daylight.*

One of the most substantial – and most thoroughly investigated – cases was the crash of a two metres long, winged object in small Lake Kölmjärv in the very north of Sweden, on 19 July 1946.[11] It was 11.45 am when farmer Knut Lindbäck and his maid Beda Persson were working by the lakeshore. The sky was clear and the sun was boiling hot. 'Suddenly I heard a humming sound from the sky' Lindbäck recalled. 'I looked up since I thought it was an airplane. Instead, I spotted a rocket-like device diving towards the lake.'

In the company of Beda he watched the ashen-grey projectile fall into the water about one and a half kilometres away. A tall column of water emerged, soon followed by yet another cascade. 'I'm sure it was a solid object' he said. 'It was two metres long and had a snub nose, while the stern was pointed. I thought there were two winglike protusions on the side, but I'm not sure. Everything happened so quickly.'

Another witness, standing on the other shore of the lake, just a couple of hundred metres from the impact, also remembers the crash very well. 'The sound was horrible' tells Frideborg Tagebo 'I had never heard anything like it before – or since. Our dog went crazy and ran away. Everything was terrible. When the thing eventually struck down it was like a bomb had detonated.'

But was it really a bomb? And, if so, whose?

The next morning a company of soldiers under the command of Lieutenant Karl-Gösta Bartoll arrived at the site. Some preliminary investigations were done and the area blockaded. From a wooden raft the military searched the northern part of the lake for almost two weeks. From the raft they could easily see how stones and moraine from deeper layers had been forced up. Seagrass and water-lilies were scattered on the nearby shore. Everything pointed to an explosion below the water's surface. 'There are many indications that the Kölmjärv object disintegrated itself' says Bartoll. 'The object was probably manufactured in a lightweight material, possibly a kind of magnesium alloy that would disintegrate easily, and not give indications on our instruments.'

But if Lieutenant Bartoll's theory is right, what became of such parts as the guidance system, which hardly could be made from such lightweight material? At least some traces of the electric system should have survived the impact.

The same day as Bartoll and his men arrived at the site, two engineers from FOA, Roland Rynninger and Torsten Wilner arrived to check for radioactivity.[12] No traces of this, or the object, were ever found and two weeks of hard work ended in mystery.

The ghost-rocket 'flap' of 1946 produced some very reliable observations of which only a few became public knowledge. Following a request from the Defence Staff on 22 July, most Swedish newspapers omitted the exact locations and names of observers when printing their stories.[13] In many other instances reports were classified and, after investigation, buried in the archives.

Two of the most well-known cases from this year may be nothing but two bright daylight meteors. On 9 July and 11 August hundreds, perhaps thousands, of Swedes witnessed bright meteorlike objects crossing the sky.

On the first occasion a man on holiday at Guldsmedshyttan (about eighty kilometres west of Västerås) even photographed the phenomenon from an air surveillance tower. The picture was widely distributed, both in and out of Sweden, as the first picture of a ghost-rocket. Eric Reuterswärd recalls the event: 'It was just a pure coincidence. I was taking a picture of the view from the tower when the bright object appeared in the sky. I really didn't think I had caught it on the film.' But he had. The picture was later examined by the Defence Staff but no conclusion was ever presented to the public.

Other events were more convincing, however:

On **14 August** a Swedish air force lieutenant, and his flight observer, observed an unknown, cigar-shaped craft during a training flight from Västerås. The rocket-like object appeared near the horizon, three or four kilometres away. 'It was not an airplane' the pilot recalls, 'It definitely was a cigar – or a disc seen from its side.' The pilot accelerated his B-18 in an attempt to get closer but instead the torpedo sped away, out of sight. 'When I tried to increase my speed it just flew away. I hadn't a chance to get any closer.' This case was investigated by the committee. No natural explanation was ever found.

On **22 August** the managing director of a Gothenburg-based chain of camera shops was on his way to Stockholm by car when he and his three friends

stopped for a rest near Norrköping; he unpacked his
film camera.

> 'All of a sudden one of my comrades shouted and
> pointed to the sky. Out from a cloud came a smoking
> torpedo dashing over the blue sky towards another
> cloud. I switched to the telephoto lens and turned the
> camera to the object.
> I could see the object clearly in the camera as I
> filmed it. It disappeared into the cloud, came out again
> and eventually we lost sight of it somewhere in the
> north. Not a sound was heard.'

After the sighting, and thoroughly shaken, they
resumed their journey to Stockholm, where they
turned the film over to military authorities. 'Then we
were summoned to a dark room where the film was to
be shown, but it was all blank! I must have forgotten to
switch the aperture and overexposed the whole film.'

One of the committee members still alive is Eric
Malmberg, once secretary of the 'ghost rocket'
committee. He makes this summation, some forty
years afterwards:

> 'I would like to say that everyone on the committee, as
> well as the chairman himself, was sure that the
> observed phenomena didn't originate from the Soviet
> Union. Nothing pointed to that solution.
> On the other hand, if the observations are
> correct, many details suggest that it was some kind of a
> cruise missile that was fired on Sweden. But nobody
> had that kind of sophisticated technology in 1946.'

UFOs – A GLOBAL PHENOMENON

COMPILED AND EDITED FROM SEVERAL
ARTICLES SUBMITTED BY ANDERS LIL-
JEGREN, CLAS SVAHN, BRONISLAW RZEPECKI,
KIM MOLLER HANSEN AND PAUL NORMAN

Those of us who live in English-speaking countries are more likely to hear about UFOs seen in other English-speaking countries, and our idea of the phenomenon is liable to be based on those cases, most particularly on cases from the United States. However, are such reports typical of experiences throughout the world?

By and large, the answer seems to be: yes. Different cultures may report UFOs differently, describing them in their own language, in terms which are meaningful according to their beliefs, but it seems the phenomenon itself is much the same wherever it occurs.

At first sight this seems a strong argument for the view that UFOs really exist as an objective physical phenomenon. But the fact that UFO reports are much the same everywhere could simply reflect the fact that human beings themselves are fundamentally the same everywhere, and liable to the psychological delusions, or to make the same kinds of misidentification.

The selection of cases which follows illustrates both the overall similarity of the phenomena and the local differences.

OTHERWORLDLY OCCUPANTS IN SWEDEN, 1958

Two young men, Stig Rydberg and Hans Gustavsson, were returning by car from a dance on 20 December

1959. Near Domsten, in southern Sweden, they stopped to look at a strange light in a glade. They saw a saucer-shaped object, about five metres in diameter, illuminated from within, standing on three 'legs'. Suddenly they were grabbed by several small lead-grey, jelly-like creatures who tried to drag them towards the light. After a desperate struggle, one of them reached the car and blew the horn. The second man was then released and the otherworldly UFO occupants ran back to their craft and flew away.

This case, which was probably the most widely publicized 'saucer story' in Swedish media history, was investigated in depth, and doctors who used hypno-analysis on the witnesses vouched for their integrity. Official investigation was carried out by the 'Fst/FL' group of the Aviation and Air Defence department of the Defence Staff at the request of the witnesses; eventually they dismissed the case on the grounds that the witnesses were less than reliable, one of them having been relieved from military duty due to a tendency to phobia.

SPIRAL UFO IN CHINA, 1981

Probably no UFO has been seen by a greater number of people than the spiral object which appeared over China in the hours before midnight of 24 July 1981. Many of the sightings occurred to several people – in some cases hundreds – at a time; independent witnesses established consecutive sightings of what seems beyond question the same object.

A typical report is that of tobacco farmer Tian Jinfu who was drying tobacco leaves at about twenty past eleven on his farm in the province of Guizhou. At first he saw a round 'star', about the apparent size of the moon, lighting the northern sky. Two minutes later a luminous 'tail' appeared to left and right of the object; this tail continued to extend, forming a five-ring concentric spiral round the original object. In true Chinese tradition, Tian Jinfu compared it to a dragon, the central core forming the head and the spiral the body and tail. When fully formed, it moved slowly away, sometimes passing behind clouds but reappearing before vanishing completely.

Several sightings came from people watching open-air movies, so that hundreds saw it at a time. Naturally, many were frightened; at Zigong people shut themselves up in their homes. But most were pleasantly excited, and particularly those already interested in UFOs. Wang Aining, of Loyang in Henan, who admitted to being 'passionate about UFOs' was just going to bed when he heard neighbours shouting 'Flying Saucer!' He rushed outside to see what the fuss was about, and was rewarded by seeing something like 'a washbasin', of a diameter he estimated at about twenty metres, spinning and throwing out flashes of brilliant blue light as it silently crossed the sky, surrounded by misty white swirls of foggy white. He and his neighbours watched it for fifteen minutes before it vanished in the distance; they agreed that it was neither a satellite, nor an aircraft, nor a weather-balloon, nor a shooting star.

Many observers started by looking for natural explanations. Li Zhengaï of the People's Army for the Liberation of China assumed it must be the moon – till he realized it was in the wrong part of the sky. Those who called the meteorological office were told patiently that, yes, they *had* seen the object but no, they *couldn't* say yet what it was.

It was a university professor who supplied the most specific description. Shi Zunsheng, Professor of medicine at Kummin, had hitherto been a severe critic of UFO believers; but after examining that night's object for ten minutes through his telescope he had to admit 'it's true, it's a UFO – there's a row of portholes!' His drawing shows a domed disc, convex below as well as above, ringed with a line of windows.

Accounts differed as to the direction in which the object was moving, and also as to its movements; but considering it was seen over so wide a geographical area, the reports are satisfyingly consistent. Several photographs were taken; most show a glowing nucleus with a hazy luminous surround. Only one shows the spiral described by so many, and that one is suspiciously 'tidy', giving every sign of retouching if not outright faking.

By any standards, this was a remarkable set of sightings; but what emerged during investigation made them more remarkable still. *They had been predicted!*

A month earlier, a twenty-four-year-old astronomer from the Observatory of Yun'nan, Zhang Zhousheng, announced that between 10 and 30 July UFO activity would intensify, with particularly good chances of a sighting from the 24th to the 29th. It would appear to the north, and should be visible all over China. Its apparent size would be somewhat larger than that of the moon, if small it would appear to be a disc, if large, a spiral. It would rotate slowly clockwise, and consist of a bright centre with a cloudy, faintly luminous surround. If seen by day it would be silver; if by night, it would show colours. According to the time of the observation, it would move off in different directions. The sighting should last for about ten minutes if there were no clouds.

It was not psychic powers that enabled Zhang Zhousheng to make so precise a prediction. Meteors become visible as they pass through Earth's outer atmosphere. The sheet of ionized gas by which they are surrounded can, under the influence of Earth's magnetic field, make spiral movements, while impact between the electrified particles can produce luminous effects. The total effect seen from Earth would be a disc surrounded by a slowly rotating spiral. Since such objects can be tracked, it was possible to make a rough estimate when this particular one would become visible.

In an official statement in August 1981, the

Zijingshan Observatory said that three explanations remain open: (1) a new kind of terrestrial scientific experiment; (2) a natural phenomenon of unknown type; (3) a UFO. While the explanation offered by Zhang Zhousheng, backed by his impressively accurate prediction, points clearly towards a natural phenomenon of some kind, it is clearly a very rare kind.

CLOSE ENCOUNTER IN POLAND, 1954

This case came to light only in 1986, thirty-two years after it occurred; consequently it was impossible to find traces, or additional witnesses. Even the main witness doesn't recall many details, because at the time she was only eleven years old and didn't make much of the case herself. In 1986 accidental talk reawakened the memory and made her speak of her adventure.

She was on holiday on Wegierska Górka in July 1954, when together with other children she went to the woods to pick mushrooms. She felt subconsciously attracted to some nearby cliffs. Suddenly, between the trees, about fifty metres from her, she noticed a yellowish-white oval-shaped light; it was above the ground, as if supported by the cliff, but actually it was not supported at all.

She approached the light, which strangely attracted her. As she came close she saw a 'door', and close to it a figure. This being stood sideways to her, but with its face towards her as if watching her. She approached along the path, and climbed the four 'stairs' which led up to the open rectangular door. She didn't have to bend her head to go in.

Inside, she saw four more beings, standing with their backs to her, facing the walls. They were not standing in line, but 'accidentally' about the 'room', which had a cylindrical pillar in the centre. These four beings were about twenty centimetres shorter than the one who had been standing in the doorway.

The taller figure was wearing a close-fitting suit, the

lower half light red and transparent, the upper half intensive red; a kind of 'mist' surrounded the lower half. There were no zips or buttons. On its head the being had a 'chimneysweep's cap'; on its back there was some kind of swelling, resembling a hump. Its hands were humanlike, with fingers. The skin was the same colour as human. Instead of a mouth there was a straight narrow fissure; she could see no nose. The eyes were rather small, but wider than ours, becoming narrower towards the temple. The figure was as tall as an average man – about 170cm; the girl's head reached its waist. She felt the beings were male.

The girl felt an 'inner voice' instructing her to sit down on the glittering floor. She did so, leaning her head against the wall, and promptly fell asleep.

The next thing she recalls is being shaken by the shoulder by one of the boys, and the group of children standing around her. She was sitting on the ground beside the cliff. The children shouted at her, asking where she had been for so long a time; it was seven hours since they had seen her last. They had been searching for her in the forest, and several times had looked in the place where she was eventually found. And what had she been doing? The other children had baskets full of mushrooms, but her basket was empty!

She had a vague memory of flying with somebody, but did not tell her adventure to the other children. Only when she got home did she tell her mother, who told her 'keep silent, it was only a dream ...'

That is the sum total of the facts. It is likely that hypnosis would enable further recall, but unfortunately this is not possible. One detail is particularly interesting: the hump on the being's back. The witness, who has no interest in ufology, is not likely to know that in several other cases, such as Emilcin, 1978, and Czluchów, 1979, entities with humps have been reported.

UFO LANDING IN KUWAIT, 1978

When UFOs threaten oil production, even governments have to take notice. In January 1979 a telex from the American Embassy in Kuwait stated that alleged UFO sightings were causing security concern in that country.

The first sighting took place at the Kuwait Oil Company's Gathering Centre No 24, near Umm Alaish, to the north of Kuwait City, on the night of 9 November 1978. Employees had reported seeing a 'flying saucer', and their sighting had been confirmed by colleagues at Centre No 15, who claimed that when it came under observation, the object extinguished its lights and vanished.

The following night employees at Umm Alaish had a second sighting, this time of a much more dramatic nature. Seven workers, including one American, witnessed a huge, cylindrical object, larger than a jumbo jet. It had a dome and flashing red lights. It landed silently close to the installation. The witnesses were afraid to approach it, but watched it for seven minutes, after which time it took off and disappeared rapidly.

The strangest part of the story, however, was the effect the object had on the oil company's equipment. A standard feature of such equipment is that it will automatically shut itself down when some failure occurs which could cause serious damage to the gathering and transmission system; after which it can only be restarted manually. At the time of the UFO landing, the pumping system automatically shut itself down, indicating that some interference had taken place; but when the UFO left the scene, the equipment did the seemingly impossible and restarted spontaneously!

An official investigation was carried out with commendable promptness by the Kuwait Institute for Scientific Research, assisted by police and military personnel. A search of the alleged landing area was conducted, and cameras were distributed to fieldworkers, in the hope of obtaining some more tangible evidence.

The plan seems to have been successful, for one of the recipients, an employee at Al Sabriyan oil field, near Kuwait's northerly border with Iraq, claimed that in the early morning of 21 November, between five thirty and six, he had seen and obtained photographs of an object which flew over a six metre high water tower, then hovered for half an hour. This should have been long enough for even the most nervous cameraman to steady himself sufficiently to obtain successful pictures, but if such photographs exist they have never been published. However, the sighting was confirmed by other witnesses; though the presence of the UFO interrupted long-distance communications – presumably radio – it did not affect local services, and the staff were able to alert the supervisor, who saw the object for himself.

Altogether, eight sightings were reported, the last being on 14 November. A few weeks later, on 20 January 1979, the investigation committee of the KISR released its report. It concluded that the objects were not espionage devices from a neighbouring power; but they would not commit themselves to the suggestion that they might be extraterrestrial. Their spokesman, Ratib Abu Id , said that the scientists did not know enough about the phenomena to rule out the possibility that they might be 'spaceships'. The committee recommended that official action be taken to protect Kuwait's vital oil installations.

Whether any such action was taken, and if so, what form it took, has not been disclosed. UFOs have been seen sporadically since then over Kuwait and neighbouring countries; in 1980 another official American document revealed that on 20 June an aircraft of Kuwait Airways had encountered a 'ball of light' on its return flight from Cairo. But so far as is known, the oil fields have witnessed no further landings.

A POLICEMAN'S ENCOUNTER IN DENMARK

'I was driving in my patrol car at approximately ten thirty pm, when suddenly the engine stopped, and all the lights of the car failed. At the same time the car was surrounded by a bright bluish-white light. I tried to call the police station in Haderslev, but the radio was dead. The temperature inside the car was increasing. After a while it was as if the light was rising upwards from a circle which it was forming on the ground around the car. When I was bending myself forwards and looking up, I was able to see the light cone terminated at the bottom of a huge, greyish object hovering right over me. When the light had disappeared into the object, this started moving and disappeared in a few seconds – vertically in the air. Immediately before this I had stepped out of the car to look at this thing. When the object had disappeared all the electrics in the car were again working normally.

Before I stepped out of the car I had taken three pictures with the automatic camera fastened in the car, and afterwards I took three more pictures of the road, which was lit up by the headlights.

The object was round, approximately ten metres in diameter, and with a hole in the bottom from which light was projected. In addition, the object had two dome-like structures at the underside.'

In this way police officer Evald Hansen Maarup tells his famous experience of 13 August 1970 in southern Jutland. The pictures Maarup was able to take with his automatic camera unfortunately show only a point of light. The pictures, and the witness himself, were examined at Skrydstrup AFB, but they were not able to explain his experience or his photos.

AUSTRALIA: THE FREDERICK VALENTICH
DISAPPEARANCE

During my travels and correspondence, I have found many false stories circulating the world regarding this most important case. Here are the facts. During the evening of 21 October 1978, twenty-year-old Australian pilot Frederick Valentich disappeared over Bass Strait, while flying from Melbourne's Moorabbin Airport to King Island, off the coast of Victoria. His last communication was twelve minutes past seven in the evening, during the largest UFO flap in Australian history. No trace has ever been found of either the pilot or his blue and white Cessna 182.

Frederick Valentich was not the only person who reported a strange object over and near Bass Strait that day and night. Researchers, from the Victorian UFO Research Society (VUFORS), have found over fifty reported observations in that area which occurred before, during and after his disappearance.

At first this incident was treated as an ordinary lost aircraft. It could not be hidden since several other pilots flying at the same time were tuned to the same radio frequency and heard the communications. The world first learned that a UFO was involved when one of those pilots tipped off the press. On Monday 23 October front page headlines on the incident led the news of the day. VUFORS telephones were ringing constantly for the following three days. Switchboards were flooded at radio stations, television stations and newspapers.

The most outstanding UFO case in Australia is also the greatest mystery in Australian aviation history. The Frederick Valentich incident has done more to change the attitude of Australian officials towards UFOs than any other event. This became obvious when, just twenty-two days after the Valentich disappearance, an RAAF official actually contacted a witness for his permission to be interviewed by the press in the hope of encouraging other reports from reliable witnesses. This reliable witness was an active master mariner with thirty-five years of responsible seagoing experience. Even earlier, immediately after the pilot's disappearance, we know of other behind-the-scenes official activity, such as the Forestry Commission telephoning instructions to fire tower lookouts to report unidentified flying objects. Police officers at various locations were instructed to interview witnesses who had reported unusual sights and sounds on that date in their areas. Aircraft pilots were called upon to report sightings of unidentified objects and lights in the sky. Instructions were given to pilots, who were flying at the same time and utilizing the same radio frequency, not to divulge any details of their communications. Attempts were made to make it appear that pilot Valentich was not where he reported his location, and that the report of the encounter itself was no more than a fabrication.

Actual Verbatim transcription of Melbourne Flight Service: The transcript portion of the communication between Valentich and Melbourne Flight Service, as released by the Australian Department of Transport follows: (FS – Flight Service, DSJ – Frederick Valentich aircraft designation)

1906:14

DSJ   Melbourne, this is Delta Sierra Juliet. Is there any known traffic below five thousand?

FS   Delta Sierra Juliet, no known traffic.

DSJ   Delta Sierra Juliet, I am, seems to be a large aircraft below five thousand.

1906:44

FS   Delta Sierra Juliet, What type of aircraft is it?

DSJ   Delta Sierra Juliet, I cannot affirm, it is four bright, it seems to me like landing lights.

1907

FS   Delta Sierra Juliet.

1907:31

DSJ   Melbourne, this is Delta Sierra Juliet, the aircraft has just passed over me at least a thousand feet above.

FS   Delta Sierra Juliet, roger, and it is a large aircraft, confirmed?

DSJ   Er – unknown, due to the speed it's travelling, is there any air force activity in the vicinity?

FS   Delta Sierra Juliet, no known aircraft in the vicinity.

1908:18

DSJ   Melbourne, it's approaching now from due east towards me.

FS   Delta Sierra Juliet.

1908:41

—   (open microphone for two seconds).

1908:48

DSJ   Delta Sierra Juliet, it seems to me that he's playing some sort of game, he's flying over me, two, three times at speeds I could not identify.

1909

FS   Delta Sierra Juliet, roger, what is your actual level?

DSJ   My level is four and a half thousand, four five zero zero.

FS   Delta Sierra Juliet, and you confirm you cannot identify the aircraft?

DSJ   Affirmative.

FS   Delta Sierra Juliet, roger, stand by.

1909:27

DSJ   Melbourne, Delta Sierra Juliet, it's not an aircraft it is (open microphone for two seconds).

1909:42

FS   Delta Sierra Juliet, can you describe the – er – aircraft?

DSJ   Delta Sierra Juliet, as it's flying past it's a long shape (open microphone for three seconds) cannot identify more than it has such speed (open micorphone for three seconds). It's before me right now Melbourne.

1910

FS   Delta Sierra Juliet, roger and how large would the – er – object be?

1910:19

DSJ   Delta Sierra Juliet, Melbourne, it seems like it's stationary. What I'm doing right now is orbiting and the thing is just orbiting on top of me also. It's got a green light and sort of metallic like. It's all shiny on the outside.

FS   Delta Sierra Juliet.

1910:46

DSJ   Delta Sierra Juliet (open microphone for five seconds) It's just vanished.

FS   Delta Sierra Juliet.

1911

DSJ   Melbourne, would you know what kind of aircraft I've got? Is it a military aircraft?

FS   Delta Sierra Juliet, confirm the – er – aircraft just vanished.

DSJ   Say again.

FS   Delta Sierra Juliet, is the aircraft still with you?

DSJ   Delta Sierra Juliet, it's (open microphone for two seconds) now approaching from the south west.

FS   Delta Sierra Juliet.

1911:50

DSJ   Delta Sierra Juliet, the engine is rough-idling, I've got it set at twenty-three twenty-four and the thing is coughing.

FS   Delta Sierra Juliet, roger, what are your intentions?

DSJ   My intentions are – ah – to go to King Island – ah – Melbourne. That strange aircraft is hovering on top of me again, (open microphone for two seconds). It is hovering and it's not an aircraft.

FS   Delta Sierra Juliet.

1912:28

DSJ   Delta Sierra Juliet, Melbourne (open microphone for seventeen seconds).
(No official conclusion has been given for the
strange sound which was heard that interrupted the pilot's last statement.)

Additional UFO reports flood investigators: During
this communication, abruptly terminated by a strange
sound, twenty people in different locations around
Bass Strait observed a green light in the same direction
and at the same time as Valentich reported the
approach and description of an object with a green
light.

In addition, other reports have been forthcoming,
such as: in the southern suburb of Frankston, a mother
and four teenagers reported what appeared to
resemble a sky rocket, although the object was
stationary. The colour appeared to be a mixture of
red, pink and white. The witnesses estimated the object
to be a quarter-size of the moon. The mother said that
she did not realize it was a UFO until she learned later
that other people had seen the same object. At the
same time, a bank manager and his wife, while driving
on the highway west of Melbourne, observed a
starfish-shaped object out over the Strait. They noticed
green flickering lights at the ends.

Another sighting was reported from Ormond, a
suburb in southern Melbourne, at seven fifteen, when
lights were noted in a cigar-shaped arrangement. The
lights were described as looking like 'silver rain' as they
appeared to fall or else were turned off from top to
bottom.

Two lads were out in the street communicating via
walkie-talkies when they saw a star-shaped object
appear at a low altitude over their heads. It was moving
slightly faster than an aircraft as if on an approach run
to an airport. During the observation, both witnesses
recall a sound like a low pulsating hum associated with

the object. Each of the walkie-talkies first became jammed with static, then communication was lost altogether, even though the lads were only a short distance apart. Communication was restored when the UFO flew away. Their description was of an object with bright white lights placed intermittently at each tip of a starfish-shaped object and at various points along the arcs to the tips.

Many other similar reports reached VUFORS of flying objects throughout southern Victoria during that same day and night, continuing for several days following the disappearance.

Government co-operation improves: Three and one-half years after this amazing incident, the Australian Department of Transport released its final report concerning the Valentich encounter. The bottom line read: 'Cause of the disappearance is unknown.'

Since that time, there have been several meetings between various officials and ufologists in Australia. Discussions during these meetings concerned various cases where veteran investigators have been involved over the years. The current situation has improved as some reports have been declassified and made available for further studies. However, certain unclassified reports still remain in official files. Some of them concern cases where we were personally involved in the investigations. We are grateful for this better co-operation and will not argue the case, although the Freedom of Information Policy is now in effect in Australia. After all, we also have confidential reports not available for publication and we will not betray that confidence. Unfortunately, the person most responsible for this better co-operation is not available to receive credit. He is Frederick Valentich, who disappeared over Bass Strait, during an encounter with a UFO.

PART II
CONTACT WITH UFOs

CONTACT WITH UFOs – INTRODUCTION

Seeing may be believing, but we are not usually convinced of the existence of something until we have physically touched it. Unfortunately, opportunities to touch a UFO are few and far between, and there are often good reasons to question the word of those who claim to have had such opportunities.

So most contact with UFOs has been solely visual, and generally at considerable distances; often, too, in conditions which make for uncertainty and ambiguity, such as when waking in the middle of the night or while driving alone in remote places.

Many witnesses claim, nonetheless, that even under these circumstances contact of a special kind is established: they report a sense of being in mental or telepathic contact with the occupants of the UFO. Sometimes this generates fear, but more often it is reassurance, peace, even love, that is communicated. Unfortunately, such emotional responses are no guarantee that the UFO is what it seems to be: they have been known to occur even when the alleged UFO can be positively identified as a natural or manmade object.

We have witness reports ranging from those which leave room for doubt to those where it seems no doubt is possible:

* A witness sees a distant light of no discernible shape, but whose behaviour is inconsistent with anything he knows.
* A witness sees a distant object of ambiguous nature.
* A witness sees an object clearly enough to recognize that it is a structured craft.
* A witness sees a structured craft close to or on the ground, or otherwise interacting with the environment, and perhaps sees its occupants.
* A witness touches a structured craft, and perhaps meets its occupants.
* A witness enters a structured craft, voluntarily or involuntarily, and perhaps interacts with its occupants.

At one end of this spectrum, misperception is possible: the distant light may be a satellite, the ambiguous shape may be a balloon, the structured object may be a helicopter seen under unusual circumstances.

At the other end of the spectrum, misperception is not possible. Clearly a witness can't be mistaken about a UFO which he can touch and enter. At this end of the spectrum, therefore, if we are to question the reality of his experience, it must be by premising something in the nature of a hallucination.

It follows, therefore, that the way we evaluate a witness' testimony will depend on the kind of contact he is claiming. Faced with an account of a distant light, we shall seek to establish just how strange its behaviour really was, and whether we can account for it by reference to a natural phenomenon such as a planet, satellite or aircraft. Similarly, when we are given a description of an ambiguous object, it is not its existence we question so much as the interpretation we put on the sighting.

Up to this point, there is no need for us to question the integrity or the credibility of the witness: misperceptions and misinterpretations are something we all do from time to time.

It is when we come to reports that allow for no

ambiguity that evaluation of the witness becomes an essential item in the investigation procedure. That an advertising plane, seen under unusual circumstances, should be mistaken for something more exotic, is an error any of us might make: but it does not involve reality testing. The thing is there: the question is, what is it? But when someone claims to have been taken aboard an extraterrestrial spacecraft, the question becomes not one of *what* happened, but of *whether* it happened. What, if any, was the reality of the event?

Unfortunately, this is something that is well-nigh impossible to establish. The fact that the witness can produce no supporting physical evidence, such as a souvenir of his encounter, or an unambiguous photo or physical trace, must make his story less probable: as does the fact that there is never any convincing supporting testimony from other, independent observers. But unless we can prove beyond doubt that his experience never occurred, there is no way we can prove it was nothing but illusion or fantasy.

At the same time, we all know how many and how varied are the circumstances under which someone may see something that 'isn't really there'. Sickness or drugs, fatigue or lack of sleep, sensory deprivation or sensory overload, the wrong diet or not enough food, stress of many kinds – these and many other factors can lead to a condition in which a person will have experiences that, while they may be real enough to him, have no reality outside his own mind.

Evaluating a contact claim, then, involves a process of escalating sophistication in the questions we ask, to match the escalating strangeness of the claims. It is not enough that we be familiar with the many natural phenomena and man-made artifacts that can cause misperceptions: we must also be alert to the infinite complexity of the human mind.

DISTANT CONTACT: RADAR/VISUAL ENCOUNTER AT BENTWATERS

Martin Lawrence Shough

At nine thirty pm 13 August 1956, Bentwaters USAF/RAF air base, a few miles east north east of Ipswich in Suffolk, would have betrayed no sign of unusual happenings to the casual passer-by. But radar operators in the airfield's Ground Controlled Approach (GCA) unit were by this time alerted to something strange on their scopes. At a displayed range of twenty-five to thirty miles, out over the North Sea, a target was picked up on the ten centimetre CPN-4 surveillance radar. It was on a west north west heading into the airfield. The rate of closure was measured with each four-second scan of the radar antenna: each sweep showed the target between five and six miles closer. The target looked like a normal aircraft echo, but within about half a minute the target had crossed the centre of the scope (Bentwaters) and was lost fifteen to twenty miles inland. Airman John Vaccare's estimate of thirty seconds' total transit time, if rationalized to a multiple of the four-second scan rate – thirty-two seconds – suggests a speed of 4500–5000mph. The most accurate measure is likely to be the distance covered from scan to scan, leading to a mean speed of 4950mph. The consistency of these figures argues against careless observation. Vaccare, no doubt conscious of the difficulty of precise measurement with a target of such unprecedented speed, settled for a cautious approximation of 4000 mph in the intelligence report sent to Project Blue Book, the US government study of UFO reports at the time.

The sightings: At about the same time another group of targets was noticed at a range of eight miles to the south west and moving towards Bentwaters. These 'appeared as normal targets' on the GCA scope manned by Training Sergeant Whenry, (whose detailed report forms the basis of the account of this event appearing in IR-1-56). Some twelve to fifteen echoes were approaching in a cluster, spread over a six to seven mile area and preceded by 'three objects which were in a triangular formation with an estimated 1000 feet separating each object. Moving at speed varying between 80 and 125mph, the group crossed the centre of the scope and proceeded north west, giving consistent returns, for a distance of about forty miles, fading somewhat as range increased. During this time 'normal checks made to determine possible malfunctions of the GCA radar failed to indicate anything was technically wrong', so a T-33 of the 512th Fighter Interceptor Squadron which was returning to Bentwaters from a training flight was vectored to the area and asked to search for the targets. The Lockheed trainer, unaided by airborne radar and without the benefit of height-finder information from the ground, searched the area visually at an unknown altitude without finding anything. Meanwhile, the target-cluster was forty miles north east, at which point it converged to form a single echo with a presentation several times the strength which would be given by a B-36 (one of the largest production aircraft ever built) under comparable conditions. This very strong echo now stopped its motion to the north east and maintained station for ten to fifteen minutes, after which it began to move again, still to the north east, for a further five to six miles, before once more coming to rest, this time for only three to five minutes. Then it picked up speed once more and moved off the scope to the north.

A few minutes after this target had disappeared a blip appeared at 2200 hours due east of Bentwaters at thirty miles range; it was a high speed target similar to the first one detected thirty minutes earlier, crossing the screen at a speed estimated by Whenry as 'in excess of 4000 mph'. The return appeared, once again, 'normal' and resembled that of an ordinary aircraft except for its remarkable speed. Twenty-five miles west of Bentwaters the target 'disappeared ... by rapidly moving out of the GCA radiation pattern'.

For a further fifty minutes or so, nothing further happened at Bentwaters. At this time no visual sightings had been made, from the air or the ground. Staff Sergeant Lawrence S Wright, the control tower shift-supervisor, had seen nothing but Mars low on the eastern horizon. He watched the bright planet through binoculars as it rose. He didn't know that it was Mars, and reported it in case it might be relevant to the radar tracks. But he described it perfectly, so we can identify this light with confidence.

Suddenly, however, at five to eleven, three events happened simultaneously. According to telegraphic report BOI-485 radar recorded another high speed target, this time between 2000 and 4000mph. This time something definite was seen from the ground: control tower personnel saw 'a bright light passing from east to west over the field at terrific speed at about 4000 feet altitude' while simultaneously the pilot of a transport aircraft (identified by the Lakenheath ATC supervisor as a C-47) which was flying over the field saw a bright light 'streak under his aircraft', again at terrific speed. This independent visual corroboration seems to have stimulated Bentwaters personnel into action. A phone call was placed almost immediately to the GCA facility at Lakenheath 'to determine if unusual sightings were occurring'. *Thus began one of the most remarkable radar-visual sequences on record.*

At Lakenheath, GCA personnel in turn phoned GCA at Sculthorpe RAF Station in Norfolk, some miles to the north. Whether anything was seen at Sculthorpe is not known as we have no access to documentation. However, either Sculthorpe GCA or Lakenheath GCA then notified the Air Traffic Control unit at Lakenheath and the Watch Supervisor there, although initially sceptical, 'immediately had all controllers start scanning the radar scopes.'

Lakenheath Air Traffic Control Centre, five to eleven GMT 13 August 1956. Training Sergeant Forrest D Perkins, Watch Supervisor, is at the Supervisor's Co-ordinating desk. The four or five other controllers on this five to midnight shift are keeping only a casual eye on the scopes. Things are quiet, with 'very little or no traffic' at this time. A phone rings; a controller answers and passes the call to his Supervisor. Because the call is routed through the Sculthorpe switchboard and because Perkins has missed the caller's introduction, he believes the message is from Sculthorpe RAF Station and will not discover his error for another twenty years. But the content of the message overshadows its origin: the caller asks whether Lakenheath ATC gave any 4000mph targets on their scopes!

Sergeant Perkins is understandably sceptical of this report, but instructs his controllers to start keeping a close watch, with all the scopes set on different range scales from 10-200 miles radius. All the scopes are using a moving target indicator (MTI) circuit, an analogue delay line which enables the frequency of successive reflected radar pulses to be compared and filters out returns from targets which are stationary (or nearly so), thus clearing the screen of inconvenient 'clutter' due to ground reflections. For 'ten or perhaps twenty minutes, certainly no more' the controllers watch for the reported high speed targets, seeing nothing. Then, at about five past eleven, one controller notices something different, but almost equally strange: about twenty to twenty-five miles south west radar shows a stationary target which, with MTI switched in, should not be there. Having satisfied himself that this target appears 'on all the different scopes' Sergeant Perkins calls the Lakenheath Ground Controlled Approach (GCA) unit, who confirm that the target is 'on their scope in the same geographical location.' Twelve years later, the SECRET intelligence teletype BOI-485 will confirm this simultaneous detection and Sergeant Perkins' memory of the target range and azimuth, adding that GCA radar had tracked this target to its present position from a position only six miles west of Lakenheath (where it would have been within the minimum range of the CPS-5 ATC radar).

After several minutes ('five minutes' – BOI-485) the target begins to move, without any perceptible acceleration, at a speed between 400 and 600 mph to a position some twenty miles north north west of Lakenheath, where it suddenly stops. At this time, about ten past eleven, Perkins sets in motion a standard alert procedure. He calls the 7th Air Division Command Post, London, the 3rd Air Force Command Post, the Base Commander, and his Air Force Communications Squadron Commander, all of whom are hooked into the ATC switchboard. An RAF Liaison Officer is also patched in, together with 'possibly others' whose identity Perkins is 'not aware of'. A busy conference line is thus established at Lakenheath, with Sergeant Perkins as its eyes and ears, relaying the situation as it develops and fielding questions and theories. The conference line authorities receive 'a detailed report on the target's movements and location' as it continues its high speed, straight line movements around the area at 600 mph, punctuated by stationary periods of between three and six minutes. Finally, at about eleven forty, 'after, I imagine, about thirty to forty-five minutes', Sergeant Perkins is made aware that a decision has been reached in consultation with the RAF to intercept the target; at this point the RAF coastal air defence and Ground Controlled Interception (GCI) radar at Neatishead, Norfolk, some forty miles north east of Lakenheath, enters the picture. Neatishead, however, is not the only RAF facility contacted.

In the underground concrete complex at Neatishead, the Chief Fighter Controller, Flight Lieutenant FHC Wimbledon, looks out from the controller's desk flanked by radar displays and communications equipment, through a glass partition and down on the large plotting board below, which shows a map of the north-eastern coastline of Norfolk. On the far wall an indicator board is ready to display details of any aircraft airborne, and the nature of the sortie. Off this room to the Controller's right are two isolated interception cabins, each equipped with a duplicate set of radar consoles fed from the cluster of radar antennae rotating ceaselessly above ground. Just after eleven forty Flight Lieutenant Wimbledon receives a call informing him of a situation at Lakenheath and the decision to scramble an interceptor. The controller relays the scramble authority to the duty airfield this night, RAF Waterbeach near Cambridge, mans both radar cabins with their four-man interception teams, and waits. The target, which they have taken no notice of before since their concentration is on the possibility of inbound targets to seaward, is clearly visible on their scopes. It will be some minutes before the aircrew at Waterbeach can run up the engine, get airborne and establish VHF contact with Neatishead, because of the airborne radio's poor range performance at low altitude and the unfavourable windward take-off pattern (a south-westerly climb and turn) which will take the aircraft initially in the opposite direction.

Meanwhile, the various authorities who are coordinating their reactions to this event through the

Lakenheath RATC centre switchboard have a separate problem. In routine airspace-penetration situations the primary concern is defence. On one level the detection of an unidentified intruder has to be an air defence issue, but the normal *operational* utility of interception procedure may not satisfy the needs of *intelligence* on another level. In the case of a 'UFO' which is clearly not a hostile or stray foreign aircraft in the usual sense, the usual strict rules for engagement will be subsumed by those of a more open-ended intelligence situation.

At Lakenheath in 1956 the concerns of USAF intelligence, RAF intelligence, and more especially the CIA, conflict with the air defence responsibilities of Neatishead GCI and Fighter Command, in as much as the narrowly defined role of the GCI system makes it useless for the purpose of gathering real-time intelligence. Neatishead's function is simply to guide the interceptor onto the tail of its target with only the bare minimum of radio communication; a different responsibility has been levied on the intelligence agencies, and so a different channel of communication must be set up.

At some time around eleven forty-five, a phone rings in the Operations briefing room of RAF Waterbeach. Outside, the crews of the night duty Flight of 253 Squadron, No 11 Group, Fighter Command, wait out the night in the cockpits of their aircraft, ready to press the starter buttons and take off at a few minutes notice. They are oblivious to the situation now being explained to the operations controller, who, almost certainly, is given no idea of the significance of the instructions he is receiving. The controller puts the phone back in its rest and switches on the telebriefing microphone, which connects the briefing building by a secure landline to the aircraft waiting at the operations readiness platform. In one of the eight de Havilland Venom NF.2a night fighters standing ready-fuelled on the dark airfield, the pilot and radar operator are startled by a warning lamp on the port-side instrument panel, and the voice of the operations controller in the pilot's headset instructs the pilot to pre-select a frequency on one of the Venom's two ten-channel VHF units, then stand by for further instructions. Moments later the controller's phone rings again, and the Chief Fighter Controller at Neatishead authorizes a scramble. Immediately, the operations controller gives the Venom pilot his interception frequency, advises him on the special discretionary use of his second frequency, and clears the aircraft for take off. The telebriefing landline connection, which automatically disconnects the Venom's VHF transmitter for security, is automatically released as the jet moves away from the operations platform towards the runway.

By eleven fifty pm the Venom is airborne to the south west of Waterbeach and executing a climb and turn back towards the north east in the direction of Lakenheath. Because of the limited range of the VHF transmitters at low altitude the pilot is not yet able to talk to Neatishead, over seventy miles away, so he takes this opportunity of using his discretionary frequency to get more information. Lakenheath ATC established radio and radar contact with the Venom inbound from the south west at a range of thirty to thirty-five miles and 2-3000 feet altitude. At this time Sergeant Perkins gives the pilot 'all the background information' and relays the current movements of the target. The time is eleven fifty-two.

Four minutes later the Venom is approaching the area of Lakenheath and its range and altitude permit the pilot to talk to his interception controller at Neatishead. The pilot flicks his VHF selector switch to the second of his pre-selected frequencies and opens the channel to Neatishead. However, because neither Neatishead nor Lakenheath can hear anything unless the pilot depresses his press-to-transmit footswitch, regardless of the frequency to which he is tuned, there

is no way for the Lakenheath controllers to tell that the
pilot has ceased listening to them, nor any way for
Neatishead to tell that the pilot was recently listening to
somebody else. Nor will either party ever be told; it is a
question of having no 'need to know'. Consequently,
Sergeant Perkins and his team continue to issue
headings to the interceptor in the belief that they are in
control as they watch the blip on their screens closing
towards the UFO under the real direction of
Neatishead GCI.

At midnight, the pilot has visual contact with a
'bright white light' (BOI-485) and calls Neatishead:
'Contact'. Shortly afterwards the code 'Judy' informs
the interception team that the Venom's radar operator
has the target firmly on his own scopes and requires no
further help from the ground. Following instructions,
the pilot is now free to open his radio channel to
Lakenheath; this is of no importance to the radar
operator, since his instructions to the pilot automatically override the VHF link when he presses the
intercom press-to-talk switch. As the Venom closes
rapidly on the now-stationary target, the pilot has time
only to report to Lakenheath: 'I've got my guns on
him', before his transmission is interrupted by the
radar operator reporting the sudden loss of the target
from his radar. This pause is noted by Sergeant
Perkins, who then hears the pilot say: 'Where did he
go? Do you still have him?' The reply goes back:
'Roger, it appeared he got behind you and he's still
there.' The swift circling of the UFO target behind the
interceptor has also been seen by the interception
teams at Neatishead, to whose frequency the pilot now
switches back for fresh instructions in order to evade
his pursuer. (The Lakenheath air traffic controllers
are neither trained to deal with this sort of situation
nor are they properly equipped to do so, lacking the
vital assistance of height-finding radar). The terse
message, 'Lost contact – more help' alerts the
Neatishead controller to the pilot's need for guidance;

the controller confirms the new situation, and for the next five minutes the pilot tries to shake the target from his tail, without success. A second Venom is now scrambled from Waterbeach, but it will not arrive in time to make contact with the target.

At about five minutes after midnight the Neatishead radar scopes lose the target in a manner which the Chief Fighter Controller interprets as a rapid descent out of the radiation pattern.[1] The target is not seen again by GCI radar, and shortly the interceptor is released from its mission. But Lakenheath is at this time still painting both the UFO and the interceptor, because Lakenheath's low-altitude radar coverage in its own immediate vicinity south of the field (the area of the chase) is far better than that of Neatishead, many miles to the north east. Thus, whilst for Neatishead the incident is over within five minutes, at Lakenheath Sergeant Perkins estimates a duration nearer ten minutes because the target is still visible during the time the Venom breaks off the action and starts on the journey home. At this time, the Venom pilot calls Lakenheath for the last time, informs them that he is returning to base and requests that they let him know if the UFO is still following. On the ATC scopes, the controllers watch the target tail behind the departing Venom on a south south west heading for a 'short distance', then stop at a position ten miles south of the field.

It is now ten minutes past midnight on the morning of 14 August, more than an hour since the target was first detected at Lakenheath. In the air traffic control centre the midnight relief shift have joined Sergeant Perkins' team in watching the radar scope. In the controller's headsets the voices of the two Venom pilots, one still inbound, the other on his way home, are heard in conversation: 'I saw something, but I'll be damned if I know what it was ... It's the damnedest thing I've ever seen.' The radar operator in Venom number one depresses his press-to-transmit footswitch and adds: 'Clearest target I've ever seen on radar' (BOI-485). The second Venom crew are denied the opportunity to see for themselves, however; as far as Neatishead GCI is concerned, the incident is over.

Shortly, the target begins to move. At a steady 600mph it crosses the scope in a northerly direction, finally being lost at a range of about fifty to sixty miles. An image on a radar scope, seen by few human eyes, has vanished; and all that is left of the Lakenheath UFO is the product of investigation, debriefings – reports and analyses that few will ever read. Years later, but for one chance letter, it would be as though the whole affair had never happened.

The implications: To study a case such as Lakenheath is now a kind of historical enquiry. Not exclusively, for we can discuss the details with some of those who were present and there is quantitative information in contemporary documents; but the meaning of the recorded facts will forever remain rooted in an historical context to which we cannot have direct access. There can never be direct experimental proof of the Lakenheath UFO, no matter how suggestive the *prima facie* evidence may be. Does this make the case useless as scientific evidence?

Oddly, the inevitable missing fragments and apparent contradictions which show up in enquiries of this nature can *increase* our confidence in the source material. Many small problems may take a great deal of painstaking trial and error to resolve, rather in the manner of reconstructing a jigsaw puzzle. Some pieces are found to be missing and the process is often frustrated by the discovery that some interpretation of a sequence of events fails to fit other parts of the picture. But twenty years later enough of the pieces can now be assembled to convince us that they are parts of an intelligible picture.

Many UFO puzzles do *not* work when we try to fit the pieces together but in the case of Lakenheath, the emerging picture begins to look very much like the picture on the box.

If the *prima facie* story hangs together well, what does it tell us about the UFOs? Can they be explained? There is no space here to attempt a detailed analysis of the many factors involved in interpreting radar-scope images or to embark on a critique of the arguments of the last twenty years; these technical issues are more fully addressed elsewhere. But we will touch on some of the less implausible interpretations here, and summarize the reasons why the Lakenheath case is held to be of rare scientific importance.

Firstly, the events at Bentwaters. Close study of the eleven-thirty slow cluster of targets has been made in terms of the following hypotheses: aircraft, birds, insects, balloons, surface vehicles/anomalous propagation, orbital bodies, meteors, microscale clear air turbulence, ionization phenomena, precipitation cells, sidelobe returns and multiple reflects effects, radio-frequency interference, electronic countermeasures techniques and spurious internally generated signals. None of these hypotheses can explain the reported target behaviour. The only hypothesis so far considered which can claim any degree of plausibility is that of reflections due to waves propagating across an inversion surface under the influence of winds, but this too requires considerable violence to be done to major features of the description.

An inversion is a stable, layered automatic structure capable of reflecting radar waves and giving an illusion of movement. However, in the case of the Bentwaters targets there are discrepancies of direction, moreover the two stationary episodes during which no movement was observed for a total period of many minutes are unintelligible in terms of such reflection. Most serious of all, is the objection that the signal strength of returns due to partial reflection is *inversely* proportional to elevation (and thus proportional to range), so that such echoes drop below the noise level of the receiver at close displayed ranges, becoming stronger as range is increased. In this case the targets were first noticed at close range, crossed the site with the appearance of 'normal' echoes, then began to fade as they *receded*. This type of behaviour is much more understandable in terms of real, radar reflective point targets (such as aircraft) than in terms of inversion reflections.

The three rapid targets detected at Bentwaters are equally difficult to explain, bearing no relation to known types of propagation anomaly. The speeds are an order of magnitude too high for meteorological explanations and unattainable by any known aircraft. The possibility of returns from the ionization wakes of meteors has been considered, but the geometry of the tracks, the improbability of three *radial* overflights on two *different* headings, and the simultaneous visual confirmation of the last track from above and below, all make this hypothesis extremely unlikely. Only a very brilliant fireball would have much chance of being detected at all on the CPN-4 in a radial orientation, and if such a fireball was somehow responsible for the five minutes to midnight radar visual report it is curious that not one single report of it is known to have been generated elsewhere in the UK. It has been pointed out that the event took place close to the maximum of the Perseid meteor shower, but the celestial co-ordinates of the Perseid radiant for that date and time are nowhere near the azimuths of these radar tracks.

Another possibility which deserves close attention is that of spurious internal signals which have been known to create fast tracks on radar scopes, but it can be shown that such an effect is essentially impossible for 1950s analogue technology.

When we come to the Lakenheath events, the multiple radar combined with visual contacts makes any hypothesis other than a 'real UFO' almost impossible to support. In the early stages, correlating returns were displayed on ATC and GCA radars of different design whilst ground personnel reported 'round white lights' displaying 'substantially the same' behaviour (which, they were careful to point out, bore no relation to the Perseid meteors simultaneously visible). When Neatishead was alerted a further ground radar channel was introduced, and the GCI system itself is a multiple radar array using different frequencies and pulse rates. At this stage, the added confirmation of the Venom interceptor's airborne radar, plus the pilot's eyes, seems almost superfluous. There is also a report from civilian observers on the ground at Ely, a few miles west of Lakenheath, of what may have been the object and the Venom in pursuit.

By any ordinary standards of evidence, the probability that something was in the air over Suffolk that night must be rated very high. Its scope presentation was strong and consistent, comparable to that of an aircraft, according to both USAF and RAF sources, and correlating returns on radar scopes of different characteristics many miles apart rule out any other currently available theory. The same very singular sequence of manoeuvres was watched on these radars, perfectly matching the simultaneous experience of the intercepting aircrew. Every significant aspect of the case so far investigated is consistent with the reality of the UFO, and it is impressive that this consistent picture emerges as the confluence of independent and corroborative sources of testimony. This corroboration exists *in spite of* what they themselves might feel to be fundamental *disagreement* on certain issues, and their testimony is supported with quite remarkable exactness by contemporary documents of which neither had any knowledge.

After twenty years of study and debate, no serious doubts have been cast on the credibility of this case; on the contrary, new information has increased its significance very considerably, and Thayer's 1968 conclusion now seems more apt than ever: 'The apparently rational, intelligent behaviour of the UFO suggests a mechanical device of unknown origin as the most probable explanation of this sighting.'[2] In a purely logical way this conclusion ought to be easy to accept. But the astonishing implications of accepting it, as well as the courage needed to accept it, may for a long while to come remain beyond our grasp.

THE LEGEND OF THE CRASHED SAUCERS

Andy Roberts

The belief that some governments have in their possession at least one crashed UFO is a prevalent one amongst many contemporary UFO researchers. A typical crash-retrieval scenario is this: a UFO crash-lands, invariably in a remote desert or mountain area. It and its alien crew are immediately recovered by government forces and taken off to an air base for study. Any civilian witnesses are silenced with threats or appeals to their patriotism. The crashed UFO is then held at the air base, rumours of its retrieval, arrival and study periodically leaking out to ufologists via sources which are almost always unavailable for checking.

The study of UFOs is full of far-fetched stories, hoaxes and unsubstantiated facts, and the crash/retrieval accounts contain elements of all three and are amongst the most bizarre of all. The very idea of crash/retrievals reads like science fiction.

The crash/retrieval story really begins in the last century. As with most of the components of ufology, crash/retrievals have a history which long predates the 1947 origin of the modern UFO era.

One of the very first accounts dealing with the retrieval of a UFO comes from 1884; it was reported that four cowboys had witnessed the crash of a cylindrical object in Nebraska. They allegedly found pieces of machinery and cog wheels which were glowing with heat. Thirteen years later there is a more detailed but no less fantastic account from Aurora, Texas which took place during the great airship wave of 1897. On 17 April 1897 an airship was seen to pass over the small Texas town of Aurora. It was travelling slowly and losing altitude, eventually crashing into a windmill, scattering wreckage over a wide area. Upon inspection by the citizens of Aurora it was found that the airship was constructed of an unknown metal resembling aluminium or silver, which proved very strong. Paper was also found, upon which undecipher-able heiroglyphics were drawn. Most significant, in the light of the post-1947 crashes, was the fact that a pilot was discovered amongst the wreckage and was identified by a US Army signals officer as being a 'Martian'. The 'Martian' was duly buried in Aurora's cemetery and the Aurora incident went down in UFO legend, featuring in several books about the UFO phenomenon.

Both these incidents have been subsequently proved to have been hoaxes, two of the many perpetrated by bored wireless telegraphers and journalists of the time, spreading 'tall tales' via the fast spreading communications network. Hoaxes or not they are significant precursors of the modern crash/retrieval accounts.

Within one month of the famous Kenneth Arnold sighting of 1947 it was claimed that the US military had recovered a crashed flying saucer. With the Roswell Incident the contemporary crash-retrieval tale was born.

The Roswell Incident has been the subject of a book and numerous magazine articles and has received a great deal of in-depth research. Although this has produced no physical evidence of any kind its proponents contend there is enough strong circumstantial evidence to suggest that the crash and subsequent retrieval of a 'flying saucer' did happen.

The events which took place at Roswell may have begun on 2 July 1947 when a bright disc-shaped object was observed passing over Roswell to the north west. A violent storm was in progress and several people heard a loud bang which they attributed to an explosion, later connected with the crash of the UFO. The following morning the debris of an object was found seventy-five miles north west of Roswell, New Mexico, beginning a saga of events which continues to this day.

The wreckage was discovered by W 'Mac' Brazel, a local ranch manager, and his son and daughter. Due to the remoteness of the area the discovery was not reported to the authorities until a few days later, when Brazel went into Roswell for supplies. During this time the wreckage was seen and handled by several people who described it as looking like aluminium or lead foil and being unbreakable or undentable (although according to Brazel's son it could be wrinkled). Other portions of the wreckage consisted of small beams made of an unknown substance similar to balsa wood and covered with 'hieroglyphics'. In addition to this, witnesses described seeing parchment-like material, silk-like threads and a metallic black box with no apparent opening.

Brazel informed Roswell's Sheriff of his find, who in turn contacted Roswell Air Forces Base. Two intelligence officers, Marcel and Cavitt, undertook a preliminary investigation, recovering some of the wreckage. Marcel is alleged to have told Brazel at this time that the object was 'not made on this Earth'. This seemed to be corroborated when, after returning to Roswell, an official press statement was released stating that the wreckage of a crashed disc had been recovered by the Air Force. This statement was issued by the direct order of Roswell Air Base Commander Colonel William Blanchard and was featured in many of the world's newspapers, including the London *Times*. The wreckage was then loaded onto a B-29 and flown to Wright Field Air Base (now Wright-Patterson AFB) for investigation, with a stopover at the headquarters of the 8th Air Force at Fort Worth, Texas.

Upon its arrival at Fort Worth General Roger Ramey took charge of it and orders were issued to the B-29 personnel not to speak to anyone about the incident and another press release was issued. This contradicted the first one and said there had been a mistake and what had in fact been recovered was a wrecked weather balloon with a tin foil radar target attachment. The wreckage was then flown to Wright Field AFB under armed guard. A photograph was issued to the press picturing General Ramey with the wreckage of a weather balloon.

Meanwhile intelligence officer Marcel returned to Roswell, where Brazel was held incommunicado for almost a week as the site of the crash was cleared of all debris. As this was taking place a press wire announcement from Albuquerque giving details of the crash of a 'flying disc' was stopped by the transmission being interrupted, and the radio station concerned was warned not to broadcast that particular item. The press accepted the story that a crashed weather balloon had caused all the fuss and the incident was forgotten. For the time.

The Roswell incident has since entered UFO lore and remains, for the crashed saucer proponents, their best available evidence.

That an event took place is indisputable, even the USAF admit that. What is disputed is the nature of the object. Although belief in the reality of the Roswell retrieval is widespread, a few points bear inspection. The appearance of wreckage which was discovered and handled does seem to fit that of a balloon and radar weather target more than that of a 'flying disc'. Pieces of a foil-like substance, threads and thin balsa-like struts are all consistent with the construction of a weather balloon and target. As there is no flying saucer yet available for study it would be unwise to state that that type of material is or is not used in their construction. Secret balloon launches were taking place at that period and there seems no good reason to suspect anything other than a secret test object of balloon type was retrieved. The actions of the military in clearing the area meticulously and their treatment of Brazel, who later said he was surprised at the fuss created over the incident, would seem in line with the testing of some type of secret device.

Whilst the Roswell incident cannot finally be proven true or false by ufologists the same cannot be said of the other major UFO crash/retrieval of the time, the Aztec case. This account came to light through a book written by newspaper columnist Frank Scully. In his 1950 book *Behind the Flying Saucers* he alleged that a flying saucer had crashed on a remote desert plateau to the east of Aztec, New Mexico. The saucer, he alleged, was ninety-nine feet in diameter and contained the bodies of sixteen dead aliens. Scully had not seen the crashed disc himself but was relying on accounts given to him by two men, Silas Newton and Leo Ge Baur, also known as 'Dr Gee'. The book became a bestseller despite the fact that no factual evidence was brought forward to support Scully's claims. Two years after the book's publication the story was discounted as a hoax in an article in *True* magazine written by investigative reporter J P Cahn. Cahn exposed Newton and Gee as skilled and convicted confidence tricksters. The story of the Aztec crashed disc was a combination of opportunism on Newton's part coupled with Scully's credibility and both of the men's desire to make money. There were also connections with film makers in Hollywood and the Aztec story has undoubtedly been the base from which many of the current crash/retrieval stories have spread throughout the years. From the Aztec/Scully case it is apparent that even in 1949, when Scully first heard of the crash, there was a well known set of details in circulation describing the circumstances relating to a hypothetical crashed UFO. Whether this narrative stemmed from the Roswell accounts or, more likely, from a combination of the Roswell case and the earlier nineteenth-century hoaxes, it is obvious that a myth was in the making.

One of the stories most frequently encountered in 'crash-retrievals' is that of the 'pickled alien'. Several of Stringfield and Moore's (the two leading US crash/retrieval researchers) informants have given accounts that aliens recovered from the crashed discs were taken to various US Air Force Bases for storage and study. Quite a few of these accounts mention that the bodies are stored either on ice or in 'pickle jars' to preserve them. The Air Force base most often referred to in these accounts is Wright Patterson AFB, whither the debris from the Roswell crash was destined. If the crash/retrieval accounts were true then Wright-Patterson would appear to be the main centre for the collection of extraterrestrial debris and bodies in the USA, with at least sixteen aliens and three UFOs being stored there. Supporters of the crash-retrieval syndrome back this up by the fact that US Senator Barry Goldwater, who has an interest in the crash/retrieval accounts, attempted to gain access to the room at Wright Patterson Airbase where some of these bodies are allegedly stored but was denied access on security grounds.

A further embellishment to the crash/retrieval syndrome is the photographs of dead aliens which are produced from time to time. Of the three most widely featured in the UFO literature one has been proved to have been an April Fools' joke in a German newspaper and another is obviously the remains of a dead airman, spectacle frames being clearly visible. Although the third photograph, which shows the 'alien' being held between two men has yet to be proved or disproved, a Swedish UFO magazine shows how it could be the retouched photograph of a baby in a pram and others have suggested it is the corpse of a monkey used in rocket tests — both more realistic explanations than that of an alien corpse. It is noteworthy that there are no photographs which purport to be of crashed saucers, no doubt because they would easily be discounted as fakes, being complex to stage.

As the crash/retrieval accounts have proliferated claims have also been made that aliens have on a few occasions been recovered alive from crashed saucers but have died shortly afterwards. In one instance it has been alleged that a unit of the US armed forces engaged a group of aliens in combat in the years 1966-8, resulting in the live capture of one alien. The alien put up a struggle and was sedated, which unfortunately led to its death. This capture of a live alien which subsequently dies of terrestrial causes occurs in at least three contemporary crash/retrieval accounts including one from the Soviet Union where an unfortunate alien infant is said to have died of a disease contracted after it was rescued.

Physical evidence not being forthcoming and the Aztec case being easily discredited, very little research into crashed discs was undertaken until the 1970s. This was probably due to the fact that most ufologists were not prepared to devote any time to the study of such a bizarre event and it was not until large numbers of UFO occupant and abduction accounts began to appear that UFO researchers considered the crashed saucer hypothesis worthy of attention. In the 1970s research and investigation into the possibility of there being crashed saucers and aliens in government custody was begun by various researchers which culminated in Leonard Stringfield's series of papers delivered to the MUFON Symposia, the book *The Roswell Incident* by Moore and Berlitz, and Moore's subsequent research papers. Stringfield, Moore and their colleagues have devoted a great deal of time and money to their research into crash/retrievals.

Besides the accounts themselves, the evidence for the veracity of crash/retrieval cases is slim especially if the hoaxing and contradictory nature of the Roswell and Aztec cases, together with the vagueness of the other crash/retrieval, is taken into consideration. At the same time, despite the lack of physical evidence there still remains a steady trickle of supposedly well placed military and government agency personnel who are coming forward and giving accounts of crash/retrievals to UFO researchers. Many of these accounts, from people who seem to have little knowledge of ufology, and of each other, corroborate. For instance, several of Stringfield's informants have given accounts of a crash-retrieval which took place in a desert area of Arizona in April/May 1953. The accounts in all cases are corroborative and suggest that *something* did really happen. One informant even produced his diary for that period in which he had noted he was going on a job the next day 'about which I cannot speak'.

In addition to this there have been several government documents which have been unearthed via the Freedom of Information act and other sources which, it is claimed, suggest that crash/retrievals have taken place. However, these are vague and as large portions of text have been censored one can only speculate at the type and quality of information which has been deleted. Contradictory statements can be found indicating a lack of interest in the whole UFO phenomenon, and not one of these documents refers unequivocally to the existence of a crashed disc or an alien corpse. A school of thought believes that this escalation in the release of documents pertaining to extraterrestrials is a part of what is known as the 'Education Programme' whereby we are being slowly fed more and more information, eventually leading up to the admission by our governments that we are not indeed alone in the Universe.

It is an article of faith amongst many UFO researchers that the US government is conducting a cover up and a conspiracy to keep the truth from the public. It is an interesting and, if true, disturbing idea, and one which deserves some examination. But it is here that, combined with others factors, the many flaws in the crash/retrieval hypothesis begin to appear.

If a conspiracy of silence about crash/retrievals is in operation then it must be a very good one. To work effectively a conspiracy must be restricted to a very small group of people. Clearly with crash/retrievals this cannot be the case. The number of people who must have had at least first hand dealings with the crashed discs and their occupants is enormous. Even the elite 'Blue Beret' unit which is alleged to perform the actual recovery and guarding of the discs must have had hundreds of men pass through its ranks since 1947. In addition to this there is the vast array of scientists and professionals who would be needed to conduct study on both saucers and aliens. At a higher level there are a number of US government officials and several Presidents. If the bodies and craft of extraterrestrials really were being held then surely no amount of threats and coercion could prevent a large proportion of these people from telling their family, friends and colleagues, who would in turn inform others. Furthermore, it is highly likely that, with so many people closely involved, some artefact of unquestionable extraterrestrial origin or an unambiguous photograph of craft or occupants would have come to light.

In addition to the above it is worth noting that despite the many UFO books and magazines which have appeared over the years 'exposing' the crash/retrieval syndrome, no government or its agencies has ever yet attempted to prevent the 'truth' getting out. Contrast this with the petty squabbles which take place between governments whenever some ex-agent threatens to reveal all about MI5 or the CIA in their memoirs, (none of which incidentally mention crashed saucers!).

Perhaps the greatest argument for the non-existence of crash/retrievals is this: If any government on Earth really were in the long-term possession and knowledge of an alien technological device and alien biology, whichever government had access to this information would have by now managed to use at least some of it in its defence. This has patently not occurred. No world government has displayed any aspect of technology which can be said to have come from the study of an alien craft or its occupants.

Seen in a wider context, the similarities between accounts of contemporary and nineteenth-century crashes are remarkable. (1) In both cases the crashed object is described in terms of the futuristic aeroforms of the time, many of which had been described in science fiction stories. Airships for the nineteenth century, flying discs for the twentieth. (2) Occupants are present in both sets of accounts. The 'pilot' found in the Aurora crash was alleged to be from the planet Mars, whereas nowadays the visiting aliens always come from a far galaxy if not another dimension. (3) Incredibly strong aluminium-like material and strange heiroglyphics are present in both the Aurora crash and many of the contemporary accounts including Roswell, Aztec and others.

All the nineteenth-century crashes have been determined to have been hoaxes and yet they contain numerous features found in the allegedly true modern retrievals. The inference is obvious.

Why, then, do these crash/retrieval stories originate and spread and why do they appear to be backed up with documentary proof? Besides hoaxes there are several possible explanations.

One possible reason is that of a long-term intelligence exercise. It makes sense that the intelligence agencies of the US and other governments would seize on the opportunities that the UFO age offers. It is a simple task to manipulate a myth such as that which the UFO affords to create belief amongst a group of people who in turn inform the public. This has happened with respect to UFOs in the Soviet union where information was fed to ufologists stating that several secret space and military launches were in fact UFOs. The benefits of this type of operation are obvious. The CIA, or whoever, observe the reactions of military personnel when confronted with a 'truth' such as that of crash/retrievals and in turn the reactions and attitudes of the American people. Also crash/retrievals also give the opportunity to cover up embarrassing secret military tests which go wrong. On this point it is worth noting that most of the alleged crash/retrievals take place in the south-western states of the USA, close to sites where secret weaponry, air and spacecraft are tested. Elements of this theory in action can be seen in the 1980 Rendlesham forest affair, Britain's own supposed crash/retrieval, where witnesses came forward stating they had seen a flying saucer in an underground room at RAF Bentwaters. Jenny Randles, who has thoroughly investigated the case, suggests that this misinformation trail has been laid to cover up a terrestrial event. Investigation is continuing, although as with all the other crash/retrieval accounts, no physical evidence is forthcoming.

This 'intelligence hypothesis' could also account for exactly why documents have been revealed indicating the reality of crash/retrievals. This scenario would require a minuscule number of people to carry it out, even over a number of years: the UFO community would act as unwitting dupes, fuelling the confusion which already surrounds the subject.

A further and complementary explanation is that they are contemporary folklore. The way in which the accounts of the crash and retrieval of aerial objects has developed and spread is seen by some researchers as fulfilling all the requirements of a folktale. In line with older folklore accounts the crashed saucer stories are largely based on rumour and verbal transmission, different versions of the same unsubstantiated story occur and the accounts are usually anonymous. To add to this we already know that some of the crash/retrievals at least are hoaxes on which future stories will have been based. This type of folktale is self-perpetuating, helped in its development by the beliefs of the UFO researchers, the sensationalism of the media and the false information fed by the intelligence services.

The crash/retrieval syndrome has, as yet, no one satisfactory explanation. As far as its proponents are concerned it can never be disproved, only proved, and the longer governments refuse to admit to possession of a crashed UFO the more the cry of 'cover-up' is heard. However, as with so much of ufology, there remains an unresolvable dichotomy between the event as reported and the tangible evidence available, and this can and should lead researchers to be highly sceptical.

THE DEVELOPMENT OF UFO OCCUPANTS

Peter Hough

Reports of 'entities' or 'occupants' sighted in or near anomalous craft, and accounts of contact with and abduction by alien beings, form the High Strangeness band of the UFO Spectrum.

A newcomer to the subject might logically assume that interaction with these occupants would be the key to explaining the UFO enigma. A guided tour around a UFO would be even better. The occupants could be asked who they were, where they came from, and what their purpose was.

In practice, it doesn't work out like that. A newcomer to ufology would study case report after report where people have allegedly sighted occupants, communicated with them (often telepathically), and sometimes been snatched from their motor cars for physical and psychological testing. From this study he would come away more confused than enlightened.

There is an almost total lack of *consistency* in reports of alleged contact. Occupants are variously described as tall, small, thin, fat, human-like, grotesque, saintly, covered in fur, hairless, with long arms, short arms, hands, claws, large heads, headless, friendly, indifferent, aggressive, appear 'solid', able to pass through walls, levitate ... and that is before we even consider the multitude of conflicting pieces of information the occupants impart to their human contacts.

On 3 September 1976, at nine pm, two women, one aged eighteen, the other sixty-three, were walking past waste land in the mining village of Fencehouses, County Durham.[1] A strange object sitting atop a mound of earth caused them to stop. It was five foot long and three and a half high, oval shaped with an orange dome, the entire object seated on runners similar to those on a sleigh.

The women seemed to enter a state of altered consciousness as they were drawn closer to the thing. All exterior sound diminished. Then they were startled by the appearance of two strange entities; eighteen inches tall, with long white hair parted in the middle, framing eyes much larger than those of a human. In fright the women closed their eyes, the occupants entered the UFO which then took off, making a humming sound.

UFO researcher Coral Lorenzen reports a sighting made by a woman friend which occurred in early June 1960. Here is an extract from the witnesses' verbatim account.[2]

'Joe, I and the two children were on our way to California. It was about midnight and we were about fifteen miles east of Glebe, Arizona, heading west. Joe was asleep beside me and the kids were fast asleep. I was driving through hills through which the road winds and drops.

At about twelve fifteen I began pulling round a right turn and when I straightened out, my headlights hit a small figure about one hundred yards away on the right edge of the highway. My immediate reaction was to let up on the accelerator, and the heavy car slowed immediately as we were on an upgrade. Simultaneously, the figure turned and ran off into the brush out of range of my lights and off the road.

The second I saw that thing my heart came up in my mouth and my stomach turned a flip-flop. I called out to Joe and he sat bolt upright. Then I told him what I had seen: The little figure, no more than twice the height of the posts which held the metallic reflecting roadguards (about three feet the thing was) was small, broad-shouldered, with long arms, dark in colour, and it had a head shaped somewhat like a flattened ball – almost like a pumpkin. In this head were two yellowish-orange glowing "eyes". I recall that when it was in side view, there was a light beaming out beyond the face. I saw no nose, or mouth or eyes. The body was not as well defined as the head, and I got the impression of hair, or fur.'

Lorenzen compares this entity to other creatures described in Venezuela, conjecturing that although in this instance no craft was seen, it was still a bona fide UFO occupant.

A case which did include the sighting of a structured disc, and the abduction of three adults and two children, occurred along an isolated road in Oxfordshire on 19 June 1978.[3] Typically, the family remembered seeing the UFO, but little else, until they noticed a time lapse and the manifestation of strange dreams. Hypnotic regression uncovered a story notable for its triteness and banality. But of interest here is the description of the aliens – because that was what the occupants claimed they were – extraterrestrial refugees from a dead planet.

One of the children, Natasha, described a small goblin type creature with large ears, but the others were dealt with by fairly normal looking humanoid entities – not too surprising, as they claimed to originate on Earth in the first place. They were tall, the men at least six foot, fair with blue eyes. One of them styled his hair in a crew cut with short sideboards. All wore close-fitting silver suits and black shoes. Their only non-human attribute were larger than normal ears.

In the 1955 Kelly-Hopkinsville landing, a family shot at several entities about four feet tall. They had elephantine ears, large slit-like mouths, and long arms ending in claws. They were also able to 'float', remain unaffected by shotgun fire and seemed to possess a macabre sense of humour.

On the night of 16 November 1963, two courting couples received a terrible fright near Sandling Park, Saltwood, Kent, which had nothing to do with their own nocturnal activities. After observing an oval-shaped 'star' descend then hover near some trees, they described a human-sized black figure, headless, with webbed feet and wings like a bat, coming towards them.

This 'monster' report had been compared to the 'Mothmen' sightings of West Virginia during the 1960s.[4] People claimed to have experienced a nightmarish entity variously described as brown, grey, headless, glowing red eyes, as tall as a man, one was 'about as big as a Piper Club aeroplane'. Incongruously, most of these Mothmen did not use their wings in flight.

There are also occupants who fit a subservient robot-type role, seemingly programmed to carry out specific tasks and no more. Indeed it has been speculated that some of the monsters cited above are biological constructs sent out from UFOs to scare away the natives from the landing sites, though they would be more likely to attract attention to the landed object.

These hundreds of conflicting descriptions weigh heavily against the supposition that many UFOs are space craft piloted by extraterrestrial visitors. For this would imply that Earth is some sort of Galactic Mecca for hundreds of different space travelling civilizations. Yet it is the occupants themselves who encourage this unlikely myth, with alleged messages on the lines of: 'We are aliens from planet X, friendly and concerned for the well being of your world. Stop tinkering with nuclear energy before it is too late ...'

During the alleged abduction of the Day family an alien named 'Uxiaulia' claimed to be one of ten million refugees fleeing from their home planet of 'Janos' which had been destroyed by debris from a disintegrating moon which set off a chain of nuclear explosions after a power station was accidentally hit.

The 'Janos people', currently in orbit around the solar system, await a time when coexistence with ourselves might be possible. One condition would have to be our discardment of nuclear toys. George Adamski's blond-haired Venusians were similarly concerned over nuclear power in the 1950s.[5]

During the spring of 1964, a Mrs Lainchbury was disturbed during the night by an orange glow illuminating her bedroom. Through the window she saw a bright sphere *silently* explode 'into a million pieces'. Shortly afterwards she heard voices in the darkness of the back garden, which looked out over fields, speaking in an unknown language.

Two months after this experience an occupant appeared in her bedroom. Humanoid, about five foot tall, it was wearing a suit covered in grey circular rings. It informed the elderly woman it was from the 'ship' she had seen explode, and was now stranded on Earth, awaiting rescue.

On a second occasion three figures materialized. She asked where they came from, and several letters formed in the air, spelling PLUTO. She consulted a book and discovered it was the ninth planet of the solar system, also the Greek god of the underworld.

All these occupants seem to be ignorant of one another. Another strange thing is that as our own space explorations have shown our planetary neighbours to be inhospitable places for life as we know it, so the occupants who used to say they came from Venus, Mars etc, now claim home worlds in as yet unexplored areas of the galaxy.

It would be dogmatic to rule out the 'occupants' as 'space aliens' theory absolutely, but an objective look at the evidence hardly points in that direction.

Yet, the United States, mother of the term 'flying saucer', brimming with contact stories when this aspect of the subject was virtually unknown in Britain, never really has let go of its belief in the extraterrestrial theory. While researchers here have been examining ancient legends and folklore, psychological and sociological ramifications, the Americans have stood firmly by the side of ET. Testimony which does not fit is often ignored or dismissed.

Veteran ufologist Walt Andrus, director of the Mutual UFO Network, announced in 1987 that after studying 'thousands of cases' the organization had concluded there were just four types of alien visiting the Earth; the small humanoid, the experimental animal, the human-like entity and the robot. Precise physical descriptions were given for each of these categories.

These four categories might be acceptable as rough guidelines of description, although the appendages 'experimental' and 'robot' should be dropped in the interests of objectivity. But as we have seen, there are very many variations; to select only four as some sort of yardstick is scientifically illegitimate and useless in practice.

The most recent development, seen most clearly in the United States, is that researchers have vectored their attention onto just *one* category of alien – a small being, usually under five foot, with emaciated arms and legs, bulbous head, minuscule nose and mouth, earless, hairless, with large black almond-shaped wrap-around eyes. Interestingly, this occupant crops up especially in cases where hypnotic retrieval methods are used.

Betty and Barney Hill were driving back from Canada over the border into the USA on 19 September 1961, when their car was ambushed and they were forcibly taken aboard a UFO for examination.[6] Under hypnosis, the Hills' described their abductors as about five foot tall (although significantly, perhaps, the 'leader' and the 'doctor' were taller). Betty described the head shape as 'mongoloid' – round face and prominent forehead – hairless with blue/grey skin.

They had deeper chest cavities and larger chests than is found in humans.

In the 1975 Travis Walton affair, a young Arizonian forestry worker was allegedly abducted in front of six colleagues in Sitgreaves National Forest.[7] Walton reappeared six days later and described occupants less than five foot, pale, with large domed heads, enormous eyes, small noses, mouth and ears. Their bodies seemed very emaciated. Ambiguously, four normal looking humanoids were also described by Walton.

A similar description was obtained from Betty Andreasson in 1977, South Ashburnham, Massachusetts.[8] The occupants who entered her home were three and a half feet tall, with pear-shaped heads – broad at the forehead and narrow towards the chin. The nose was reduced to two small holes, and the mouth a simple horizontal slit.

Researcher Budd Hopkins has many similar descriptions gleaned from witnesses under hypnosis. The latest of these was fantasy writer Whitley Strieber, who recounts his experiences in his 1987 book, *Communion*.[9]

Strieber believes that during his life he has been contacted and abducted by 'non-human beings' for experimental purposes. He describes his captors as being small, with large domed heads and black almond-shaped eyes. He received the impression that individually these beings were afraid of him because of his physical superior strength.

To his credit, Strieber has shunned attempts by the media to force him to go along with the idea he was abducted by 'extraterrestrials' and taken on board a 'space ship'. He cannot go along with this *because he does not know*. However, a large number of American ufologists are confident this case *is* a further example of extraterrestrial intervention. Even those who strayed from the fold for a while in the 1970s, dabbling with a broader paranormal answer, have come back to ET.

These domed-headed, large-eyed, emaciated occupants look almost like the human foetus. This 'coincidence' is surely too close to be ignored, suggesting that deep psychological overtones are at work. Could it be that 'the Phenomenon' has found this occupant type to be the most effective in North American society?

In sceptical Britain, however, the formula is not proving successful if 'the Phenomenon' exists it is now in disarray, perhaps in the process of regrouping for another assault on our perceptions with a different 'image', a rewritten script. Both our psychological and sociological beliefs affect how 'the Phenomenon' is perceived.

Prior to the present 'space age', for example, they masqueraded as creatures suiting the expectations and technological status of the era. When, during the pre-World War I era, from around 1880 to 1913, America and Britain were plagued by sightings of phantom airships, the occupants were perfectly normal looking men and women, wearing clothes compatible with those times. Often they claimed to be 'secret inventors' or military adventurists.

Researcher Jacques Vallee uses the 1961 Eagle River case to make a historical comparison. Joe Simonton, a sixty-year-old chicken farmer, discovered a saucer-shaped object hovering outside his home.[10] Three men were inside 'resembling Italians'. They were five foot tall with dark hair and skin, wearing blue knitted outfits styled with turtle neck tops and knitted helmets.

One was cooking on 'a flameless grill of some sort', and after expressing an interest in food, Joe was given three small flat cakes. At their request, and in return, Joe gave them a jug of water.

Two of the cakes were tested in the Food and Drug laboratory of the US Department of Health, Education and Welfare, at the request of the USAF. The cakes contained terrestrial ingredients but, surprisingly, lacked salt.

Vallee points out that during encounters with fairy folk, small cakes were often said to be exchanged for water, and the 'Gentry' could not abide salt, as apparently neither could Joe Simonton's alien visitors.

American author Evans Wentz quotes a Manx witness: 'There are as many kinds of fairies as populations in our world. I have seen some who were about two and a half feet high, and some who were as big as we are.'[11]

T C Kermode, member of the Manx Parliament, related to Wentz a personal experience:

'One October night, I and another young man were going to a kind of harvest-home. My friend happened to look across the river and said: "Oh, look, there are the fairies." I looked across and saw a circle of supernatural light, in which spirits became visible. The spot where the light appeared was a flat space surrounded on the side away from the river by banks formed by low hills; and in this space around the circle of light, I saw come in twos and threes a great crowd of little beings. All of them, who appeared like soldiers, were dressed in red. they moved back and forth amid the circle of light, as they formed into order like troops drilling.'

Wentz was also told the following by what today we would term a 'contactee':

'They are able to appear in different forms. One once appeared to me and seemed only four feet high and stoutly built. He said, "I am bigger than I appear now. We can make the old young, the big small, the small big".'

In short, the Gentry could appear in any manner of appearance or size, exactly like today's UFO occupants.

In the last forty years or so, UFOs and their occupants have developed in the public consciousness as being synonymous with space craft and extraterrestrial aliens. The occupants themselves encourage this assumption, to great effect still in the USA, perhaps the last bastion of the extraterrestrial hypothesis. But are the occupants the fairy folk of yesteryear? Are modern abductees no different to the People Evans Wentz heard about who were taken to Magonia, where time ran at a different rate to the world of men?

If the entire business is an as yet inexplicable relationship between human psychological processes then it makes sense that occasionally the mask might slip, and a confusing demonstration of mixed metaphors be displayed.

In Pernambuco, Brazil, a saucer-shaped object was seen flying over the area on 26 October 1965. At about noon, Jose Camilho, a mechanic of good repute, was passing along a road through a belt of scrubland, when he saw two small people sitting like children on the stump of a fallen banana tree.

As he approached, they jumped to their feet, and he saw they were less than three foot tall, with shrivelled brown faces, white hair, round disproportionately large heads, and slitted oriental eyes. One had a sparse beard and wore a dark peaked cap. Camilho noticed one of them carried a rod-shaped object and 'looked so astonished it seemed his eyes would leap from their sockets', then indicated to the Brazilian it was a weapon of some sort.

The second entity was much calmer and wore shirt, trousers and footwear similar to tennis shoes; the most astonishing feature was a luminous belt, featuring an array of bright flashing lights. Between the little 'men' stood a cylinder as tall as them. The entity with the flashing lights staggered off with it, comically colliding with his nervous companion, almost falling to the ground.

Colleague Arthur Tomlinson helped me investigate another curious encounter again suggesting mixed metaphors.

Canteen assistant Mary Kent, lived on a Lancashire

council estate surrounded by hills of reclaimed land seeded with grass, bushes and trees. On a May morning, Mrs Kent decided to visit her daughter's house, just a short distance away, before she went to work.

It was six fifteen, quiet, bright and sunny, as she walked along the only road at the edge of the estate. Suddenly she stopped. There was a figure staring intensely down at her just beneath the brow of a nearby hill. Although it resembled a man, there was something very peculiar about his clothes, and his unnatural unmoving posture transmitted a feeling of intimidation.

'He' was wearing a one-piece silver suit with a cloak tied at the neck, and raised pointed lapels. On his head sat a cone-shaped hat, and boots were just visible above the line of the grass. Then something else took her attention away.

To the right, and behind the figure, stood a large silver spherical object which cast a bright beam of light down the hillside.

Numbed, Mrs Kent hurried on to her daughter's house but said nothing. On her return, a few minutes later, the phenomena were still there, so she took a different route back to her house. 'Just in case', she told us 'he might have seen where I lived'. There was nothing on the hill when she turned out for her bus at six forty-five.

What on Earth was an 'elf' doing standing beside a 'space ship'? What are 'gnomes' doing in Brazil, wearing 'space age' garb and carrying 'futuristic' artefacts? Did someone slip up sorting through the costume chest? Was the Phenomenon trying to show us that 'fairies' and 'extraterrestrials' are one and the same thing. Or is it all part of some gigantic cosmic joke of which we are barely just aware.

At the heart of this box of perpetual conjuring tricks, we seem to have a phenomenon which is truly alien – perhaps *totally* beyond our means of comprehension. The occupants are on the front line; sometimes comical, sometimes serious, sometimes benevolent, sometimes uncaring, sometimes sinister, but always outrageous, because to our computerized and regimented way of thinking, in the final analysis, it all appears insane …

Across the entire spectrum of entity/occupant manifestations, including the ancient gods, angels, apparitions, spirit entities, fairies and ufonauts, we seem to be dealing with the same phenomenon; a huge confidence trick on a grand theatrical scale.

THE CONTACTEE ERA

Dennis Stacy

Probably ninety-five per cent or more of all UFO reports have been transient atmospheric events that involved a handful of people at best, and more often than not only one or two eye-witnesses. But for the first few years of their post-Arnold existence they were rarely seen up close or on the ground. Rarer still were those instances in which someone claimed to have actually seen or encountered occupants in association with a landed UFO.

There are two ways of looking at what happened next: either the UFO evolved from a passive phenomenon to an interactive one, or, given human nature, it was inevitable that someone, somewhere, sooner or later, would claim contact with the alien beings aboard a flying saucer. The dubious distinction fell to a Polish immigrant George Adamski (1891-1965). Despite the lack of a formal education, Adamski seems to have been entirely self-sufficient and perhaps a little charismatic. After a couple of duty tours in the Army, he eventually settled in southern California around the time of the Great Depression. At some point he began promoting himself as 'Professor' G Adamski, an authority on Eastern esoteric religion and author of a sixty seven-page pamphlet 'Questions and Answers by the Royal Order of Tibet'. By 1944, he was living on the southern slopes of Mount Palomar, seven miles from the Hale Observatory, home of a 200-inch telescope that was the world's largest. Whether deliberate or merely fortuitous, this association with the frontiers of space science seemed to have weighed heavily in Adamski's favour. Two years later he had written a science-fiction novel, *Pioneers in Space*. Neither of his literary works paid the bills; for that Adamski worked in what one UFO historian described as 'a four stool cafe', flipping hamburger patties.

According to *Flying Saucers Have Landed* (1953), coauthored with the English writer Desmond Leslie, Adamski saw his first saucer on October 1946, almost a year before Arnold. In August 1947, on a single night, Adamski watched starstruck as a stream of saucers – a total of 184 by his count – streaked overhead. Not surprisingly, since he was seemingly acting like a lodestone for such things, Adamski began trying to photograph the objects. By 1953, he had logged some 700 tries, a record that would stand for almost thirty years, until superseded by Eduard 'Billy' Meier of Switzerland. Meier, with only one arm, boasts that many *good* pictures. Adamski using both hands, could manage but a meagre eighteen good ones. Still, they sufficed. By then Adamski was on the burgeoning UFO lecture circuit, selling copies of his prints, and publishing articles in *Fate* magazine. But better things lay ahead.

Near Desert Centre, California, on Thursday, 20 November 1952, in the company of six other witnesses, including the late and enigmatic George Hunt Williamson, Adamski claimed contact with beings from beyond. First, a large, cigar-shaped craft hovered overhead before sailing out of sight behind nearby mountains. Then came a 'flash in the sky' which resolved itself into a 'beautiful small craft'. The second ship also disappeared in the mountains. Adamski next saw a figure approximately 500 feet away, which waved him on. Approaching alone, he encountered a 'man' with long, blond hair who stood about five foot six inches tall, and weighed about 135 pounds. Dressed in a chocolate-brown uniform of glossy material with no visible zippers, seams or pockets, he appeared to be in his late twenties. 'The beauty of this form', Adamski said, 'surpassed anything I had ever seen ... [I] felt like a child in the presence of one with great wisdom and much love.' Adamski's visitor, who communicated both telepathically and by means of sign language, turned out to be from Venus. He indicated he and his people were concerned 'with radiation going out from Earth', a fallout of our nuclear weapons testing.

Although not allowed to photograph the Venusian himself Adamski was free to take pictures, both inside and out, of the space ship. The visitor even borrowed a roll of film after promising to return it later. Adamski's photographic bad luck held; one camera was out of focus, while the other malfunctioned, leaving him with but a single, blurry shot.

Near the end of their conversation the Venusian informed Adamski that others of his kind lived among us, disguised as human beings. Adamski asked if they ever abducted humans, to which his extraterrestrial interlocutor only 'smiled broadly,' stepped into his space ship and flew away, leaving behind only his footprints in the desert sands.

Already a success on the saucer circuit, Adamski became somewhat of a national celebrity following the publication, in 1955, of his second book, *Inside the Space Ships*, in which he told of further contacts and adventures with benevolent beings from above. Since they so closely resembled us in appearance, Adamski simply met them in the various Los Angeles bars and cafes they frequented ('haunted' hardly seems the word) before being whisked away to the rest of the inhabited planets of the solar system via flying saucer. Given the galaxy of beings he eventually met this way, including Martians, Saturnians and Jupiterians, perhaps it was just as well Adamski was such a poor photographer. Pictures would only have detracted from the tales he had to tell about our 'space brothers' and their reasons for being here. Their elder philosopher he called simply 'the Master'. While space women served refreshments aboard the saucers, Adamski and the Master discussed the present condition of the Universe and Earth's somewhat perilous position in the scheme of things. Not only did our atomic and hydrogen bombs threaten to destroy the planet, they also threatened the others nearby. Their mission was to help us save ourselves from ourselves by spreading the message. Jesus had been such a messenger, and now Adamski himself had been selected to do the same task. The Master warned, however, that he must be prepared to face the ridicule sure to follow such an announcement.

Adamski seems to have handled the job with some alacrity. The author of two bestselling books, he went on a round of personal appearances, including both radio and television talk shows, and meeting with various other world celebrities, among them the Queen of the Netherlands and, rumour bruits it, the Pope, who bestowed a papal ring on the former Polish immigrant. The reasons for reviewing Adamski's chequered career at such length become apparent in any discussion of the larger themes that permeate the 'contact phenomenon'. In one way or another, he anticipated virtually all of them, from freewheeling rides aboard flying saucers, to near Apocalyptic warnings of man's meddling in the affairs of Nature, physically or spiritually.

First and foremost of the contactees, as they came to be called, Adamski was hardly the last. Indeed, a goodly number of his immediate contemporaries seemed to have recognized a cottage industry when they saw it. Bookstore shelves were soon sagging with the weight of similar tomes. The year 1954 saw the publication of both Truman Bethurum's *Aboard a Flying Saucer* and Daniel Fry's *White Sands Incident*, the former penned by a mechanic laying asphalt in the California (!) desert. Bethurum claimed he was awakened one night by 'about eight or ten small sized men ... from four feet eight inches to about five feet tall', well built, olive skinned and dressed in uniforms. Telepathy was unnecessary; the aliens, after a false start in a foreign tongue, spoke English perfectly.

Nearby hovered what Bethurum later learned was a 'scow', a classic, if huge, flying saucer some 300 feet in diameter and approximately eighteen feet thick. The platoon of little men invited him aboard to meet their female captain, Aura Rhanes, whom Bethurum thought 'tops in shapeliness and beauty'. Nothing interspecial happened, however. The two whiled away the hours until dawn, Aura enlightening Bethurum about the advanced society of her home planet, Clarion, perpetually hidden behind our moon. Clarion proved to be unsullied by disease, doctors, politicians or taxes, not to mention nuclear weapons. Mrs Rhanes (she was a grandmother) was also capable of passing for a human being. Truman met her once in a restaurant, sipping orange juice, but she ignored him.

Another desert locale features prominently in 'Dr' Daniel Fry's extraterrestrial escapades as well. While working at the White Sands Proving Ground, New Mexico, Fry saw a flying saucer land nearby. He approached and was about to reach out a hand, when a voice said, 'Better not touch the hull, pal, it's still hot!' No need for mental pyrotechnics here, either.

Fry's contact was named 'A-Lan', later shortened simply to Alan. He invited Fry aboard and flew him to New York City, the round trip taking less than half an hour. In flight, Alan asked Fry to pen a book about his experiences so that the world wouldn't fall into the 'terrible abyss' of a nuclear holocaust; the reason why he and his kind couldn't make the appeal in person was that the appearance of space people would upset the 'ego balance' of Earth's civilization. 'Understanding' among the Earth's peoples would solve most of our social and political ills.

In 1955, Orfeo Angelucci's *Secret of the Saucers* appeared, a book which at least returned the contact scene to its perhaps rightful origin – California, more specifically a remote field in Los Angeles. Angelucci's message was more blatantly spiritual than that of his predecessors; it also contained a prophecy with a specific deadline. His mentor, a self-described 'space brother', warned that 'material advancement' was threatening our evolution. Orfeo, too, seemed able to draw the saucers down with regularity. A few weeks later he spied another one and stepped on board for a ride. After the flight he was introduced to an ET named Neptune. They discussed the usual philosophical state of affairs and Angelucci underwent an experience akin to a mystical revelation, leaving him with a sense of fellowship with his new friends.

Subsequent meetings with the space brothers continued, often in public places, including cafes and a Greyhound bus station, the company slogan of which nowadays is 'Take the bus, and leave the driving to us!' One encounter was with Jesus Himself, who told Angelucci the incognito extraterrestrials were here to help us, adding 'this is the beginning of the New Age.' On another excursion he met the lovely Lyra and her boon companion Orion on their home planet. In another life, they explained, Angelucci had also been a space man named Neptune. Unless the Earth people worked together for their own good, they warned, a major catastrophe would befall the planet in 1986.

The fifth of the major contactees of the 1950s was self-employed sign painter Howard Menger of Brooklyn, New York. His family moved to New Jersey when he was eight, and there Menger saw his first flying saucer, in the company of his brother Alton. He was wandering in a wooded glade near his home, in 1932, when he encountered a beautiful, long-haired blonde girl, resting on a rock beside a crystal-clear brook. Through a sort of translucent ski-suit, Menger could make out the 'curves of her lovely body'. Moreover, 'a tremendous surge of warmth, love and physical attraction ... emanated from her to me'. She and her people, she explained, had 'come a long way' and 'we are contacting our own'. After a few more revelations of a general nature, she left, leaving young Menger weeping at the poignancy of it all.

Ten years later he graduated from high school and joined the Army. While stationed with a tank unit on manoeuvres in the desert south west (!) of the States, Menger began seeing saucers again. On a weekend pass in Juarez, across the border from El Paso, Texas, a taxi pulled alongside the strolling soldier. From the rear seat a deeply tanned man with longish blond hair said 'I have something to tell you, would you get in the cab?' Perhaps his parents had warned him about long-hairs. At any rate, Menger declined the offer, though he learned later from another contact that the man indeed was a space man, one who had been warned that he'd have to get a haircut if he hoped to go around meeting Earth people!

Menger's new informant told him many Mexicans were hip to the saucers and had been contacted 'long before the ... Conquistadores made contact with the Aztecs'. They had shared their secrets with many of the older Earth civilizations besides the Aztecs, but in every case the knowledge, including marvellous technology, had been lost in conquests by warlike creatures.

Stationed in Hawaii a short time later, Menger surrendered to an impulse and drove a borrowed jeep into the brush to some nearby caverns. There he met a dusky beauty done up in pink (translucent again) tunic and pants. She 'exuded the same expression of spiritual love and deep understanding [as the blonde on the rocks] ... but not without a strong physical attraction one finds impossible to allay when in the presence of these women'.

After the war ended, Menger returned to New Jersey and started his own sign painting company.

Another impulse drove him to revisit the scene of his first encounter. Disappointed at first, he was soon delighted when an immense, bell-shaped spaceship descended from the heavens, disgorging two attractive men, fair-skinned and blond, in ski-suits of a metallic colour, followed by his early temptress. 'But you are no older!' blurted Menger. 'Oh, but I am,' she cooed. 'Guess, Howard, how old I really am.' Menger could not. 'I'm more than five hundred years old,' she said.

Menger's numerous experiences with the space brothers and sisters, and they were legion, were recounted in *From Outer Space to You* (1959). Among other things he served as a sort of 'go-fer' for extraterrestrials of both sexes, going for this and going for that. One time he brought back a bundle of bras for a saucerful of girls. Tittering, they tossed them back out the door, saying they didn't wear such things where they came from. Other items on the ET shopping list included sunshades with red lenses. Apparently in exchange for his help (he also taught them English and cut their hair), the space people revealed the secrets of a 'free energy motor'. A photograph of Menger shows him holding the small device, consisting of a few ball-bearings attached by springs or arms to a central mechanism supported by a shaft passing through its middle.

From the late 1940s through to the early 1950s, the UFO phenomenon, for whatever reason, appeared uniquely American. Perhaps as the most technologically evolved nation on the face of the Earth, it logically attracted newcomers. Certainly any advanced intelligence with a modicum of surveillance and detection devices would have been attracted to the nuclear test explosions increasingly dotting the desert south west. (Within a year or two of World War II's end America's atomic bomb stockpile numbered 200. The first of the captured V-2 rockets were also shooting skyward, scaling new heights. Radio, radar and television waves were beaming into space. In terms of electromagnetic and newfangled nuclear technology activity, the United States was unambiguously 'where it's at'. Ravaged Europe was only beginning its remarkably fast-paced recovery).

The Land of Opportunity beckoned even on a cosmic scale. The roots of democracy, the natural if sometimes dinosaurlike enemy of class consciousness and tyranny, grew deep and spread wide. In a country where every young boy (or so went the myth) could aspire to the Presidency, they could just as easily be chosen as contacts by the envoys of a cosmic brotherhood (and *were*, apparently!). None of the five major American contactees – Adamski, Bethurum, Fry, Angelucci or Menger – boasted pretensions to class, culture or schooling. Adamski was apparently self-taught to some degree; the others, for the most part, came out of the massive manual labour force in America that had survived the war. Of course none of this prevented their hobnobbing with royalty and the Pope, as in the case of Adamski, when the occasion arose.

Even when a foreigner did enjoy extraterrestrial attention, the major pieces of his (or less frequently, her) make-up seemed cut from the same classless cotton. A case in point here being the career of George King, a former London taxi driver. In May 1954, while washing dishes in his unprepossessing flat, King heard a voice declare 'prepare yourself, you are to become the voice of Interplanetary Parliament'. King went on to found the Aetherius Society (named after his prime communicator of ethereal wisdom), slipping into public trances during which he acted as a medium for the incoming messages. His mother, Mary, also became involved, and the taxi driver did little to dissuade acolytes who drew any 'Mary, the Mother of King (Christ)' parallels. Eventually, however, King saw the light himself, moving the Society to southern California, where it probably properly belonged.

While it would not be proper to call the contactee

club a conspiracy, or even a close-knit coterie, they did come in casual contact with one another, either meeting at various saucer conventions, once the rage, or in the course of talk show appearances. As pies went, theirs was a relatively small one, but competition for its parts remained mostly crass-free. Adamski, by virtue of having been the 'firstest with the mostest', was awarded the lion's share and the topping. The others behaved, at least in public, like perfect gentlemen, often going so far as to support one another's claims in their writings.

Inexorably, the contactee craze had an effect not only on serious UFO research, but on the public perception of the phenomenon as well. So suspicious were the early civilian saucer groups of such claims that, for the most part, they refused to even consider cases in which a supposed UFO occupant, or humanoid, had been reported. The contactee stigma extended to include 'repeaters', too, people who had seen UFOs other than the one (no matter how reliable) they were reporting. In fact, the Repeater Syndrome is still often considered the kiss of death, especially among sceptics. And since debunkers employ it regularly to shoot down cases, as was done most recently with the Japanese 747 captain who reported a spectacular sighting over Alaska, UFO investigators tend to shy away from such stories. This tendency was also evident in the handling of Betty Hill, a celebrated abductee from the 1960s, who has since gone on to report a neverending series of UFOs at a New England 'landing site' near the scene of her original encounter and abduction.

For the contactees and their followers, the effects were even more pronounced. Cults grew up around most of the major figures (we have hardly touched on them all) not dissimilar to those surrounding the Eastern gurus of the 1970s and 1980s, and not to mention their earlier predecessors in this century. The reasons are not hard to fathom. Though their contacts hailed from the stars (well, the other planets in the solar system, actually), their concerns and subsequent preachings were decidedly human, if spiritual, in nature. Like their earthbound coreligionists, the space brothers were worried primarily about Good and Evil. Love and brotherhood, of course, fell into the former category, materialism, war and atomic bombs into the latter. By most accounts, citizens from the stars also worshipped the same God, and the same Son of God, we did. Women, be it noted, remained much the same objects of male fantasies they had always been, even when given to philosophical or spiritual rhapsodizing.

Putting oneself out on such a limb, as it were, entailed personal consequences, too. Menger, for example, divorced his wife after meeting an attractive woman named Marla while on a lecture tour. Although the fact was unbeknown to Marla herself, Menger immediately recognized her as a fellow space person and proposed (successfully). Most of the lifestyle changes, of course, involved their newfound status as cosmic celebrities, a role that Adamski in particular seems to have relished to the end. Menger started a mail order course based on the space people's teachings and King founded what amounted to an interplanetary ministry, replete with reams of spiritual transmissions. Menger took his friendly competition a step further; besides a second book, *The Carpenter Returns*, and the famous free energy motor, he also proffered up a 'Lunar potato', reportedly six times more protein potent than the terrestrial variety. Once, in an isolated cabin in the woods, he met a Saturnian inside, playing the piano. Returning home, Menger found he could play the same music and eventually released a commercial record album of same.

An unconscious, darker side surfaced in contactee literature and preachings, too. These heavenly gods, for such they were, were invariably clothed in the physical raiments of a fair, white skin, crowned with flowing blond hair. Conversely, their counterparts, the mysterious 'men in black', who reportedly intimidated UFO witnesses and some researchers, just as invariably had dark skin and Oriental features. It would take a Jungian analyst to weave archetypal sense out of all the contactee stories, but it becomes obvious that the unintentional undertones were both racial and Aryan in nature.

Had the complex of UFO phenomena as a whole remained static, the contactees and their devotees might be but an interesting sociological footnote. But, like the invisible Devil of Devonshire, events were afoot. During the 1954 wave of UFO sightings that struck France, a disproportionate number involved reports of humanoids seen either immediately beside or in close association with landed UFOs. Though the impact was hardly instantaneous, growing numbers of even the most serious and objective of UFO researchers were forced to pay lip service to, in retrospect, the logical notion that if flying saucers were extraterrestrial space craft, then obviously they were piloted by either (1) remote control, or (2) real, live extraterrestrials.

Unfortunately, the evidence from the French Wave was paradoxical and hardly as clear cut as ufologists could have hoped. Reports of accompanying figures fell into two broad categories: those that closely resembled human beings, and those that clearly did not. The latter group consisted predominantly of dwarf-like creatures, about three to four feet tall, usually clad in what looked like a deep sea diver's suit. Customarily, the little men were grey, not green, and their proportions somewhat resembled those of a foetus, with a large, bulging head looming above small shoulders. Eye-witnesses also remarked on the size of the alien dwarfs' eyes; they were quite a bit larger than what would have been expected. Nose, mouth, ears, when mentioned, were frequently vestigial, almost as if the facial features had been pencilled in by a clumsy cartoonist who could draw eyes but little else.

Begrudgingly, the humanoid cases were slowly accepted among the growing curiosities of the UFO canon. By the end of its first decade, the UFO phenomenon had evolved from distant nocturnal lights and daylight discs, as well as an occasional cigar and other odd shape, into apparent nuts'n'bolts, craft, glimpsed close up on the ground, and occupied by alien crew members. The reports also reached out democratically from America and Europe to encompass the rest of the world's nations. If the phenomenon was playing games, or something more serious, it was the only one laughing. Indeed, the image that comes to mind is that of Lewis Carroll's enigmatic Cheshire Cat, its sliver of a toothy grin hovering in the air like a mockery of our own increasingly advanced technology. Adamski, remember, had asked if Earthlings were ever kidnapped. His informant had only 'smiled broadly'. Soon, he would be grinning from ear to ear.

INVESTIGATING THE ABDUCTEES

Budd Hopkins

In the fall of 1966 *Look*, a popular American weekly magazine, carried a story by journalist John Fuller documenting the apparent 1961 abduction of Betty and Barney Hill, residents of Portsmouth, New Hampshire, by the occupants of a landed UFO. This article, a shortened version of the book *Interrupted Journey* that Fuller published later that year, marked the introduction to the general public of this type of bizarre report. It was read, argued about, attacked and defended, but it remains a watershed event in the history of our awareness of the UFO phenomenon as something intimately connected, for better or worse, with the human race. What the Hills described was a kind of involuntary seizure and forced physical examination, as it were, by small, grey-skinned beings who communicated with them telepathically; other accounts such as those involving police officer Herbert Schirmer and Brazilian farmer Antonio Villas Boas, were published in more marginally accessible places. But not until 1973 was the general public again aware of a vivid UFO abduction account – the Pascagoula, Mississippi, kidnapping of Charles Hickson and Calvin Parker. In this widely publicized event the terrified abductees described more mechanical appearing, more robot-like figures, but other details, such as the enforced 'physical examination' and the general time frame, seemed quite similar to the earlier cases.

In 1975, the Travis Walton abduction near Snowflake, Arizona, again put the issue back into the newspaper headlines, and thus into more general public awareness. Five of Walton's companions witnessed the initial moments of the encounter and shortly afterwards passed lie detector tests on the crucial detail of their having seen a UFO hovering a few yards away from Walton shortly before he disappeared. A few other abduction accounts from 1975 made this another watershed year, and from then on this type of account has appeared from time to time in the tabloids, though rarely in the more conservative press. Contrary to public perceptions, only one commercial movie has ever been made on the abduction phenomenon per se – a film version of John Fuller's book on the Betty and Barney Hill case, entitled *UFO Incident*. Despite literally hundreds of investigated UFO abduction reports, only a tiny handful have ever become well known, due largely to the general neglect of the subject by investigative reporters. A number of books of varying merit have been published on abduction cases, however, but few of these have had wide readership. Internationally, writers such as Charles Bowen, David Haisell, Cynthia Hind, Jenny Randles and Antonio Ribera have made valuable contributions to the subject. In the United States, most books on UFO abductions have tended to concentrate on single cases, such as Raymond Fowler's two studies of the Andreasson affair and those by Travis Walton, Ann Druffel and Scott Rogo, Charles Hickson, Bill Barry, Whitley Strieber and Ralph Blum. A key synthesizing account was Coral and Jim Lorenzen's 1977 *Abducted!*. In this important book the authors put together seven abduction reports and attempted to find parallels among them, an effort I have tried to continue in my own work.

In 1975 I had begun my own investigations into the

UFO phenomenon and by 1977 was concentrating my attention on abduction reports. Because of certain discoveries I made in the course of these investigations I felt that I should publicly present my findings. *Missing Time* was published in the spring of 1981. I have received hundreds of letters in response to my note at the end of the book requesting 'anyone who thinks he or she might have had such an experience to write to me in care of my publisher'. The case of a woman I shall call 'Angie' provides an example of such a response, and will serve as a typical abduction account. In 1983 when she first wrote to me, twenty-eight-year-old Angie was serving in the armed forces, and held – and still holds – a high security clearance. Her letter explained that she had lived in a rural area in the state of Pennsylvania, and had always loved to walk in the woods. However, at some point in the mid-1970s she began to be very frightened whenever she was alone there which she attributed to an unusual experience. In 1976 she saw a very large light hovering silently at tree-top height near her house. She alerted her father and her younger brother, and they all agreed that the object was not a police helicopter as they had assumed at first. While they watched in fascination, Angie blinked her flashlight several times at the glowing oval, and it flashed back in the same sequence. At this Angie's brother panicked and begged his father to take him back into the house. (He was too afraid to walk the hundred feet by himself.) The object then moved off, and a little later Angie's father also went back inside, leaving her alone, waiting to see what would happen next.

After a short while the object returned and once more hovered above the trees towards the back of their land:

'I walked to the edge of my property and just looked at it. I was sort of scared, especially since I was alone. All the wood's noises had stopped (or else I just quit hearing them). I remember that all the houses were dark, and I couldn't hear any traffic. I remember something about not being afraid. I don't recall if I heard it or was hoping the light wouldn't be. I don't remember if I shined my flashlight at them or not, but I seem to recall being really nervous when it looked like they were coming towards me. I remember a flash, and the next thing I knew I was running around the corner of our garage. Once I thought it was safe I peeked around the corner. I don't know if the light was gone or not. I went inside and everyone was in bed asleep, so I went to bed. I think it was after two am, but I'm not sure.

Angie added an interesting note. 'I also have this weird little scar on my left thigh ... It is round, almost perfectly round, about the size of a quarter. It feels different than the surrounding skin. I've asked both my parents if they can recall me ever receiving a wound there. They both say they don't remember a time when I was hurt there, and I don't either.' She closed her letter with a variation on a refrain I have read scores of times: 'Well, sir, that's about all I can give you without getting into a bunch of maybes or guesswork. I don't know if I'm more afraid of being ridiculed for this or of finding out that more happened than I thought.'

One of the fortunate aspects of this case is that Angie informed me, during a subsequent conversation, that she kept a diary. During a later trip back home she located some highly suggestive passages from three successive days. The 14 August 1976 entry describes her father, brother and herself sighting the object, and flashing her light at it. 'Chuck got scared and Dad took him in. I wasn't afraid. I even tried thinking at them. I chickened out and went in. I'm so tired! I'd like to read but I think I'll go to sleep. Got church tomorrow.' August 15: 'Skipped church today. Went to evening service. Mom asked about the UFO. Dad and Chuck helped tell about it. I told how I got scared and hid by the garage. Dad didn't laugh. He knew it wasn't anything Earthly ... Chuck was embarrassed by his being scared last night. We listened for anything on the news. I was going to go out again but I changed my mind ...' August 16: 'Had a bad headache today ...' August 17: '... Man, I can't sleep tonight! Wish there was a movie or something! I must have insomnia or something.' These diary entries implied that the UFO sighting had been quite important for Angie, and that her normal sleep habits had been subsequently disturbed. Reading between the lines can infer a certain degree of fear informing her behaviour: 'I was going to go out again' – presumably to look once more for the UFO – 'but I changed my mind'.

The various gaps and confusions in the sequence of events described in the original sighting, the odd phrasings in Angie's account, were all immediately suggestive to me. Who were the 'they' whom she tried 'thinking at'? Again, who were the 'they' she felt were coming towards her? What did she do between nine or ten o'clock when Chuck left in panic, and two am when she finally came in herself and went to bed? I had learned that gaps were not only very common in a subject's recollection of a UFO abduction experience, but also oddly unpredictable. The evidence suggests that these memory blocks are externally imposed, but their duration and effectiveness vary immensely. In a number of cases abductees have recalled nearly the entire range of events, the way one might remember a mugging or an accident, and in other cases, when very little conscious recollection remains, hypnosis has been used to restore forgotten details. In Angie's case it seemed that if she had been abducted that night she was recalling her *responses* – fear, the desire to signal, to communicate – but not the specific *causes* of these responses – what 'they' looked like, what 'they' did during the period of apparent missing time, and so forth.

Eventually Angie visited my studio in New York. She was hypnotized first by Dr Don Klein of Columbia Presbyterian Hospital, and later I carried out the regressive sessions myself. Under hypnosis she recalled walking into the woods where she met a small, grey-skinned figure, about as tall as her shoulder. Seemingly without volition she continued to the cornfield behind the woods where she could see 'some kind of ship'. I ask if it's up in the sky. She answers that it is not, that it is on the ground, the cornfield. She walks towards it. There are three small figures standing beside the large, oval craft, which glows without lighting up its surroundings. Again without being able to exert any will of her own she walks up a ramp and into a brightly lit interior. Ultimately she is put upon a table and made to feel very tranquil while a series of physical operations take place. A circular incision is made on her thigh, cut painlessly into her flesh by a 'tulip-shaped' implement, apparently a coring device of some sort. After the operations are completed she is taken back into the woods and walked home; her conscious memories return when she sees the flash by her garage.

Subsequent investigation of Angie's case has uncovered at least three other abductions which occurred at intervals from her earliest childhood on, and it seems clear that her mother and possibly her sister have also undergone UFO abduction experiences.

These assertions are fully consonant with the patterns that I and other investigators have uncovered. When I wrote *Missing Time*, my first book on the subject, I had made three basic discoveries. Most central is the idea that the amnesia usually encountered in these cases can sometimes block almost *every* memory of such an experience. In the Steven Kilburn case the only indication that such an event might have occurred was his fear of a certain stretch of highway, and the vague feeling that this fear might somehow involve a UFO. Unlike Angie or the Hills, Kilburn did not recall having sighted a UFO or noticing a gap in his recollection of the time sequences. And yet, under hypnosis there emerged a UFO abduction experience extraordinarily similar to theirs. This meant that almost *anyone* can have suffered such an experience and yet be totally unaware of it for all practical purposes. What before was thought of as a very rare event might be infinitely more common than anyone had supposed.

My second discovery was the fact that many – and now I believe most – abductees are first abducted in childhood, and are then systematically reabducted in some kind of ongoing study. It is not, apparently, a random phenomenon, but rather a methodical one. Third, I discovered that many abductees, particularly in childhood, are marked by incisions made by their captors, possibly for some kind of cell sampling purpose.

A few statistics are called for. At this point I have investigated eighteen cases in which the subjects, under hypnosis, have described operations in which these incisions were made. I have worked with another twenty individuals who have such scars and associate them with abduction experiences, though they do not recall specific operations or sensations; they merely recall that immediately after their return to normal consciousness they notice these fresh wounds. The thirty-eight individuals bear on their bodies forty-one suspicious scars which are distributed in the following way: eighteen scars are located on the lower leg, often at the back of the calf. Nine are located on the thigh, and two in the region of the hip. Six are on the back, one on the chest, one on the wrist, two on the abdomen, one at the waist and one is on the forehead. When the operation inside the UFO has been recalled there is usually a memory of an odd, low-level sensation; only a few abductees remember the experience as causing much pain. In a number of these cases I have been able to interview the subject's parents and have found that the origin of the scar is something of a family mystery. Often the injury was high on the calf or thigh, yet there was no tear in the trousers the child had been wearing. That fact, plus the lack of extensive bleeding, pain or other clues as to what caused the cut, serves to create a genuine enigma, and the incident finds its way into the family folklore. And if the cut occurred during a period of time when the child was actually lost and being searched for, the mystery is forever ingrained in the parents' memory.

In 1983 I received an intriguing letter from 'Kathie Davis', who lives near Indianapolis, Indiana. She described a strange series of events which involved members of her family, and she enclosed some photographs of what seemed to be a classic UFO landing-trace on her father's property. This letter launched me into an investigation which has now extended over three years, and which led to my writing the book *Intruders – The Incredible Visitations at Copley Woods*. The details which emerged, when seen against the background of twelve similar cases I've investigated along the way, persuaded me that we have discovered what is most likely the central purpose of the UFO abduction phenomenon.

Apparently it works this way: human beings are first abducted when children, and a cell sampling operation ensues. Then, it would seem, after these samples are analyzed, certain individuals are followed closely and after puberty ova and sperm cells are taken from them. (This detail turns up in the early case of Betty and Barney Hill). The goal of these procedures, the evidence suggests, is the merging of human and 'alien' genetic material for the production of a hybrid race. In some cases women are abducted and artificially inseminated, and within a few months reabducted so that the developing embryos can be removed. These hybrid embryos are apparently brought to term in a laboratory inside large UFOs. (I have several congruent descriptions of these 'nurseries' which I have not yet published. I am withholding these and other details as a means of verifying any new accounts which might come to light). Most bizarre of all, the humans –

male or female – who have involuntarily provided cells are later abducted yet again and shown the results – tiny hybrid infants or children. In fact, they are asked to pick up and hold their 'offspring' in a kind of bonding experience! I am the first to admit the sheer outrageousness of such ideas, but outrageousness doesn't mean untruth. I find the evidence, unfortunately, compelling; I have every reason to conclude that these 'impossible' breeding experiments are actually taking place. Recently, several abductees have recounted these procedures to me clearly and precisely, without the use of hypnosis, describing particular details that I had deliberately concealed, and thereby establishing to me their veracity. I have no idea what might be the final purpose – or 'place of residence' – for the hybrid individuals produced in this manner, but I am convinced that, for good or for ill, these genetic procedures are at the heart of the UFO abduction phenomenon.

I am confident that we have made a major leap forward in our knowledge of Unidentified Flying Objects and the reasons for their presence on our planet. For years investigators, myself included, have patiently logged UFO sightings and noted down descriptions of airborne craft. It was as if we were trying to record the licence plate number on the getaway car without having understood what the crime was. Now we know what the occupants of those craft have been up to, and we can proceed accordingly. Through patient investigation the enigma is finally, slowly, yielding its secrets.

LIVING WITH A CLOSE ENCOUNTER

Jenny Randles

Shortly after becoming a UFO investigator I was visited at my home by a seriously distressed young woman. She trembled, shook and fought with a volcano of emotions. Clearly she desperately wanted to talk to someone. Equally clearly she felt a barrier preventing her from sharing her burden.

It took the best part of an evening to get a semi-coherent account from her lips. Through tears and a voice strained by panic she poured out what was unquestionably real terror associated with a UFO sighting in September 1976. Not only had she seen something unidentified at that time, but now she was convinced it was going to come back and kidnap her!

The sighting itself was not the most dramatic that a seasoned investigator will come across. An oval 'craft' with yellowish lights at each end had risen, apparently from a landed position, inside a clump of trees. It had climbed into the sky early one morning, in full daylight, and right in front of the eyes of the terrified observer.

I could not possibly explain to this distraught woman that the degree of emotional trauma which she was displaying is usually consistent with a far stranger encounter. It normally suggests that something happened which the witness has forgotten. Something that sits inside the mind, like a caged animal trying to get out – although in almost every case they have no comprehension of why they feel so worked up about what may not be recalled as any more than a light in the sky.

This seemingly straightforward case opens up many questions. It also forced me to face up to some of my responsibilities as a UFO investigator. In this situation I had to *lie* to the woman, or rather I had to obscure my suspicions that there might be more to her story – a repressed memory of a possible contact or abduction experience.

To have suggested that under the circumstances would have been disastrous. The temptation to propose regression hypnosis was great, urging the witness to try to relive the experience and see what else might emerge. But it was obvious she was in no position to cope with such a process.

I gently reassured my frightened visitor that UFOs do *not* kidnap people. Having one close encounter in your lifetime is good fortune. The chances of having more are astronomical. Even if it were to happen, there would be absolutely nothing to fear.

I met the woman quite by chance in the supermarket some weeks later. She was a different person, happy and confident. The encounter with the UFO was still a part of her life, but she had successfully integrated it. It was just 'one of those things', to be filed and forgotten.

I do not think I had any real choice in this particular case, but I still ask myself if I did the right thing and wonder if there is a part of that woman's life that will reveal itself one day. I am well aware that some people feel I should have sent her to see a doctor or psychiatrist. But where would this have led her, save to ridicule and even more confusion? Nobody in the medical profession (particularly in Britain and a decade ago) had (or still has) the experience and expertise to handle something like this. UFOs to most professional people do not exist outside the imagination, so naturally these non-existent things could not possibly kidnap people. To tell anyone in this woman's position, however carefully, that all she experienced was a product of her mind would, in my judgement, have been counter-productive.

What this story does show is, firstly, the need for a code of practice to govern the behaviour of an investigator and, secondly, the alarming lack of an adequate, honest response by the UFO community to the basic needs of the witness.

It was a relatively simple task to correct the first problem. By 1982 BUFORA, for instance, had legally vetted and published a code of practice, subsequently adopted by other organizations.

The second problem is not so easy to deal with. The experience of novelist, Whitley Strieber is pertinent: In his non-fiction book, *Communion*, Strieber claims that he has been the subject of lifelong abductions. In newspaper interviews, and on national television, he heaped scorn on what he labelled 'UFO buffs' who did not put the interest of the witness ahead of all other considerations and who sometimes tended to abuse them.

Whilst there is a degree of substance in what Strieber says, he is also well aware that the very book which led to his 'discovery' of his abduction *Science and the UFOs* contains the BUFORA code of practice. Also, having seen Budd Hopkins in action, Strieber must have realized his concern and compassion for witnesses.

Of course, most UFO investigators know nothing of psychology, and this should be rectified. A team of close encounter counsellors should be on call, ready to respond to witnesses in a given area. Their task would be to enable witnesses to come to terms with what might well have been one of the most devastating events of their lives. Such teams would need to combine both careful UFO investigators and psychologists, working with one common aim.

There have been steps in this direction. In 1980 I

contacted Dr John Shaw, a professor of psychology at Manchester University. His knowledge of UFOs was limited, but he was a willing listener and he proved helpful on one abduction case. Gradually a rapport developed, although he was reluctant to be publicly associated with a field hardly noted for its restraint. In 1985 he and I worked together at a university seminar where some of the issues were discussed and the role of UFOs in modern psychology was established. Our plans may achieve the rudiments of close encounter task forces, but their success will depend upon the desire of other doctors and qualified specialists to learn, listen and help.

In the next forty years there seems little doubt that the CE 4 (abductions) will prove to be the most important 'growth area'. It may be that some other UFO phenomena will be understood quite soon, in particular Unidentified Atmospheric Phenomena. However, the CE 4 *appears* to be different. It is in the abduction cases where the alien nature of the subject manifests; whether they ultimately prove to have any actual substance or whether they represent something else (eg a bizarre mental process) which is no less fascinating or significant.

Study of CE 4s began after an incident in the White Mountains of New Hampshire, USA, with the sighting of a light by Betty and Barney Hill in 1961, (this case is examined in detail elsewhere in this book – Ed) but was slow to catch on in Britain, partly due to greater scepticism and the lack of willing doctors or psychiatrists. But quite a number of CE 4 cases do now exist in British archives, as in the records of UFO groups all over the world.

But how does an investigator (or witness) recognize a potential abduction case?

Firstly let us look at a case which was *not* a CE 4, although it might have been.

Gerry Mitchell, former RAF pilot, now a businessman, was driving near Carrington, Lancashire, one evening, when several balls of green fire whizzed by. There was a slight loosening of his grip on reality, but it was all over in seconds. What we had, then, was an interesting sighting by a credible witness of some UAP over an oil refinery complex. (The green fireball phenomenon is, in fact, one that has been reported many times, often in connection with power sources such as nuclear energy stations, or radar systems.)

Gerry Mitchell was put under regression hypnosis by a qualified doctor in Manchester. No deeper memory emerged, just a reliving of the sighting in graphic detail. Evidently this was *not* a CE 4.

This is by no means the only occasion where hypnosis has failed to reveal a deeper abduction memory. Sceptics propose that hypnosis creates a climate in which the witness is encouraged to recall more and more and does so to satisfy the researchers. Failed cases prove this to be erroneous, as indeed do those cases where a recall is spontaneous and requires no hypnosis to trigger it.

What factors distinguish Gerry Mitchell's type of case from those like Betty Hill's? If the differences are chiefly those of personality, perhaps the CE 4 is a psychological phenomenon. If there are differences in the form of the experience itself, then the CE 4, on some level at least, is perhaps real.

Gradually we have recognized a set of common factors which tend to be present on the surface of a UFO sighting hinting at something else beyond the threshold of awareness of the witness. I have examined twenty-eight British CE 4 cases, many of which I was involved with to some extent. Six main factors are common to each, and the evidence suggests these may also be present in CE 4 cases all over the world.

Missing time: In October 1974 a family of five returning from a night out in their home village of Aveley, Essex, observed a bluish light, which was accepted as a UFO before it vanished. Next they drove through a strange green mist, seeming to take only a moment to do so. Arriving home a few minutes later they were astonished to discover that between one and two hours had been lost somewhere on the short journey. Under investigation by Andy Collins, Barry King and London dentist Dr Leonard Wilder (using hypnosis), attempts were made to retrieve the missing time. This produced a supposed on board abduction, medical examination and lengthy discussions with tall, silver-suited aliens and small grotesque 'robotic' servants.

This time lapse is the single most consistent factor in such cases. Fifty-four per cent of the cases evidenced it, and it features in classic reports, including the Hill and Schirmer cases. The length of missing time varies between a couple of hours and fifteen minutes.

What is this missing time? It might literally be what it appears to be, a period that is blocked from memory whilst the abduction occurred and which is often only partially retrievable by techniques such as hypnosis.

If so, how does the induced amnesia arise? If 'aliens' are responsible then this implies that 'aliens' exist *and* that they abduct humans. Equally, we might suggest that the shock of the encounter is the real cause of the memory loss.

Reality blinks: Alan Godfrey, a police officer of Todmorden, West Yorkshire, saw a UFO on the road ahead, and sketched it in his accident report pad as it hovered – then suddenly found himself further down the road with the car engine in a different gear (for a fuller account see my book *The Pennine UFO Mystery*). I call this type of experience a 'reality blink'. Careful reconstruction revealed to field investigators (and to Alan's surprise) a quarter-hour time lapse. Resultant hypnosis by several doctors and psychiatrists in Manchester revealed a supposed memory very like that of the Aveley family, where Alan was hit by a beam of light, taken aboard for a medical examination by small robot-like creatures supervised by a taller figure in a long, white robe.

This sudden switch in scenes is also found in dreams, and this may be relevant to the proposition favoured by some researchers (including myself) that the event (*whatever* it is) happens during an altered state of consciousness similar to, though not identical with, dreaming.

The Oz factor: Besides the symptoms of missing time and reality blink, there is a third syndrome, which I call the 'Oz factor', that seems to imply distortion in time or space. For instance, an Essex man reported that when he saw the UFO it was like being inside a closed room. After it had gone it was as if he had stepped out into an adjacent room where a party was going on. In other words, the Oz factor often manifests as like being inside a protective bubble, with just the witness and UFO linked together and everything else being outside time and space.

The Oz factor again suggests that the CE 4 is occurring in an altered state of consciousness, and makes one wonder if, in a situation where a witness is supposedly abducted from his car (eg police officer Alan Godfrey), they ever *really* get out of the vehicle at all.

Nightmares: Jenny had an awful, recurrent dream about UFOs and a silver-suited figure. But later, when put under hypnosis by a CE 4 researcher, she did not recall any such dream. A colleague of the researcher, himself a witness to a close encounter, prompted her (still under hypnosis) to find a memory that might be thought of as a dream but was in fact real. Instantly the floodgates opened!

Behaviour changes: After a close encounter witnesses sometimes alter their behaviour patterns in quite remarkable ways. Here are some examples:

A Spanish witness hit by a lightbeam 'fired' by an 'entity' spent some days in a military hospital suffering from shock. According to bizarre evidence that later surfaced he developed an incredible expansive knowledge of science.

In South America, a poorly educated man began to discuss astrophysics and deep philosophical matters after his encounter, as if knowledge had been planted inside his head.

Meanwhile a British family stopped eating meat, took a deep interest in conservation and ecology, and were 'different' in the eyes of even close friends. Others have developed obsessions with nuclear energy. Some have even started to try to build UFOs in their bedrooms!

Sudden PSI abilities: The final factor is allied to the last one, but even more likely to be offputting to the average, cautious citizen. However, it cannot be dismissed because of that. It happens with alarming frequency.

Witnesses who claim psychic experiences tend to be more likely to have a CE 4. Even those who have not had any psychic experiences (PSI) often find these stimulated by the close encounter.

We might argue that the state of consciousness demarked by the Oz factor, in which CE 4 cases are most likely to happen, is one where PSI is also facilitated. Others may suggest that 'aliens' chose to contact individuals with a capacity for PSI, because they use telepathic means to communicate (almost every CE 4 case refers to the entities 'speaking' without moving their mouths). Also, if the planting of images into the mind and the imposition of some kind of mental block are both important in the design plan of the abduction, it would make sense to work with humans who are psychic or suggestive.

Twenty-nine per cent of the British cases talk of psychic events in the wake of their CE 4. These include out of the body experiences (another version of the floating/levitation trick), seeing apparitions and being able to move objects by thought alone (psychokinesis). Premonitions are also common.

In the wake of a close encounter, witnesses have to live with many problems. There are three main areas that the conscientious investigator must be on guard for.

Physical illness. Does the investigator or the witness visit a doctor and explain that they have seen a UFO and fear it might have had associated radiation? There is no doubt from the evidence which investigators possess that radiation *is* emitted in certain UFO cases, so this is no academic matter. Some doctors (through their ignorance) might consider that there is no cause for a full medical examination and suggest psychiatric care instead! But if nothing is said, can we be sure that proper screening for radiation effects will be given?

Even in the absence of physical consequences (found in nearly half of our CE 4 cases) the witness will still face **psychological problems**. As already suggested the victim has been in a situation not unlike a mugging or rape, terrorized by an assailant. However, they are in an even worse position because at least the nature and purpose of rape or mugging is understood. A UFO abduction is an assault by something unknown, from who knows where, and may even leave the witness with just a partial memory of what occurred.

The sense of intrusion and upset in the flow of one's life can be immense, and it is made all the harder because most people can neither comprehend nor even *believe* the experience.

This leads to the third consequence of a close encounter: **social stigma**. Even in the case of merely *seeing* a UFO an element of that remains. It is infinitely worse if you proclaim a contact or abduction by strange beings. Indeed many well-qualified and respectable people (exactly those whose testimony would be most evidential and influential) think out what might occur and decide to avoid going public with their story.

To experience an abduction or contact, survive its aftermath and then report it (even just to a UFO researcher) takes guts. To go public requires great strength of character. But it is fortunate that we do have people, such as police officer Alan Godfrey, who are willing to take that chance. Without him and the handful in Britain (or a few dozen world wide), who have come forward with courage and credibility, the abduction scenario would remain a myth instead of the thought provoking and deeply disturbing phenomenon that it is.

Coming to terms with a close encounter can take years. The case of Shelley, from Lancashire, shows this clearly. Her experience was in January 1976, when she was just seventeen. The pressures put on her at the time were enormous. The police (to whom she spoke in confidence) *gave* her story to the local press (sadly far from the only time such a disturbing thing has occurred). She resisted all the offers to sell her story or appear on television, because she was neither interested in self-promotion nor able to handle the way her story had become in demand. She spoke to a UFO investigator at the time, but withheld details which she felt might make him keen to question her further (such as the difficulty she had understanding where fifty minutes of time had vanished to).

After eight years, now more confident and eager to understand, Shelley called me and asked for help. Gradually, thanks to the assistance of other professionals, we worked through her story and began to find out what might be the missing link. But it was 1986, more than ten years after her encounter, before Shelley was ready to talk openly. She consented to be interviewed by me for a radio documentary on UFOs. However, this was with the mutual agreement that we talk only of her conscious memory and not of the supposed abduction which was revealed under hypnosis (interestingly most witnesses are cautious about accepting the evidence of hypnosis).

Although Shelley was not identified on my radio programme she did receive an invitation to appear on a major TV show. However, she would not agree to this and subsequently, when she allowed a freelance writer to do a story on her in a woman's journal, she began to fear that she had made a mistake. Even a decade was too short for her to fully accept what had happened to her.

The typical close encounter witness is torn between three extremes. They desperately want to know what happened and why it happened to them. In the search for this they seek out someone who can give them the answers (although those answers usually lie inside themselves). They also feel that they owe it to the world to report what to them is a major, earth-shattering, universe-altering experience. The knowledge that we are *not* alone. Yet they also worry endlessly about the risks of talking. What will it do to their marriage, their family, their careers?

These are the problems, but what are the solutions? In the UK some abductees have been brought together in loose self-help networks. In the USA, Budd Hopkins has created formal self-help groups of CE 4 witnesses, who meet to talk over their difficulties with the only other people who can possibly help. At the University of Wyoming, Dr Leo Sprinkle (another abduction specialist of many years' standing) brings dozens of contactees together (from the serious and stable, to others who barely qualify for that description.) These 'conferences' are hosted each summer in the hope that something fruitful might emerge from such a gathering.

Such answers have been worked out separately by the researchers concerned, although they are actually quite similar in outlook. Support groups do appear a genuine way forward, even though it may prove hard to establish a kind of 'Close Encounters Anonymous'.

In conclusion I present a six point plan which I believe we should adopt as fast as we can:

(a) We must teach people how to recognize the symptoms that *might* suggest their UFO sighting has hidden depths. But there has to be a telephone number they can call in total confidence.

(b) The facts and the cases must be presented objectively and carefully. It is too easy for the media to trivialize and sensationalize the UFO subject.

(c) UFO task forces must be set up to handle the close encounters. These should comprise a balance of medical doctors, psychologists, psychiatrists and experienced field investigators. Each can contribute to the overall aim, which is principally to *help* the abductee but also to learn more of what is happening in the CE 4 phenomenon.

(d) The use of support groups. Only a person who has themselves experienced a close encounter can truly aid a witness.

(e) The choice of hypnotic regression by qualified exponents should be available to witnesses *if* they want it.

(f) Finally, if a witness is ready to go forward with his story, then he must be given adequate counselling so he can appreciate the dangers and the advantages of this course of action.

EVALUATING THE ABDUCTEE EXPERIENCE

John Rimmer

Within a few years of Kenneth Arnold's 1947 UFO sighting people began reporting encounters with the ostensible pilots of the strange craft that were invading the world's skies. People like George Adamski and Howard Menger gave accounts of their meetings with friendly extraterrestrials – the so-called space brothers – who usually imparted some fairly banal gems of cosmic wisdom. Often the people so contacted were taken aboard the aliens' crafts, usually to be shown the splendours of the visitors' home planet, or given a rapid trip round our neighbouring planets. Instead of the barren wastes we now know them to be, these were inevitably lush semi-paradises. Some of these 'contactees' were later exposed as phoneys, some went on to form UFO-based cults, such as the Aetherius Society. This combination of fraud, cultism and backyard philosophy repelled serious ufologists who felt that it lessened the chance of having ufology taken seriously as a scientific discipline.

However there was another type of contact. Some witnesses claimed to have met not the tall, god-like aliens of the cultists, but more grotesque, truly alien creatures. These were small, gnome-like, with over-sized heads and thin spindly bodies. They did not hold forth to the witnesses on the state of the universe, but most likely ignored them, or treated them with mild curiosity and occasionally hostility. Although many ufologists still rejected *all* contact cases, others were impressed by these more objective-sounding reports. By the mid 1960s the space brothers had become an historical curiosity, but the alien creatures were becoming a major part of the UFO mystery. The earlier, more mystically inclined contactees went aboard their visitors' ships voluntarily. Some of those who met the newer type of alien also went aboard the strange craft – but not of their own volition!

The first abductions: In October 1957, Antonio Villas Boas was working on his brother's farm in Minas Gerais, Brazil. It was the southern hemisphere summer, and the heat was so intense that it was easier for them to work in the late evening. At eleven on the night of the fourteenth they gave up their ploughing after becoming rather unsettled by a light which seemed to follow them around. The following night Antonio was out working alone when the light appeared again. This time it came closer and hovered near him. He uncoupled his tractor's ploughing gear and tried to head home, but his alarm grew when the tractor would not start. Suddenly the light swooped to the ground a few yards away from him and two figures emerged. These were small entities, dressed in what appeared to be helmeted 'space suits' with some sort of breathing apparatus attached. They seized Villas Boas by his arms and frog-marched him into their craft.

It was here that the most sensational aspect of the abduction took place, for the space-suited aliens were not the only occupants of the craft. Villas Boas was stripped naked and left in a small compartment; here he was joined by a woman, blonde, about four foot eight inches tall, and also completely naked. At the woman's urging the couple had sex twice, and although Villas Boas quite enjoyed the experience (so, it appeared, did the woman) he was rather repelled by the gutteral, barking sounds she made. Afterwards one of the other aliens returned his clothes and he dressed. He was then taken to other parts of the craft and allowed to see what appeared to be a control room. He tried to remove a clock-like item of equipment, but was foiled by his captors, and was later deposited back at the farm.

The Villas Boas case was not the first abduction to gain widespread publicity, nor, as it turned out was it particularly typical of other incidents. The most widely publicized abduction, and perhaps more typical of the genre, was the Hill abduction.

Betty and Barney Hill were returning from a holiday in Canada in 1961. They were driving through the White Mountains of New Hampshire when they saw a strange light in the sky. Like Villas Boas' light, this eventually transformed into a large craft with windows and occupants. At this point something happened which has become the pattern for many subsequent cases – nothing! The Hills remembered nothing of subsequent events, and it was only in the months following that odd memories began to come to mind. A Boston psychiatrist hypnotized the couple, and under hypnosis the following missing memories began to flood back.

After the initial close sighting of the UFO, Betty and Barney were taken aboard the craft, where they were both given a form of medical examination. Betty apparently had a long, needle-like instrument inserted through her abdomen – some researchers later thought this might be a form of pregnancy test. Similarly, Barney Hill was subjected to some form of examination of his genitals, which may have involved taking a sperm sample.

The Hill abduction has become almost the archetype for later cases. There are three particular aspects that have recurred frequently in later abductions.

The car ride: A great number of abduction cases seem

to begin with the abductee driving along a lonely road late at night. There is some ambiguity as to the significance of the car ride in abduction reports. Those who support the idea that UFOs are extraterrestrial in origin would say simply that most UFO activity takes place under the cover of darkness in lonely places and that people out in lonely places after dark tend to be in cars. Others claim that people driving cars at night, especially for long periods, can fall victim to a sort of self-hypnosis, producing a mental state in which they can start seeing things that are not there.

Missing time: In the majority of abduction cases the people involved do not seem to have any conscious recollection of the experience. After their 'release' they often just drive home apparently unaware of their ordeal. It is only later that they realize a substantial period of time is missing from their lives.

The fact that so many abduction stories have been revealed through hypnotism has been a matter of considerable controversy. Some claim that the hypnotic techniques bring to the surface memories which have been hidden either by the trauma of the event or deliberately by the aliens. The alternative argument is that the stories might themselves be the product of hypnosis.

The medical examination: A West Yorkshire policeman, Alan Godfrey, became an abduction victim in the early morning of 28 November 1980. After encountering a UFO during his patrol car rounds, he was hypnotically regressed to recall the full details of his abduction. He too was apparently given a medical examination whilst lying on a table in a sort of laboratory. There was a bright light over his head, and pieces of equipment were placed on his arm – he describes it as 'like a blood pressure test'.

It seems that we can almost create an identikit abduction case. It may not correspond exactly to every case on record, but several elements from it will be present in almost all the cases in the literature:

1 A driver on a lonely road at night
2 is followed by a mysterious bright light.
3 The light gets closer, resolves itself as a metallic craft and lands.
4 The witness remembers seeing figures coming from the craft
5 then drives off home. On arriving home an hour or more is missing.
6 The witness is hypnotized, regressed to the time of the UFO encounter, and more details emerge.
7 After the initial approach by the figures the witness recalls being taken on board the craft,
8 He is shown around the craft, meets other 'occupants', sees details of control panels, crew 'living quarters', etc.
9 He is subjected to a medical experience, which may involve the taking of blood samples, or some form of sexual examination.
10 He is given an enigmatic message, or shown images on a TV screen before being returned to his car.

This pattern seems to be consistent with the idea that the abduction experience is the result of a programme of examination of the human race by a civilization from another world. The 'medical examination' in particular looks very much like part of a biological study. When we compare this with non-abduction UFO close encounter cases where entities have been seen gathering samples of soil, plants or even small animals, the evidence for extraterrestrial visitors would seem very strong indeed. But there are other facts and alternative viewpoints that make the issue seem much less clear-cut.

Although the era of UFOs can be said to have begun with Kenneth Arnold, and the abduction phenomenon with Villas Boas and the Hills, these were not the first instances of people seeing strange objects in the sky, or being abducted by unearthly beings. You will read elsewhere in this book of the 'pre-1947' UFOs – the ghost rockets, the mystery airships, phantom planes and ghostlights – but consider here this abduction case.

A doctor travelling home at night after treating a patient reaches a crossroads. Here he is suddenly blinded by an eerie blue light, whereupon he loses consciousness. When he awakes he is in a vehicle, surrounded by hideous beings with faces like grotesque masks. He is threatened and instructed not to tell anyone about his experience, then dumped from the vehicle. The next thing he remembers is being back in his own bed.

But this was not an abduction by the occupants of a UFO in some remote location in the American boondocks. This took place in Haiti in the 1940s. The doctor was a witch-doctor, a voodoo magician, and the vehicle was not an extraterrestrial spacecraft, but a *motor-zobop*, an unearthly motor car, which travelled the suburbs of Port-au-Prince at night.

But we can look back further than voodoo-haunted Haiti of the 1940s to find evidence of alien abductions. We can find them in the myth and legends of many (perhaps all) cultures. Our history and our folklore is full of stories of contact between humankind and other entities. Although these stories are now seen as little more than a naive branch of literature, and tend to be treated as stories rather than experience, they do in fact represent the experiences of the common people throughout history.

A frequent feature of the folklore of the Celtic lands is tales of people who have been 'taken' by alien races – the *sidhe*, the little people, the fairies – and are shown round their alien realm just as the UFO abductees are shown around the 'space ships'. These folk tales have many similarities with the stories that are told to us by the UFO abductees. Perhaps one of the strongest links is the curious distortions of time which occur in both sets of accounts.

We have seen the 'missing time' factor in UFO cases, but the folklorist Edwin Hartland knew nothing of UFOs when he wrote about 'the supernatural lapse of time in fairyland' in his book *The Science of Fairy Tales*. He quotes a Welsh story about a boy who had disappeared. His mother had long given him up for dead when nothing had been heard from him for two years, until one day she found him standing at the door with a bundle under his arm, looking just as he did when she last saw him. 'Where have you been all this time,' she demands, to be told, 'Why, it was only yesterday I went away!' He described how he had been taken by 'the little people', and danced with them by a stream.

In January 1982 a young soldier was found to be missing from his post near Kuala Lumpur. There had apparently been a number of similar disappearances before in the area, and the local belief was that they had been abducted by beings known as the *buni* people. The victims usually turned up after a few days, with reports of having been taken to a distant place and given marvellous food. Unfortunately most of the abductees were violently sick, and the 'food' found to consist of grass and worms!

Another case which provides a link between UFO cases and the traditional elements of folklore took place in Brazil in 1969. An off-duty soldier, Antonio Da Silva, was fishing at a lake near the town of Bebedouro. During the afternoon of 4 May he heard voices and saw figures moving around near him. Suddenly he felt his legs being burned by a blast of fire from a weapon held by one of the figures. His attackers were four feet tall, stockily built, helmeted humanoids, who dragged him off to a peculiar craft resembling a tumbler between two saucers. He was forced into the craft and a helmet rammed uncomfortably over his head. After a journey which seemed to last for several hours, he was blindfolded and marched off. When he could see his surroundings and captors again he was in a strange room whose walls appeared to be made of stone. The creatures revealed themselves behind their helmets to be bearded – their long beards fell below their waist – with bushy eyebrows, big ears and apparently toothless mouths. He was most alarmed to see what appeared to be four dead human bodies lying on a low shelf in the room. The dwarfs (they seemed to resemble the traditional images of dwarfs quite closely) examined the contents of his pockets and pack, and attempted to communicate with him by sign and gesture. Da Silva thought that they were asking him to be their spy on Earth. Eventually they began quarrelling amongst themselves over a rosary Da Silva had, behaving in a childish and irrational manner, until a human figure appeared and spoke to Da Silva in Portuguese. After this, the small creatures took Da Silva and dumped him two hundred miles from his starting point.

Tales like this – story-book dwarfs in stone spaceships who panic at the sight of a rosary – seem to make no sense in terms of contact with advanced extraterrestrial civilizations, but provide a contemporary version of folktales of human beings coming into contact with subterranean fairy folk.

It would appear that throughout history humankind has been plagued with abductions of one sort or another conducted by small and/or grotesque creatures; abductions in which our understanding of time can be distorted, and in which our bodies are examined or abused. Some would derive from this evidence that UFO entities have been visiting our planet for centuries, in earlier times these visitations were interpreted as supernatural events while now we can see them for what they are. More sociologically inclined interpreters would reverse this, saying that throughout history we have feared being abducted from the safety of our familiar world, earlier generations have expressed this fear in terms of 'the little people', in a more technological age we describe craft from another planet.

This brings us to the fundamental question about abductions (and UFOs in general): are they reports of the intervention of some alien force (not necessarily an extraterrestrial one) into human lives, or are they a psychological phenomenon, which involve only the person making the report. Are abductions real?

At first sight this might seem an absurd question with hundreds, maybe thousands, of such reports. Some of them involve two, three or more people, and there is no evidence from the published reports that any but the tiniest minority of the people involved are in any way mentally unbalanced. So, QED, the abductions are real.

But it's not as easy as that. Firstly, all the abduction reports we have are just that – reports. No one has yet produced a piece of hardware from a visited craft. We heard how Antonio Villas Boas attempted to remove an instrument from his captors' vehicle, and how they reacted to this with a great deal of annoyance. Few other abductees have shown even this degree of initiative. There is a certain amount of so-called physical evidence which has been brought forward to back up claims of UFO sightings and close encounters – pieces of metal, landing traces, even, according to some accounts, crashed saucers. These are described elsewhere in this book. There are hundreds of UFO photographs, some of them are downright fakes, others misinterpretations or photographic accidents, there are even a few genuinely puzzling shots which appear to show structured objects.

Unfortunately even with the wider UFO phenomena, none of this physical evidence can be said to be totally convincing.

The situation is even worse for abductions. There are no photographs, no pieces of metal, no extraterrestrial artefacts. Why should this be, when our witnesses are not just standing looking at the UFO, but are actually in it, often apparently for several hours, walking around and examining the craft? There seems to be a comparison again here with some of the abductions in folklore – gold and treasure brought back from fairyland turns out to be dead leaves and chaff, exquisite supernatural food is revealed as grass and worms.

So what other 'physical evidence' can be offered as proof of a physically real abduction? Perhaps the best evidence is that which is left on the abductees themselves, the various marks left on their bodies by the ordeals they have undergone.

Two young men, identified only as 'P' and 'W' underwent a traumatic abduction near the mobile home they shared in Maine. Both had night jobs, so were awake and listening to music at three am, when they heard an explosion outside. They decided to drive around in their car. Soon they found themselves in the midst of a display of vivid lights moving around them. Some time later 'W' underwent hypnotic regression and told how he found himself in a cone-shaped room, where he was joined by peculiar creatures with 'mushroom-shaped' heads, and dressed in sheets. After a struggle in which he hit one of the creatures he was stripped and forced to lie on a table where he was given a 'medical examination' with the aid of a square instrument with gauges and controls. A blood sample was also taken, using a long needle-like instrument. Later he was allowed to dress, and found himself back in the car.

The 'physical evidence' for this account took the form of a variety of physiological symptoms which were later displayed by both the men involved. They included burning eyes, skin discolouration and soreness. Villas Boas, after his encounter with the seductive alien in Brazil suffered almost identical symptoms, and they have cropped up in several other abduction and UFO close encounter cases. These certainly seem to be significant of the fact that *something* traumatic happened to the people involved, but it would be difficult to tie it in exclusively to their abduction.

Proponents of the extraterrestrial theory have suggested that these symptoms may be caused by radioactivity aboard the craft, and certainly they do resemble some of the reported symptoms of radiation burns. On the other hand they also tend to resemble the sort of symptoms that can be brought about by certain nervous conditions, along with such symptoms as hair loss and difficulty in breathing. No one doubts that an abduction, whatever it may be, must be a very traumatic event and one that could well precipitate the physiological effects described, but these symptoms do not allow us to get behind the event to see what may be causing it.

If there is no physical evidence which may be examined at leisure after the event, do we have any cases where independent witnesses might be able to give confirmation of the reality of the event? The evidence is ambiguous. We have a number of multiple witness cases – the two young men in the Maine case, mentioned above, or a rather similar case at Pascagoula, Mississippi in 1973, where two fishermen, Calvin Parker and Charles Hickson, reported a close encounter with a strange craft. Subsequently Hickson was hypnotically regressed and came up with a 'classic' medical examination abduction report. Parker however was never hypnotized, and was only able to confirm the first part of Hickson's story – the encounter with the 'craft'.

One case that has been put forward as a multiple-witness abduction event was that of Travis Walton, a forestry worker from Arizona. In 1975 Walton was a member of a forestry gang clearing brushwood in the Apache-Sitgrave National Park in Arizona. With his six workmates he was driving back to base after the day's work, when they all saw a large glowing object over the trees to the side of the road. Against the objections of the others, Walton jumped from the truck and ran towards the object. There was a sudden flash of light and he fell to the ground. The men in the truck drove off in panic.

Walton was missing for five days, eventually turning

up in a telephone booth in the nearby town of Snowflake. Subsequent hypnotic regression revealed about an hour from the missing five days, including an encounter with small, chalk-white creatures, with huge eyes, no hair, small mouths, and wearing red coverall suits. He also met a tall, human figure, with blond hair and tanned skin. A major controversy involving rival UFO groups and investigators erupted over Walton, the six coworkers in the forestry truck being held up as eye-witness confirmation of Walton's claims. In fact the others only saw Walton walking towards the aerial object and falling to the ground after a flash of light. They did not see him being seized by creatures, or enter the object of his own accord. Despite claim and counter-claim, it is still unclear as to what exactly happened to Walton in his missing days – was he in fact held captive by alien creatures; did he wander the inhospitable forest in an amnesiac state after encountering an unknown natural phenomenon, as some researchers have claimed; or did he just sneak off and hide away as part of a hoax? Sceptics have claimed that the whole event was set up by the forestry gang to excuse their lateness in completing their government contract.

This lack of witnesses seems to be more than just an unfortunate coincidence. If we look at those cases where there are two or more witnesses we see either that there is confirmation only of the initial, non-abduction, part of the story; or, as in the cases of the Hills or the Avis's, the people involved are married or closely related. In these circumstances there are many reasons why the couples confirm each others' stories – there are endless opportunities for the parties to discuss the case and subconsciously influence each others' memories. The couple will have a certain shared background of experiences which may influence the way they see or perceive events or indeed, one may just not want to make the other out to seem a liar or a lunatic.

The apparently obvious solution to the question of abduction events is that they are the result of intervention by some alien force from elsewhere in the universe. We have accounts, often remarkably similar, of the appearance of structured, metallic craft, landing and taking off from the surface of our planet and we have accounts from dozens of people of apparently identical contact with the operators of these craft. It would even appear, from recent investigations by researcher Budd Hopkins, that this investigation involves some form of genetic experimentation. This is also suggested by the experiences of Villas Boas and the Hills.

But how well does the extraterrestrial hypothesis (ETH) explain cases such as that of Antonio da Silva? His captors at Bebedouro at first appeared to be extraterrestrials like the creatures Villas Boas met – small figures wearing 'space helmets' and breathing apparatus, but soon who revealed themselves as irrational, squabbling, bearded dwarfs.

Can the ETH explain why there seem to be so many *different* kinds of creatures? Although there are broad similarities in many cases, nearly all are different to some significant degree: short, big-headed creatures; human figures; monkey-like aliens; one-eyed monsters; creatures with one leg; creatures with webbed fingers; some speak fluent English, others communicate in grunts and signs, others seem to be telepathic; all this without mentioning the equally varied forms of craft involved. If we take all the accounts at face value it would seem that almost every abduction has been the work of a separate race of alien visitors.

The main alternative to the ETH is that the abductions form part of a complex psychological phenomenon. We have seen that UFO abductions have interesting parallels with other forms of abductions throughout history. The present form of the UFO abduction may be a result of people's fears of science and technology. Certainly, the way abductees are treated by their 'captors' sounds rather like the way scientists treat laboratory rats: they are pushed, poked, prodded, examined clinically, treated much like laboratory specimens, then dumped when the experiment is over. Many people would see this as a way in which modern society is dehumanizing the individual.

One particular abduction report demonstrates this fear best: the case of Lee Parrish. His abductors were machine-like figures; one a huge black slab-shaped object about fifteen feet tall (rather resembling the black monolith in the film *2001 – A Space Odyssey*.) These inhuman forms prodded their victim around, and at one stage seemed to push a needle-like probe into his head. He got the feeling that this was some sort of analysis of his chemical make-up. This seems to be a particularly vivid piece of symbolism – the human being, not just as a laboratory animal, more a specimen in a test tube, picked up for analysis, and presumably flushed away down the sink when the experiment is over. The fact that this is done by machines rather than by animate humanoids seems to reflect fears of a technological and mechanized society where humans are increasingly irrelevant and redundant.

Although we must bear in mind the possibility of confirmatory evidence ultimately coming to light, the evidence so far revealed about UFO abductions seems ambiguous. There does not seem to be hard evidence of real, physical abductions by 'nuts and bolts' space ships. The experiences of the abductees seem to be linked to fears and anxieties rather closer to home than outer space. The abduction experience seems to be just one part of a large human preoccupation which has recurred in different forms throughout history. The evidence does seem to point to UFO abductions being a psychological phenomenon, the images of which are structured by the society in which the 'victim' lives.

But all these conjectures could be dismissed in a moment if the next abduction case were to produce irrefutable proof. Until then we may offer suggestions, suspect strongly, even offer tentative conclusions, but we must be prepared to admit that we just do not know what is happening to hundreds of people who have undergone this most traumatic and terrifying experience.

PART III
INVESTIGATING UFOs

INVESTIGATING UFOs — INTRODUCTION

Ufologists, like detectives, have to investigate events after they've already happened — sometimes a long while after. Which means that — again like detectives — they are almost wholly dependent on what witnesses tell them. As a result, most UFO investigation consists of checking the details of the witness's account. Does his description of a mysterious light match up with a known satellite? Could his alleged 'landing marks' be a fairy ring? Are there factors in his personal life that might make us question his claim to have been taken aboard a flying saucer?

In the early days, reports were hardly investigated at all: they were taken more or less at face value, and matched if possible to a natural or man-made explanation, more often than not with no on-the-spot investigation at all being carried out. Gradually, over the past forty years, it has become clear that no value can be assigned to a report until it has been thoroughly checked, taking into account not only the event itself but also the conditions and circumstances in which it is alleged to have occurred, and the personality of the witness himself.

In the light of today's more sophisticated approach, investigators are returning to the files to reassess the cases of past decades; often, what they find casts doubt on many long-accepted events. Thus, Spain's Vicente-Juan Ballester Olmos and Juan Fernandez Peris, in their definitive 1987 study *Enciclopedia de los encuentros cercanos con OVNIs*, found reason to reject 117 out of the 200 landing cases which had been included in an earlier catalogue!

The trouble is that a thoroughly investigated UFO report can demand as much time and generate as much paperwork as a police dossier; and while police detectives are full-time workers backed by massive and well-equipped organizations, UFO investigators are unpaid, part-time volunteers who seldom enjoy substantial co-operation from any other section of the community.

PRIVATE GROUPS AND INDIVIDUALS V. GOVERNMENTS

The investigation work conducted by governments is rarely made available to these unpaid part-time volunteers creating a duplication of effort and a lack of access to government resources. Recently, various 'Freedom of Information' acts have forced some Western governments (but not, sadly, that of the UK) to reveal details of their investigations, and in this section Bill Chalker details some of his work with official Australian government files. Much more co-operation is needed, however; as Lord Hill-Norton GCB, Admiral of the Fleet and Chief of Defence Staff 1971–3 stated in a letter to one of the editors of this book, 'The more pressure that can be put on governments about UFOs the better'.

FROM SKYWATCH TO PROJECT IDENTIFICATION

Understandably, frustrated ufologists have sought ways of remedying this situation. The most obvious method is to try to eliminate dependence on witnesses by becoming witnesses themselves. Hence, in the more naïve era when skywatching was popular, English investigators flocked to locations such as Warminster's

Cradle Hill, said to be a favourite place for seeing UFOs. The results, alas, were more interesting to the sociologist than the ufologist. More scientific efforts were made in France, where on prearranged nights ufologues throughout the country would simultaneously watch the skies in order to obtain a nation-wide view of UFO activity: the results were interesting statistically but in no other way.

More favourable opportunities arise when UFOs are reported over a sustained period of time in a specific area, so that there is a real chance that regular surveillance will be rewarded. This has been achieved in two areas: one at Piedmont, Missouri, where continued reports of mysterious lights prompted a seven-year investigation by physics professor Harley Rutledge; the other at Hessdalen, in central Norway, where a series of reports from the local farming community encouraged investigators from UFO-Norge to set up their own observation stations, continually manned over a period of weeks.

The results in both cases fully justified the effort, and though the interpretation of those results remains controversial, the existence of the phenomenon itself has been established beyond any doubt, registered not simply by human but also by instrumental observation. Both Rutledge's and Norwegian-Swedish Project Hessdalen make it clear that there exist, in close proximity to Earth, anomalous luminous phenomena whose nature and behaviour don't match anything else we know of, natural or artificial. Even if it should turn out – as many ufologists believe – that the phenomena in both cases are natural, it is clear that these pioneering efforts open up new and exciting prospects for future research.

INTERDISCIPLINARY APPROACHES

In order to be sure that we are dealing with a wholly new phenomenon, of course, it is necessary to know what phenomena already exist. From the start, it was recognized that many UFO reports were the result of misinterpretations of conventional phenomena — planets, satellites or aircraft seen under unusual circumstances, with the imagination of the witness enhancing the strangeness of the sight.

A more recent development has been to extend study from things that could be mistaken for UFOs, to things which have similar characteristics or which may be relevant in other respects. For example, Yorkshire's David Clarke and his colleagues have gathered traditional accounts of 'spook lights' and other such phenomena, and compared them with present-day UFO reports. Clearly, if today's UFOs can be seen to be the latest chapter in an on-going history, this throws doubt on such suggestions that UFOs are extraterrestrial craft, attracted here by our entry into the Space Age!

But if such findings close some avenues, they also open up new ones. Characteristic of the speculations they inspire are the various 'earthlights' hypotheses currently being proposed by such researchers as Wales' Paul Devereux, Canada's Michael Persinger and Sweden's Dan Mattson. What is envisaged by these speculations is a process that combines a natural origin — often of a geophysical nature, such as an earth tremor caused by stress in the planet's crust — with psychological effects — such as those known to be caused by changes in the atmosphere.

While no conclusive formulation of such ideas has yet won general acceptance, there is little doubt that the approach is likely to throw light on at least some aspects of the UFO phenomenon. In particular, it may prove relevant to findings such as those of Project Identification and Project Hessdalen.

TESTING FOR PARALLELS

Another promising line of research is to see whether or not the effects attributed to UFOs can be paralleled in other fields of science. The most active researcher in this field is California's James McCampbell, whose 1973 book *Ufology* marked a landmark in UFO research. What characterizes his approach is a face-value acceptance of witness reports: assuming that, by and large, witnesses have given a reasonably reliable account of what they saw, he analyzes their stories to see how the phenomena they describe might be matched elsewhere in science. As an example of how this approach pays off, he recently conducted a study of electro-magnetic effects on car radios, which showed that the oft-reported phenomenon in which witnesses claim that during UFO observations the car radio went haywire, is scientifically plausible: in his practical experiments he was able to precisely duplicate just such an effect. Thus what has hitherto been regarded as a bizarre detail becomes a scientifically significant aspect of the phenomenon.

Testing of a different kind has been carried out by investigators whose concern is with the witness rather than with what he reports. The most significant work of this kind is that of California's Professor Alvin Lawson and his colleague, Dr McCall, whose 'imaginary abductee' experiment established that under hypnosis witnesses who were deliberately fabricating stories of encounters with alien beings would come up with accounts that are virtually indistinguishable from the stories told by those who claim 'real' abductions. Such a finding is capable of more than one interpretation, and certainly doesn't prove that the 'genuine' witnesses were lying. What it *does* do is to indicate how complex are the psychological processes involved. This in turn invites comparison with other manifestations of anomalous behaviour, such as encounters with apparitions and diabolical possession.

Witness evaluation is inevitably a controversial area, because ultimately it is up to the investigator to make a subjective estimate of how much he thinks his witness can be relied upon. In an effort to put witness evaluation on a more objective basis, Austria's Dr Alexander Keul has been working with Ken Phillips, of BUFORA, to formulate tests which will provide investigators with an objective yardstick to measure witness dependability. Though seemingly far removed from the investigation of UFOs, this is a valuable first step which will help the investigator know how much he can depend on the account he has been given.

MEANINGFUL ANALYSIS

The ultimate field of investigation consists in analyzing the statistics made up of the combined reports. Only when substantial numbers of cases are compared can we discern meaningful patterns – of what is seen, how it behaves, under what conditions, and with what consequences. Dr Willy Smith's *UNICAT* project, for example, which is linked to other computer programs throughout the world, seeks to build up a file of cases that have been competently investigated and about which a reasonable quantity of information is available. Working from this basis, it is possible to make useful inferences that can both help us in the evaluation of subsequent reports and also suggest useful avenues of exploration for further research.

As we have seen, investigation can take many forms: checking on witness reports; setting up observation stations so that researchers themselves can see and instrumentally record the phenomena; comparing those phenomena with other anomalous manifestations; exploring links with other fields such as geophysics; studying the witness to see what psychological processes may be at work; analyzing the statistics to see what patterns may emerge. UFO investigation has progressed a long way from the early days; today, it is a sophisticated and scientific field of study, calling on an array of specialist skills and requiring a wide knowledge of the external or parallel factors that may be involved. We may still be a long way from

establishing the ultimate nature of the UFO phenomenon – or even if a UFO phenomenon exists as such –
but already UFO investigation has given us exciting
insights both into the natural world and into the
complexities of human experience.

INVESTIGATIONS – THE STARTING POINT

Jenny Randles

As we do not have flying saucers to examine in our workshops, we have to work from what we *do* have – the eye-witness report. This is the typical sort of UFO case that ufologists face daily:

In autumn 1981, on a Sunday evening, David, a twenty-nine-year-old engineer, and Barbara, a teacher in her early thirties, were bored and decided to go for a ride. They left their Manchester home and drove into the Derbyshire hills. It was twenty-five minutes before midnight, but the dark, deserted roads were a pleasant change from the urban scene.

Stopping at a cul-de-sac by Howden Reservoir, David (the names are fictionalized – common practice when UFO reports are published) observed a brilliant blue/white ball of light 'ten times as bright as Venus' (one of the most brilliant 'stars' in the sky). It was silent, despite the country quiet around them, and moved at a speed 'like that of a military jet'. But then it slowed down and stopped, descending vertically like a parachute before climbing again. Disturbed, the couple drove back home, but stopped at Glossop to report the matter to the police. Perhaps it was a distress flare, they suggested to the officer in charge. But he knew of no search parties or missing persons in the hills.

David and Barbara were in a situation countless witnesses face. They had seen something puzzling. It was not a giant space ship with glowing portholes, or a being from another world.

They did their best to evaluate what they saw and even came up with an explanation. Though a distress flare did not seem to fit the facts, it is important to many witnesses that the interpretation 'UFO' be a last resort. It makes sense to go through what astronomer Dr J Allen Hynek called 'the escalation of hypotheses', testing one solution after another, hoping to find something that works and this is in fact what witnesses do.

In fact the Glossop police ought to have done something about the report. There are standard procedures all police, coastguards, airports etc are supposed to follow. These include reporting the affair officially to a department within the Ministry of Defence (currently called Air Staff 2) that logs all UFOs. Proximity to reservoirs is, in fact, a key question on this list (presumably because the UFO might be a saboteur or spy plane). Of course, we do not know if the Glossop police's indifference was real or not, because if they had dutifully reported the experience to the MoD that would be the last the public would have known about it.

We do not know what the MoD do with their reports. They claim they do nothing. The Glossop police were supposedly not interested. So David and Barbara went home and tried to forget about the light. Especially when the least mention of it brought giggles or amused comments about 'little green men' from friends. Like so many others, they had to accept that to mention a UFO sighting was in some people's eyes putting their sanity in doubt.

This case would have never come to the attention of ufologists in most circumstances. There must be hundreds like it every year lost to UFO research because witnesses have no idea where to find serious investigators. Not only do investigators lack the resources to advertise in *Yellow Pages* (as some do in the USA), but there is the added difficulty for the lay person of telling which are the serious investigation groups. Anyone can set up a 'UFO group', and unfortunately many who do are often inexperienced, if enthusiastic. And to complicate matters there are cults and societies for whom UFOs are a cornerstone of their belief system. Phoning Jodrell Bank may provide an immediate answer on a strange light or occurrence, or it may get the caller referred to BUFORA – or any other group who've been in touch there recently.

There are only about six UFO investigation groups in Britain (including BUFORA, which is nationwide) which have lasted more than ten years. Some have only a handful of members, however the good sense of a group is often inversely related to the number of its members. The BBC once asked me how many members BUFORA had. When I told them two hundred and fifty I received the reply 'the Aetherius Society have thousands and so they are clearly more representative than you'. They were seemingly not bothered by the fact that 'Aetherians' believe Jesus lives on Venus and that its founder has saved the solar system from intergalactic war by commanding a fleet of Martian spaceships against an intelligent meteor that was about to devour the Earth!

A good UFO group *investigates* what people report, tries to explain what they saw and regards a failure to do so as defeat ... if an inevitable one, because some UFOs are unexplainable. The others (which includes the cults and the inexperienced) *believe* in UFOs, and consider explained sightings as an irrelevance which get in the way of their pet theory.

But how can a witness know the difference? S/he can ask about the group's aims and whether it has a code of practice (BUFORA, for example, has instigated a code that is now followed by many other groups, and its aims are a matter of public record at Companies

House). These will at least offer some indication as to whether the group wants to find answers or perpetuate mysteries.

Had David and Barbara known it, there is such a group in the Manchester area. MUFORA (Manchester UFO Research Association) was formed in 1963 and so matches BUFORA's quarter century to rank with the oldest UFO societies in the world. Yet it presently has a fairly typical complement of about nine members.

This limited membership is self-imposed. The group exists only to investigate UFO sightings and has no grand pretensions. However, it has over the years worked on some notable cases and held one-day seminars at Universities.

Being just a group of like-minded people who meet every couple of weeks to share their investigational casework in the area, has advantages and disadvantages. It means that selected cases do get handled quite well. But it means also that the group cannot cope with every UFO sighting that might come its way, so it rarely appeals for sightings publicly, having more than enough to do with those that gravitate towards it naturally, as happened when a media story was seen by the witnesses to the Howden Reservoir light and five years after the encounter they chose to write it down for a UFO investigator.

What happened next? Obviously the most important thing was to get as close as possible to an accurate account from the witnesses of their actual observation. Five years can alter the memory in subtle ways so careful questioning is called for. The next task is to look for an explanation on the assumption that there *will* be one.

Statistics strongly favour a sighting being reducible to an IFO (Identified Flying Object). Whilst most groups would not take a mundane sighting very far (resources just do not permit it) the probability of a sighting being explicable is in the region of nine to one.

MUFORA know, for example, that aircraft from

and to Manchester Airport (the biggest in Britain outside London) pass low over the region. But no records are kept longer than a few weeks and airports have other priorities besides providing lists of movements to UFO societies. In any case it might have been a light plane that filed no flight plan, in which event no airport would be in a position to provide information.

Obtaining weather data is often necessary, to assess the probability of a meteorological cause such as ball lightning or inversion layers that might cause mirages. But meterological information is difficult and costly to obtain.

Astronomical assistance is easier to come by. The British Astronomical Association regularly interface with ufologists on subjects such as satellite burn-ups (spectacular shows high in the atmosphere which trigger many UFO reports). Bright meteors are also often misperceived as strange phenomena. It is possible to access computer programmes that plot the sky at the time and place of a sighting and indicate bright stars and planets which may have been misidentified.

At Howden Reservoir there were no obvious bright astronomical sources. No weather clues emerged. Air traffic could not be checked.

It would be perfectly reasonable to conclude that David and Barbara saw an aircraft with unusually bright lights, turning, and so appearing to hover and descend. They would not be happy with such a suggestion and it cannot be proven or disproven. There is the additional complication that the Pennines have been a major source of bright light UFOs (UAPs – unidentified atmospheric phenomena) and there is good reason to speculate about geological causations inducing atmospheric effects.

Georgina Mills of MUFORA carried out the investigation. Her work was then discussed (as are all other cases) within MUFORA. Her report, when written up, contained sections devoted to the witness story, the weather, checks made to find an explanation, site maps and sketches and a review of the various possible conclusions. Ultimately the conclusion proffered by an investigator is a personal choice (forged by their experience and subjective evaluation of the subject). But a good case report should contain all that an independent reviewer would need to know, in order to formulate their own (perhaps different) conclusions.

There is a long, hard road from the original perception of a strange thing in the sky to the final investigator's case report compiled for the record.

As far as Britain is concerned most of the few serious local groups are in some way affiliated to BUFORA, the national co-ordinating focal point. In a few instances (eg WYUFORG in Yorkshire) the affiliation is as a group. In others (eg MUFORA) by way of several members also being members or responsible field investigation 'agents' for the national team. This national team essentially comprises what is called the NIC (National Investigations Committee). It has as voting members all the twenty-three BUFORA Accredited Investigators but all interested local groups are invited to the NIC meetings two or three times annually and often input their ideas.

Georgina Mills produced her report for MUFORA and it was filed with the NUFON archives. However, as a BUFORA AI also she submitted a copy for BUFORA. This not only gave national access to the data but was a useful protection in case of unforeseen disasters to any set of files.

Next time you see a UFO report think of all the hard work put into its creation by dedicated individuals, in their own time and at their own expense, in the belief that, by documenting this strange and yet fascinating phenomenon, someone, somewhere, somewhen will figure out what is going on.

THE PEOPLE PROBLEM

John A Keel

'The average UFO report isn't worth the paper it's written on' an Air Force officer in the Pentagon told me back in 1966. At the time I scoffed at the statement, assuming it was just part of the sinister conspiracy to downgrade and dismiss the UFO phenomenon. But gradually I came to realize that the statement was painfully accurate. Few UFO reports, even today, contain enough substantive information for a valid analysis. The art of writing reports is still a puzzle to many civilian UFO investigators. The result is a flood of paper and red tape which tells us nothing whatsoever about the UFO witnesses themselves and very little about the actual case being investigated. Before Project Blue Book was dismantled in 1969, Air Force investigators often dismissed baffling cases with the terse remark: 'insufficient information'.

A major part of the problem was created by the Air Force's own official questionnaire (form FTD 164) which was closely copied by most of the civilian UFO investigators and their various organizations. The form is practically worthless. It looked impressive in its seven page format but it was obviously designed by pilots and astronomers for a singular purpose: to extract only information which would make it possible to identify the unknown as a conventional object or mundane astronomical phenomenon. It asked the witness to make impossible estimates of speed, altitude, angle from the horizon, etc, without defining important factors such as the exact position of the witness and the local terrain.

Early in my own investigations I discovered that the average witness could not even pinpoint true north – even when he or she had lived in the area all their life. It is common for a witness to say that the object appeared in the east, say, and travelled to the south west when actually I found that it had appeared in the west and travelled north east! Estimates of altitude are much more difficult to make, even for experienced pilots. And at night it is almost impossible to judge the altitude of an object (usually just a light) of unknown size. Everything becomes relative. For example, a jet airliner travelling at 500mph at 30,000 feet appears to be moving rather slowly to a witness on the ground, while a Piper cub rattling along at 60mph at treetop level seems to be moving at a much faster speed. In my files, I have reports *by police officers* who claimed the object they saw must have been travelling at a speed of at least 2000mph. One report by an elderly man in Florida claimed he saw an object take off at a speed of 5000mph!

If you are a battlefield veteran you know that the experienced eye can actually see a cannon shell in flight and even estimate roughly where it is going to land. Artillery shells lumber along at a fairly slow speed – 7–800mph. Bullets and high velocity shells travel much faster and can't be seen by the naked eye. In order to see a fast moving object, particularly at night, it must either be gigantic in size or it must be a great distance from the observer. An orbiting satellite, for example, can be travelling several thousand miles per hour but is visible because it is hundreds of thousands of miles from the observer.

Therefore, estimates of UFO speeds are usually inaccurate and altitude estimates are questionable unless the object appears near something of a known altitude – such as a mountain or a conventional aircraft. The knowledgeable investigator also carefully checks direction with a compass, allowing for normal magnetic variations in the area, from the exact position of the original sighting. (It is surprising how few investigators bother to do this.) Ninety per cent of the time you will find that the witnesses were completely wrong in *all* their estimates, particularly if they were in a moving vehicle at the time of their sighting. We are on safe ground only in the comparatively rare cases in which a local radar station got a reading on the object or when, as has happened in several instances over the years, the witnesses were able to track the object with a theodolite, a surveying instrument which measures angles and directions accurately.

While Air Force investigators were bent on 'proving' that the witness had seen the planet Venus or a weather balloon, the average civilian investigator is biased in the opposite direction. He's usually trying to prove that the witness saw some type of alien space ship. This bias leads to all kinds of misrepresentation in his report. The witness may have just seen a bluish light with a red glow on the upper part but the investigator gets him to admit that the light was circular or discoid (all lights seen from a distance are circular in appearance), asks many leading questions and ultimately ends up putting together his own version of the event. The final report is apt to read: 'Witness saw a solid object surrounded by a blue haze, with a red flashing light on top.' When the report is later translated into magazine articles and books it becomes 'A disc-shaped object with blue lights and a red strobe light on the upper surface'. The strange blue light has become a metallic flying saucer from outer space!

Unfortunately, the Air Force debunkers were often correct when they claimed that a large percentage of UFO sightings were of natural phenomena – weather balloons and conventional aircraft. But, oddly, none of the astronomers and physicists associated with Project Blue Book ever bothered to study the sources of these misinterpretations. For example, a phenomenon known as noctilucent clouds has produced many spurious UFO reports – but the only real study of these clouds has been made in the Soviet Union.

Noctilucent clouds are brilliantly glowing masses of self-luminous gas which orbit the earth at altitudes ranging from 80–500 miles. Some are gigantic in size and a ground observer can easily think they are much lower in the atmosphere. They appear in a variety of shapes, from spherical to spiral to saw-toothed forms. Back in the mid-1960s Soviet scientists discovered that these clouds reflect radio and television waves. The US Air Force attempted to fire instrument laden rockets into them from isolated bases in Alaska but the results of these experiments were never released. We really know very little about how these clouds are formed. Some scientists think they are related to the Air Glow phenomenon.

What's the Air Glow phenomenon? Astronauts orbiting Earth have seen and photographed spherical glows on the dark side of this planet. These spheres are sometimes arranged in neat formations, like rows of soldiers. This phenomenon is rarely seen by ground observers, just as the huge, self-luminous brownish clouds also reported by astronauts while looking down at our planet, seem to elude witnesses on Earth. It is probable that in a few rare, isolated instances these phenomena have been mistaken for UFOs.

Ball lightning, another rare phenomenon, can also produce spurious UFO reports – especially from ships at sea. Ball lightning consists of spherical charges of electricity which appear during storms and sometimes glide along the surface until they touch something and disappear with a loud explosion. They have been known to come down chimneys, circle a room, and fly out an open window or door! In some cases, animals and humans have been killed by these discharges. Ball lightning at sea appears to be a solid glowing sphere rushing down from the sky and disappearing into the water.

Although few laymen are aware of it, lightning, including ball lightning, does not always travel from the sky to the ground. It sometimes rises from the ground or sea and races upwards into the storm clouds! This lightning-in-reverse could be mistaken for a UFO taking off and disappearing into the sky.

In the late 1940s government scientists became concerned with another kind of natural phenomenon – glowing green fireballs. They still zip across the skies in the mid-west and south west and we still don't know much about them. They are probably related to bolides – small low-flying meteors. Since they usually appear and disappear very quickly most witnesses tend to disregard them rather than report them.

Throughout the 1960s, German and American scientists launched hundreds of special rockets all over the world, which released great clouds of barium gas into the upper atmosphere. These luminous clouds slowly stretched out, following the patterns of the earth's magnetic field like iron filings clustering around a horseshoe magnet. Some of these experiments inspired erroneous UFO reports because they could be seen for hundreds of square miles.

For some mysterious reason, the UFO phenomenon has apparently taken advantage of the barium cloud experiments, particularly when the space shots were given advance publicity. In 1966, a barium cloud shot was announced for 16 August and that night thousands of people turned in UFO reports. The phenomenon was so intense that radio and TV reporters in Arkansas stood in the streets and gave their audiences eye-witness live coverage. A group of scientists in Chicago gleefully collected a large number of reports from Illinois, Minnesota and Wisconsin, believing the barium cloud shot had caused the UFO flap. The only problem was: *the 16 August shot was postponed at the last minute*! So the witnesses in five states must have been watching something else. But what? The barium cloud shot was postponed several more times and was finally held on 24 September 1966. Not a single UFO report was registered on that date!

Few serious UFO investigators have made it a point to find and read technical books about the barium cloud phenomena. Too many others, irritated by the Air Force's often absurd explanations, still continue to overwhelm the UFO reporting networks with reports of these things. Common meteors zooming across several states have also inspired waves of false UFO reports. Occasionally mischievous youngsters get into the act by releasing hot air balloons consisting of plastic bags heated by candles. Several states have now outlawed such activities because the balloons can cause fires when they finally drift earthward.

Colorado University's controversial UFO study (the 'Condon Report') admitted that genuine hoaxes seemed to be rare. Nevertheless, whenever a civilian UFO research organization came across a case containing puzzling psychic elements, it has been a long standing practice to cry 'hoax' and brand the innocent, well-meaning witnesses liars and frauds. They fail, however, to realize that the stranger the ingredients in the witnesses' stories, the more likely it is that the reported incidents are true. Modern investigators must be very cautious about crying hoax. Legally, a hoax must be proved either by overwhelming evidence or, preferably, by a written confession signed by the perpetrator of the hoax. Otherwise, both the investigator and the organization he represents can be sued for libel. In some instances, local police and reporters have deliberately labelled a case a hoax *at the request of the witness* to protect him from the hordes of amateur investigators and enthusiasts who inevitably descend upon the scene.

One of the most difficult problems in ufology is

proving the validity of UFO photographs. (This subject is covered in depth by two articles in this book – Ed.)

Many civilian UFO enthusiasts conduct conversations rather than investigations. Witnesses must be interrogated carefully by reviewing each incident and movement on the day of their sighting as well as their movements and actions after the sighting. Some remarkable, often incredible, details crop up during well conducted in-depth interviews. In a Long Island case in 1967, I learned that the witness had started the day by being followed by a mysterious car. When he parked on Main Street in Babylon, NY, the car pulled in behind him and its occupant jumped out, pointed a camera at him and took his picture. He thought this was odd but soon dismissed it. Later that same day, he saw a circular object hovering low above some trees on a lonely stretch of road. He did not think the two incidents were related, of course, but I have investigated many 'phantom photographer' cases and I believe these mysterious cameramen are connected to the phenomenon in some strange way. Other investigators have uncovered similar incidents in England and, most recently, in Sweden.

In other cases, I have found that healthy witnesses have suffered inexplicable blackouts or fainting spells hours *before* seeing a UFO. These blackouts, experienced by people who had never suffered them before, are especially prevalent in UFO contact cases.

It is also important to extract a complete biography of the witness with emphasis on any unusual psychic or occult experiences they may have had prior to their UFO encounter. I discovered that the majority of all witnesses had latent or active psychic abilities and after I revealed this in a series of articles in the 1960s other independent investigators around the world confirmed it in their own research.

Although many UFO believers choose to assume that most UFO sightings are random chance encounters, there is evidence to show that *witnesses are selected* by

Frank Scully's 1950 *Behind the Flying Saucers* was the earliest book devoted to the phenomenon. The cover reflected the hysteria of the time.
Mary Evans Picture Library

McMinville, 11 May 1950. One photograph not rejected as a fake by the Condon Committee.

Mary Evans Picture Library

Professor Hynek visits the Project Hessdalen site. From left to right: Leif Havik, Professor Jens Tellefsen, Professor J Allen Hynek, Erling Strand, Christer Nordin, Jan Fjeuander.

Project Hessdalen – Erling Strand

Kanab, Utah, 21 March 1968. Fritz van Nest allegedly photographed this classic saucer; subsequently a New Zealand researcher described in detail to one of the editors of this book how he had taken it at Coromandel, New Zealand in 1978.

MEPL

'Circles' phenomena of all shapes and sizes are one form of alleged UFO physical trace. Recent investigations suggest a meteorological origin, however. This was taken in August 1985 at Castions di Zoppola, Italy. *Maurizio Verga*

Delphos, KS, 2 November 1971. Though the case received the *National Enquirer*'s Blue Ribbon Award for the best UFO case of the year, controversy has never ceased to beset this dramatic event for which the only witness was a sixteen-year-old boy and the only substantial evidence this curious circle which, when photographed on Polaroid daylight film shortly after the alleged sighting, showed a fluorescent glow, accompanied by anomalous water-resistance in the affected soil. Nobody questions the phenomenon; but many are disinclined to accept the cause.

Trindade Island, Brasil, 16 January 1958. Freelance photographer Almiro Barauna, assigned to a geophysical research vessel, obtained controversial photographs of a disc which was allegedly also seen by many officers and men on deck. (Inset: enlarged object.)
Mary Evans Picture Library

Poster announcing one of George Adamski's lectures in Britain.
Mary Evans Picture Library

SCOTTISH U.F.O. RESEARCH SOCIETY

Only appearance in Scotland

GEORGE ADAMSKI

On a World Lecture Tour
co-author of "FLYING SAUCERS HAVE LANDED"
author of "INSIDE THE SPACE SHIPS"

SUBJECT

"Flying Saucers"

CENTRAL HALLS TOLLCROSS
TUESDAY 5th MAY AT 7.30

TICKETS 3/- NOW ON SALE
AT BOX OFFICE ONLY

EDIN. BOOKSHOP   JAMES THIN
57 George Street   55 South Bridge

23 May 1971. Rudi Nagora allegedly took photos of a daylight disc. It has been suggested that they are faked; compare this to Gerald Mosbleck's deliberately faked reconstruction below.

Gerald Mosbleck faked the above photograph of a hub-cap thrown into the air, imitating the famous Nagora photograph above.

Gerald Mosbleck

Clearly a fake. TV and film special effects expert Martin Bower shows what can be done in thirty minutes. John Spencer, one of the editors of this book, is given his own 'close encounter'!

Martin Bower

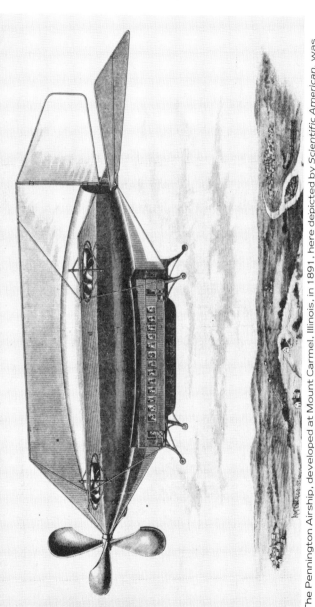

The Pennington Airship, developed at Mount Carmel, Illinois, in 1891, here depicted by *Scientific American*, was one of many projects which could have served as a model for the 1896 airship scare.

Mary Evans Picture Library

Kenneth Arnold. The man whose sighting gave flying saucers a name and ushered the 'modern era' of the phenomenon.

George Adamski with a painting of the Venusian he claimed to have met on 20 November 1952.

Mary Evans Picture Library

some unknown process and that strictly accidental sightings are rare, if not altogether non-existent.

Perhaps the greatest deficiency in the Air Force questionnaire was its neglect to extract the most basic personal information about the witness. It asked only for the witness's name, occupation, and address. However, even the witnesses birthdates can be important. (In a series of contact cases I investigated in 1967 I discovered that *all* of the witnesses had been born on the same date!) Religion can also play a part. Although we now have a huge body of many thousands of reports covering the past thirty years we find that Catholic and Jewish witnesses are extremely rare. Protestants and 'fallen Catholics' (those who have drifted away from the active practice of their religion) account for the bulk of the reports. People with American Indian or Gypsy blood in their background tend to see more UFOs than other people. If sightings occurred on a purely accidental basis, certain statistical laws should be followed. There should be more Smiths, Browns, and Joneses among the witnesses simply because there are more of them in the population. But this isn't the case. People with unusual names like Jablowsky tend to have more sightings than the Smiths. Although left-handed people are a decided minority, there are more left-handed contactees than right-handed ones. The late Ivan Sanderson once pointed out that people with red or blond hair also seemed more prone to having UFO experiences.

The selectivity doesn't end there. Occupations also are of special importance. Schoolteachers, especially those dealing with gifted or, conversely, backward children, seem to be involved in an unusually high percentage of low-level cases and incidents in which the object pursued a car. This UFO penchant for schoolteachers seems to be a world-wide factor. In my travels I found another special group not widely mentioned in published reports – police officers and night-watchmen. While the UFO observations of on duty policemen are frequently cited by reporters searching for reliable witnesses, a great many lawmen also have unusual sightings while off duty, as do night-watchmen (who are often retired cops). Finally, and most chilling of all, are men and women who are civilian employees at military bases or who work at jobs requiring a security clearance. Barbers, farmers, and auto mechanics are decidedly rare among UFO witnesses. In recent years there has been a sharp increase in sightings among doctors, lawyers, regional politicians and stubborn, sceptical newspapermen.

Obviously the UFO phenomenon has some system of selectivity, and it is highly probable that most of the people picked undergo something more than a mere visual sighting. *Something they cannot remember later*. Are their minds being reprogrammed, as many researchers suspect?

The only way we will ever learn what is really going on is by thoroughly investigating the witnesses themselves. The UFOs are so widespread and so active they must be doing something. And whatever it is, *they are doing it to PEOPLE*. Special people who have been carefully picked from the mainstream of society and chosen for special treatment. Therefore, their descriptions of what they have seen are less important than what they have experienced physically, psychologically, and mentally. The objects are merely the medium for their message, whatever it might be. The Air Force never got anywhere because it was concerned solely with explaining away the descriptions of the objects. The civilian UFO organizations have never made any progress because they have been concerned with trying to interpret the meaning of the objects, determining their source and attacking the Air Force explanations. Proving the reliability of witnesses became more important to them than learning the details of what the witnesses actually experienced.

In the post-1947 era, there were two civilian groups dominating UFO investigations in the United States.

The National Investigation Committees on Aerial Phenomena (NICAP), headed by a writer for pulp flying magazines, Donald Keyhoe, became notorious for its efforts to suppress all contact and abduction reports. But the Aerial Phenomena Research Organization (APRO) operated by a housewife named Coral Lorenzen did make an attempt to publish contact stories, particularly those from South America. But both groups were so bogged down in a hopeless battle with the US Air Force – and with each other – that they accomplished very little. Although contact and abduction cases were occurring on a massive scale most American ufologists refused to recognize such activities. They spent forty years chasing pies in the sky rather than conducting methodical research into what was happening on the ground.

It was not until 1986, when a popular novelist named Whitley Strieber underwent a long series of demonological experiences and wrote a best-selling book, *Communion*, that American ufologists belatedly began to consider abduction cases. Budd Hopkins, a commercial artist, had previously started a study of contactee claimants but, lacking the necessary historical background, he ran amok in a hallucinatory world of 'devil's marks' and classic demonological manifestations. Again, both men strained to put everything into an extraterrestrial concept when, of course, the real explanations were to be found in another direction.

The UFO phenomenon can really be divided into two completely unrelated parts. The objects seen in the sky, often passing through all the colours of the visible spectrum from ultraviolet to infrared, actually have no connection to the things – and the entities – seen on the ground. The landings, abductions and contacts and general tomfoolery are primarily part of a very ancient, very well observed phenomenon that has spawned all of man's belief systems. It has no more basis in reality than the popular Arab belief in Djinns. The manifestations behind these systems have a purpose that has been deliberately hidden from the human race for thousands of years.

The so-called New Age of the 1960s and 1970s has produced a new awareness in millions of people. Their minds have been conditioned to accept what was once totally unacceptable. Even the always pathetically conservative, foot-dragging scientific community is beginning to adopt New Age attitudes and science itself is careening towards an Age of Magic. The whole UFO phenomenon, with all the attending nonsense, is a small part of the great changes ahead. Ufology has, I have noted, been largely advocated and supported by people who are on the outside looking in. People who have really been excluded from all that has been taking place in the past two decades. And the phenomena have been leading them around by the noses, causing them to mumble darkly about alien invasions, hybrids, genetic experiments and other gross, amateurish misinterpretations. I know because I was once there. I was awed that all the contactees I came across had been born on 6 September. But I quickly learned this was the nature of the game. If an investigator sets out to find left-handed, red-haired, cross-eyed contactees they will turn up by the dozens. Author Brad Steiger has even published a series of books about 'Star People' listing criteria by which they can be identified. So, naturally enough, thousands of 'Star People' conforming to those criteria have appeared.

A few years ago Dr J Allen Hynek devised a 'Strangeness' index to compare witness reliability with the degree of strangeness in their report. Unfortunately, strangeness is totally subjective, like pain, and difficult – if not altogether impossible – to measure. What might seem incredibly strange to one inexperienced investigator might seem almost routine to a more experienced person. Reliability is also difficult to establish. The usual criterion is the person's occupation. But the history of ufology has shown that a town drunk can have a real UFO experience as well as the town's police chief. The drunk would automatically receive a very low rating on the reliability scale. The police chief might actually be a conniving, cantankerous, lying old reprobate but his occupation would give him a high rating.

Similarly, a person who has a long history of prophetic dreams and other psychic experiences might be known to the local gossips as a crackpot and would rate low on the reliability scale. But extensive UFO studies have shown that this is also the kind of person *most likely* to have a genuine low-level or landing sighting. Their psychic ability might also make them susceptible to receiving a telepathic message or undergoing something even stranger. So they would have a high strangeness quotient and a low reliability rating, thus negating their report and unfairly depriving the public of valuable information.

Witnesses should be judged only by experts trained in such matters: psychiatrists, psychologists, sociologists, and experienced journalists. An experienced lawyer can be a much better UFO investigator than an astrophysicist for example, whose training does not include dealing with – and judging – people. If nothing else, the past thirty years have taught us that technology is virtually useless in UFO investigations. Nevertheless, many civilian investigators still load themselves down with Geiger counters and other expensive gadgets. It is true that excessive radiation has been found at a few UFO sites in the past thirty years, but so few that the odds for stumbling into such a situation are astronomical. Even then, Geiger counters can only indicate the presence of radiation. They cannot give an accurate and scientific measurement of the radiation.

Today experienced investigators carry tape recorders for interviewing witnesses, and a few plastic bags for collecting samples of any substances that might be found at the UFO site. A compass, a star chart for locating the exact position of the brightest stars in the sky at the time of the sighting, and a pocket camera are the only other pieces of equipment you will really need. Elaborately outfitted expeditions lugging walkie-talkies, theodolites, flares, and firearms are a thing of the past.

Finally, what should you do with your UFO report once you have carefully interviewed the witnesses and painstakingly typed it all up? Make several copies and distribute them to more than one organization or investigative body. The national UFO organizations have a distressing habit of throwing reports they receive into a file drawer and forgetting about them. Some organizations even demand exclusive rights to all reports they receive. You might as well flush your report down the toilet.

If the witnesses don't want their names used, give their full names, addresses, etc in your report but include a notation stating that they wish to remain anonymous. If they agree to having their names used, get the agreement in writing. If you take photographs, buy a pad of model release forms from a camera store and make sure everyone who appears in your pictures has signed a release form; if your pictures are ultimately published in a magazine or newspaper you could get in a lot of legal trouble if you don't have written permission from the people you've photographed.

Back in the good old days, UFO investigating was a relatively easy task. Now ufology is slowly evolving into an exact science and it is becoming more and more complicated. The simplistic extraterrestrial hypothesis is losing ground to the complex paraphysical concept. Investigators are no longer concerned with merely proving that the Air Force is lying, or that UFOs came from outer space. We are trying to find out what is really going on, and what the ultimate meaning of the phenomenon is. So we have to approach everything with the same thoroughness that military intelligence might use in collecting evidence to find a spy in the Pentagon.

TRACES OF UFO LANDINGS?

Maurizio Verga

UFOs are a set of phenomena essentially based on witnesses' tales: hard evidence is needed to demonstrate the reality of those tales. During forty years of sightings of unusual aerial phenomena all over the world, a great deal of physical proof has been offered to show the materiality of these 'objects' and, consequently, their extraterrestrial origin. Of the three most important kinds of proof; photos, radar detections and traces, traces related to the sighting of UFO phenomena or indirectly associated with them (even though no sighting was reported) would, if trustworthy, be the most solid evidence and consequently the most convincing; it is also one of the most intriguing aspects of the whole question.

Traces imply that the phenomenon is not something perceived subjectively and pertaining only to the senses of the witness, but something with truly physical attributes. Extraterrestrialists, as support for their contention that UFOs exist as material spacecraft, rely heavily on physical trace evidence.

What is a trace case?: As many as 3000 alleged trace events have been reported in the past forty years, representing real 'trace phenomena' whose existence cannot be neglected. But this is a long way from saying it represents proof for the materiality of the UFO phenomena: on the one hand the quality of the original report is often questionable, and on the other even when the traces are unquestionably real their origin and nature may still be open to question. Physical traces are included in the so-called 'close encounters of the second kind' (CE 2) together with less frequent incidents, such as those involving physiological effects and light 'injuries' on witnesses. They form twenty per cent of all close encounter reports.

There are two kinds of traces: those directly associated with UFO phenomena and those where such an association is indirect only. The former represents about sixty per cent of the whole, and it includes explained cases too, as the selection parameter is the presence of an observed 'unusual' phenomenon in the same area where a physical trace has been found. So while we have cases such as Trans-en-Provence in France, where the witness described a strange object hovering over the place where a circular trace was later found on the ground, we also have cases presented by the press as 'UFO trace incidents' which were simple meteorite falls producing holes in the ground.

A third or so of all trace cases refer to strange marks on the ground without any related visual sighting. Their apparent strangeness, the characteristic circular shape and, often, news of UFO sightings at that same time, lead people to presume a relationship with UFO phenomena. Such is the case with the famous English 'cornfields circles' which appear each summer and which, like most of these traces, have no clear link with what we usually call a 'UFO phenomenon'.

To qualify as a 'UFO trace incident' an event would have to be associated with what is conventionally known as the UFO phenomenon, either reported or only supposed.

Such an association is open to question in two ways.

First, by considering the natural phenomena capable of producing traces. Second, by considering the facts and figures, as well as the methods of the field investigators.

There are several natural events that can produce remarkably strange trace marks under certain circumstances. These include fungi, plants and grass sickness, lightning, animal habits, whirlwinds, tornadoes, rain, helicopter slipstreams, exfoliation, geomorphological features and so on. Furthermore, the action of man on the environment can also result in traces, for example cars, mowers, fires, chemical products, etc ... Discovering such a trace after a local UFO sighting can easily lead to their connection with 'alien activity'. Even where no UFO was seen, the discovery of a trace (especially when circular) can reawaken memories in the collective conscience of stereotyped flying saucers and their alleged effects. The existence of concrete evidence tends to make any case more credible, no matter how spurious it may be. Here are a few examples of explained traces taken from the author's own studies:

— eleven (!) rings ranging in diameter from two point five to six metres were found in a wheatfield near Rossburn, Canada. Some of them were aligned directly underneath a telephone line: others ranged from nought to sixty centimetres apart. The crop was swirled and depressed to the ground in an anti-clockwise direction in most rings, though a few were swirled clockwise. An analysis of the grain showed that a peculiar darkening was not due to scorching but to the presence of mould, presumably caused by grain lying on the ground being pushed into the wet soil. Almost certainly the traces were caused by a tornado, as suggested by an atmospheric specialist: the area was relatively prone to tornadoes, and one or two months before the discovery of the rings the weather conditions were favourable to produce them. Again, a remarkable set of traces involving serious damage to some trees and a stone wall at Montauroux, France, in October 1972 was related by a UFO magazine to UFO activity, but was explained as the action of a strong tornado.

— a depression about 1.8 metres across was indented to a depth of 15.2cms with a central indentation about 45.7cms: the sides were smooth as glass. There were seven smaller holes around the edge of the central indentation. A fine powdery substance at the base of the main hole and around the hole was found to be natural salt desiccated by an intense heat. The trace was found at Boggabri, New South Wales, Australia in November 1970 and was indirectly associated to UFOs. Its origin was actually primary and secondary lightning strikes during a coinciding period of electrical storms.

— at Barbiano di Cotignola (near Ravenna, Italy) on 8 July 1974 a semicircular zone of yellowed and damaged grass was immediately related to a local UFO sighting, but later a man stated he had produced it with a mower.

— three nearly circular burned traces, placed a few metres one from the other in a straight line. Inside them, the soil and some dried shrubs were burned. Almost certainly the cause was due to picnickers. The traces were found on a mountain by a young ufologist in search of physical evidence for the sighting of a bright object seen over the mountain itself: the 'mysterious light' was identified as Venus.

Footprints and fragments: There is a particular kind of ground mark known as 'footprints': they are generally small traces supposedly left by the so-called 'entities' often seen in association with UFO landings. Usually they resemble the imprints of shoes or human feet, even though the size is often abnormal. Their number and the way they are placed on the ground is puzzling in most cases: for example, it is hard to think that they have been left by a 'living' being when only two footprints have been reported. Such 'footprints' seem to provide physical evidence for entity sightings, but the reality is quite different.

Some big 'footprints' were found after two rainy days, during the investigation of the famous Italian abductee Fortunato Zanfretta near Genoa, on 27 December 1978. One of them was 53cms long, 20cms wide and 5cms deep: the following imprint was 1.8 metres away. In fact, they were just puddles.

There have been very few instances of fragments and other unusual substances on alleged UFO landing sites: some twenty events in forty years. Most have not been subjected to an in-depth investigation and available information is often rumour with no value. To obtain a piece of a UFO is the dream of every ufologist; unfortunately those few samples subjected to analysis didn't even supply interesting information.' Their constituents were perfectly normal, even though the results were sometimes interpreted according to ufologists' wishes: for example, the long debated Ubatuba case, in which a UFO was thought to have exploded over a Brazilian shore in 1957 and some fragments then found. Following the original analysis someone stated that the metal pieces were near pure magnesium, impossible to produce on Earth at that time. Further analysis and interpretations gave different results, but it seems that the 'exceptionally strange fragments' were nothing other than parts of a projectile shot by the Brazilian artillery!

Often falls of strange objects from the sky, such as pieces of ice or metal, as well as simple meteorites, have been associated with UFO phenomena and labelled fragments. Most ufologists justly avoid considering those events as physical traces.

Psychological implications: The discovery of a trace tends to set the witness thinking in terms of a UFO.

And, of course, if there is a close encounter at the root of the discovery he will often go to the area where he saw the UFO with a view to finding evidence of the reality of the experience. This intense desire to find proof can easily lead to him discovering a myriad of insignificant anomalies (eg a broken branch, an animal mark, the remains of a fire and so on) and relating them to the UFO. This is a typical scenario for a UFO seen in the distance (where often the exact location of the landing or near landing is not known anyway).

Less common is the deliberate false linking of spurious traces with a genuine UFO, in order to make the sighting more believable, but this scenario is also feasible even for many rational people who would normally not behave in this fashion, and must be taken very seriously when investigators don't follow up the traces on site and merely rely on the word of the witness.

When enquirers do visit the site we should expect them to validate or invalidate the traces, but the reality of the matter is often rather different. Unfortunately, the UFO investigator is usually on the same level as the witness, having the same unconscious need and beliefs, maybe even more powerful due to his work. He is usually unprepared in terms of scientific methodology. He may well strongly desire to present a classic case to his colleagues. He may have a belief system which includes the material reality of UFOs, thus anticipating trace evidence. All of these things lead him to frequent and serious errors. Any sufficiently strange mark at or near the site may be seen in terms of alien activity.

Unidentified traces: There are some truly strange and apparently unidentified traces, but their number is low. In any case, doubts must remain. Natural phenomena or human activity under unusual circumstances could precipitate apparently unexplained traces. If this circumstance is rare enough the possibility of identification is close to impossible, except in a few lucky cases. Those which are investigated in enough depth form again but a fraction (perhaps twenty-five per cent). In other words, what we term the trace phenomenon is but a small residue of well investigated reports, about five per cent or less of the total.

Here is one example of a high quality case, where the reported traces haven't been explained satisfactorily:

— following the observation of a metallic cigar-shaped object taking off from a maize field, an oblong damaged area was found in the field itself. The plants in that zone were folded, without being broken, in such a way that the leaves were also laid flat. The maize cobs appeared dry on the outside, while inside they were still fresh. The squashed area covered part of three of the plant rows, two of which were folded towards the east and one towards the west. The measurements of this affected side were 6.5 × 2.9 metres and the 2.4 metres high, plants were folded at a level of 1.1–1.2 metres from the ground. It seems that in the middle of the area there was a hole which appeared to have been made by a strong stream of air.

Hoaxed traces: We must also not forget the outright hoax – faked traces accompanying UFO sightings. The pseudo-witness or other people produce material proof for creating a story where the fundamental element is the UFO or, even better, what it represents at the emotional stage. There are two groups of faked traces: (1) those produced purposely, and (2) those previously being on the site of a discovery and exploited to improve the reliability and exceptionality of the (invented) sighting tale.

Because physical evidence is a way of defending one's belief system from the sceptics, this kind of hoaxing is surprisingly widespread. Hoaxers hide themselves behind anonymity and only in very rare cases (generally after a long period of time) they confess. Most investigators aren't able to go deeply into the enquiry and though they may have doubts about the reliability of a trace case, it isn't always possible to prove them.

Hoaxes are deeply biased by the popular image of UFOs as extraterrestrial devices. Traces always present a technological peculiarity, that is they have to reproduce UFO effects produced by a physical craft during landing and take off. There are basic stereotypes in UFO mythology: the classic saucer shape associated with circular traces (found even if the observed object is shaped like a sphere or an oval!), the legs used as landing gear in accordance with the space craft of science fiction films or the US Lunar Module, the presence of a sort of propulsion or energy able to produce wide clearly outlined burnings on the ground or strange desiccations of vegetation. It is clear that hoaxers prepare the whole event (the trace in our case) using the fundamental components of UFO technological mythology: each of us perceives them in his or her own way.

The following is taken from tens of other similar events:

— in the same place where a man claimed to have sighted some strange coloured lights was discovered a five to six metre circular trace, where the soil appeared burned. The whole event was a joke by some boys on the witness, a true believer in UFOs and extraterrestrials. They traced out the circle using a motor lorry tyre, then burned the area with petrol.

Conclusion: The study of traces gives us much cause to rethink common attitudes, on two grounds:

— the explanation of most trace reports is to be found in terms of natural or identifiable artificial origins.
— many investigation reports are unacceptable as a basis for scientific data. Investigators are often guilty

of subjectivity and emotional involvement.

We are left with a small residue which seems to demonstrate the physical reality of a seemingly unknown phenomenon (although unknown does not necessarily mean alien). But, even so, we can never totally exclude rare kinds of conventional explanation due to the lack of specific information.

Consequently, as material back up for witness reports, the physical trace evidence we possess is sadly inadequate.

THE ELUSIVE PHOTOGRAPHIC EVIDENCE

Gerald Mosbleck

Detection of fake or proof of authenticity should be the prime objective when investigating UFO photographs. If eyesight alone is not sufficient, the next step is the use of magnification instruments for an analysis of the structure of the picture. The most modern way is examination by computer. The American group GSW (Ground Saucer Watch) has tried this in recent years, with varied success.

Possible causes of erroneous UFO photographs: Main causes may be clouds, birds, planes, balloons and optical phenomena. But less known photographic phenomena can lead to a misinterpretation of the image as well, eg in Hamburg a policeman snapped a picture of his patrol car at night. The blue light of his car resulted in a wonderful red UFO in the upper half of the picture. When he took the picture, the policeman had not noticed this so-called katadioptric image, whose origin has a reflection within the lens.

If you take photographs by night using a flashlight, tiny particles of dust or raindrops in front of the camera may appear on the picture like brilliant balls of light. Simple lens reflections often have the form of a flat disc. The origin of this is the lens and back-lighted exposure. If you're lucky, the source of light is discernible on the picture, but in most cases it is not, and then you can only speculate.

Faults may also appear when the photo is being developed, and may later look like UFOs. They occur especially when you develop your own pictures as a hobby, but they can also happen in professional laboratories.

Fake photographs and hoaxes: As every UFO-researcher knows, there are unfortunately many UFO photos taken by sensation-thirsty or greedy hobby-photographers. Many authors of such photographs have been found; the Swiss 'Billy' Meier is only one example. The following examples should be considered:

— a *photomontage* uses parts of different pictures and reproduces them so that the later picture shows objects that had not been visible in the originals. These manipulations show up easily by the different grain structures of the object and its surrounding.

— some cameras allow *double exposure*. The film is not wound on, allowing the frame to be exposed twice. If you photograph, for example, a forest with a lot of sky above, you may later photograph a UFO-model into this sky.

— a considerable number of tricks are possible *during the process of magnification*. The simplest way to create a fake here is to leave out parts of the picture by choosing only a sector for magnification. It is also possible to copy in objects with the *enlarger*.

— the simplest way to fake UFO-pictures is also the most common. In most cases someone throws a model into the air and photographs it. Any object of any size can appear as a giant flying object. Sometimes the object is suspended on a thread or glued to a glass pane

in front of the camera. The problem with these photos
is that you can rarely prove they're faked.

I have experimentally faked several pictures with
thrown objects and objects suspended on nylon
threads. In one there is a man standing in a meadow
with his arm held high, giving an impression of great
range. Actually the two-inch model was suspended
only three feet from the camera. Even with the highest
enlargement you'll only get the grain and not the
thread. The picture shown in this book imitates the
famous 'Nagora photos'. A hub cap thrown into the air
is identical with Nagora's flying saucer. You can prove
no manipulation in this case – there is none! A flying
object was photographed! Optical effects make it look
bigger than it is. Only because we perceive (on photos)
small near objects like far away large ones these
pictures look genuine.

Manipulation with films: On still photos, fakes are
easy to do and hard to prove, but on film there is more
to be analyzed. With a moving image it's easier to
pronounce about the size and – most of all – mass of
the object. It's a pity there are not many UFO films.
Many, such as the Utah and Montana films, show
merely undefined brilliant points of light. Others,
mainly from the USA (for example the 'lost creek
saucer', 'airport saucer' and the Menger films) are
clearly hoaxes.

Circumstances of the picture: Investigation of the
circumstances of a UFO photo are as important as the
analysis of the film material itself. Information that can
easily be verified adds to the credibility of the witness.
If a witness claims he took the picture on a sunny day,
but in fact it was a rainy day (check with the weather
report), you naturally should be cautious. You should
also examine the scenery. If you can't locate the place a
witness tells you (as in the Nagora case) you have to
doubt the genuineness of the picture. And information

about the camera is as important as information about the film.

The credibility of the witnesses will be discussed elsewhere in this book but you should look for financial motives. A photographer who has snapped a genuine UFO will make it available without looking for money from a newspaper. Films or photos offered for sale are suspect for this reason. The relatives and friends of the photographer can supply further hints about fabrication. If you find that the photographer has contact with 'UFO sects', that is a further reason to be on your guard.

Conclusions: As long as there are people who fake UFO pictures and films for money, and as long as there are no conclusive methods for analyzing these pictures, UFO research should not use photos as proof, only as further evidence in a well-researched case. But critics should consider also that the proof that you can make pictures or films of an aircraft model does not imply that no real aircraft exist!

IS A PICTURE WORTH
A THOUSAND WORDS?

John Shaw LBIPP

The title is an old and well worn expression, but never more appropriate than when applied to the UFO phenomenon. Often, UFO photographs submitted for appraisal are taken by a single witness but even in cases with multiple witnesses, they may represent the only tangible evidence of a UFO event.

As we shall see, some photographic reports turn out to be:

— *misidentifieds*, everyday objects seen from an unusual angle or under unusual circumstances.
— *Optical or photographically generated misidentifieds*, lens flares, film processing or coating faults, camera fogging or other images on the film not truly representative of the scene recorded.
— *Hoaxes*, designed to mislead;
— *natural aerial phenomena*, scientifically accepted but sometimes little-known occurrences: ball lightning, piezoelectric effects, static discharges, Sun and Moon dogs (false secondary images of the Sun or Moon seen in nearby clouds), unusual cloud formations, mirages, comets, fireballs, meteors and many others.

A very small percentage of the reports, after undergoing appraisal on all of the above, continue to remain UFOs – unidentified. These can be movie films, stills and video images of hitherto unknown aerial phenomena and in some very few instances appear to provide very strong evidence for the possibility that this planet is being visited by an extraterrestrial agency.

Perhaps the most significant development in UFO photographic research over the past forty years is in the use of the computer to enhance images of would-be alien spacecraft. The technique is a spin off from the space programme; such as the much publicized photographs from the NASA deep space probes. When applied to photographs or films of UFOs, this becomes a powerful research tool in sorting out hoaxes, misidentifieds, unknowns – leaving the UFOs. Usually the images presented are small in relation to the picture area and when enlarged, details are lost in the grain of the film. However, the detail is still there, and can, in the hands of a skilled operator, be recovered.

One investigation group, Ground Saucer Watch (GSW) of Cleveland, Ohio, has employed a computer on UFO photographs on a large scale; analyzing a thousand photographs and rejecting all but forty-five as misidentifications and hoaxes.

The technique for analyzing photographs uses a television-type camera to scan a picture and break it down into individual pixels (picture elements). In the case of GSW, this is displayed as an array of 512 columns and 480 rows – nearly a quarter of a million pixels to make up the entire picture. The scanner measures the brightness of each of the pixels and assigns a number to it representing how bright it is on a scale of nought (black) to thirty-one (bright white). These numbers are then stored in the computer's memory and can be recalled onto a television screen as a direct copy of the original. Also, they can be manipulated to increase or decrease the contrast, lighten the shadow areas of the picture while holding back the highlight or brighter parts of the picture and so retain detail in both, something very difficult to do photographically. Measurements of angles and distances between objects in the picture can be calculated very quickly by the computer and so indicate if the UFO is a real object or a model either in the camera's field of view or superimposed upon the scene at a later date.

One of the very useful effects that can be obtained is that of 'edge enhancement' whereby the computer is instructed to look for any line too faint to be visible to the naked eye, and then make it visible in the picture. For example, a thin wire holding up a model, or the faint outline of wings identifying the UFO as an aircraft.

A good example of work with computer-assisted analysis involved the classic case of a film shot by professional cameraman, Lee Hansen, while flying over Catalina Island, California. Shot in April 1966, this film withstood explanation for nearly twenty years. It showed a disc-shaped object, silver in colour, with a shadow beneath, moving about the mountains. The pilot estimated the object as moving at a speed of approximately 150 knots and about twenty metres across. On the face of it, a good, typical UFO. The film was taken to a top expert in computer enhancement, Dr Robert Nathan of the Jet Propulsion Laboratory, Pasadena, home of NASA's image-processing facilities.

A frame of the film was scanned, enlarged and displayed on a television monitor. This picture showed a fuzzy disc with all detail obscured in photographic grain. The following frame was also digitized and overlaid on the first; the two frames being averaged. This procedure was carried out with the third and fourth frame. On each pass, the grain in the picture diminished and the image of the UFO became sharper and exhibited more detail. Slowly the UFO became recognizable as a small, light aircraft, seen from about the same flight level (hence the absence of any wings seen in the film) and at three-quarter angle, which tended to obscure the tail fin of the aircraft. After enhancement even the cockpit and pilot could be discerned.

However, enhancement equipment is expensive, and GSW have to make a charge for every photograph or film analyzed, so when it comes to analyzing photographs, researchers often have to resort to less exotic means – and this leaves them susceptible to the hoaxer.

In March 1970, David Simpson initiated a photographic UFO hoax at Warminster in England which ran for two and a half years. At that time, Warminster was the UFO event centre of England and anyone interested in the subject made the pilgrimage to the hills just outside the town in the hope of seeing one or more of the many UFOs reported. It was on one such 'skywatch' one night that a group of people interested in the subject became the unwitting pawns in this event. David Simpson placed a purple light on top of a car some distance from the researchers while a colleague of his within the group appeared to take photographs of the 'UFO'. The group were not aware of this liaison; in fact the UFO had already been superimposed onto the film prior to the evening's events. The resulting film, taken away that night and processed by the group, showed two UFOs hovering above the hill.

Despite the fact that there were many inconsistencies in the witnesses' accounts of the night's events, such as two UFOs above the outline of hills in the photographs while the group observed one light below the level of hills at the time; and that a study of the previous frames showed some street lights to be on and other frames showed them to be off on the actual night in question, the photographs were extensively publicized by UFO buffs and purported to be genuine. An eminent French scientist went on record as saying that he was convinced of their authenticity. Sadly, many people interested in the subject will accept evidence on face value if it supports their case.

This sort of hoax can also be lucrative; one person who allegedly took some dubious photographs of the Loch Ness Monster fully expected an income of some £200,000 in the first six months from world-wide syndication fees.

We have seen how fakes can be produced photographically, but how feasible are they from the point of view of constructing the object to be faked? I contacted Martin Bower for his opinion on this.

Martin is one of Britain's top film/TV special effects model makers. His film credits include *Alien*, *Flash Gordon*, and *Outland*; on television, *Space 1999*, *Dr Who*, *Tripods* and many others.

Clearly, with mega-million budgets to work with model makers like Martin can produce all kinds of visual images, so is a UFO hoax expensive to stage?

'Definitely not' Martin assured us. 'Technique is what counts. Bearing in mind that the image being created is not well known the possibilities are endless.'

Martin agreed to demonstrate this, with the editor of this book, John Spencer, as witness (and, as it turned out, victim!). He deliberately faked a photograph of a landed UFO complete with alien entity giving John Spencer his own *very* close encounter. (See picture section.) This photograph would not of course pass close examination; the UFO's car hubcaps alone are very obvious and we deliberately asked Martin to make the 'alien' as ludicrous as possible to make clear the fact that the photo *was* indeed a fake.

What is important about this photograph is how easy it was to create! It took less than thirty minutes to produce the photograph of an alien actually intertwined around our 'contactee', sitting on a landed saucer in a typical desolate landing setting. And that included the time it took to make the UFO and entity models! We promised not to give all the techniques away but I can say that the 'UFO' took less than ten minutes to create (it wasn't even glued together) from the two car hubcaps, a dustbin lid and the top of a wok.

Ten minutes after the shutter clicked the hubcaps were back on the car! The camera Martin had used was the type every holidaymaker uses for his snaps.

'And bear in mind' Martin pointed out 'I'm not really trying. A properly constructed model and more attention to detail would not be difficult if I had really set out to deceive.'

I told Martin about the sort of money hoaxers hope to make, and sometimes do make. 'For that' Martin said, 'You don't have to fake, as such. Give me a few days and a reasonable budget and I'll build the full size one hundred foot craft. And I'll get it in the air for you, without wires!'

Martin agreed with me, though, that this didn't mean that all UFO photographs were useless; it just emphasized that to be really useful independent witness confirmation was required, and attention to more than just the visual image.

Therefore it must be remembered that photographs on their own are very poor evidence. So much can be done to doctor a film and so produce images of unreal objects. The camera has one lens, one viewpoint and a fixed field of view – a fact relied upon in the still and movie industries to record images in a particular way. False images can also be produced by double exposures, reflected objects and models, although a fairly close-up study of most photographs, particularly the negatives, will reveal this. For instance, with models, giveaway clues are the sharpness of the object in relation to the background – an object far away will appear 'fuzzier' than one close up due to atmospheric effects, or an object may appear sharply focused while the background is out of focus indicating that it is close to the camera, or the underside of the object may be dark which could mean that it is close to the ground. A close study of the negative will usually detect double exposures and a thorough investigation and study of photographs and where they were taken will usually detect mirrored images – for example, a view taken in daylight from inside a house through a pane of glass, may show a reflection of a room light. One hoaxer, Alex Birch, claimed to have photographed five UFOs over Sheffield, England in 1962. In actual fact the images were painted onto a pane of glass through which he took the picture. His photograph was accepted as genuine for ten years before he finally made his confession. In that time he had been interviewed on radio and television and by the Air Ministry and had even appeared at the inaugural meeting of BUFORA!

So what type of photographs would provide suitable evidence? They must meet certain criteria before they undergo complex analysis such as computer enhancement, and the ones that do not can usually be weeded out at the initial investigation stage. There should be at least one independent witness to the event, other than the photographer. The original film, negative, or transparency (slide) should be submitted. The whole film should be provided, not just the appropriate frames, as the other photographs on the roll may give clues to the operating functions of the camera, ie lens flare, light leakage, shutter operation, weather conditions and time of day as well as the characteristics of the film itself. There must be reference points in the picture, eg trees, buildings, geographical features and an horizon line. These will assist in assessing the size, shape and distance. There should be a series of pictures if possible, the more, the better. Several photographs are more valuable in providing detail than one and a movie sequence is the most valuable of all, being harder to fake than a still photograph, and it can provide information on the time elapsed during a sighting.

Recently, I was asked to comment on a photograph that apparently showed a UFO over a block of flats in South London. I was concerned that the witness had stated that he had taken the photograph looking in a westerly direction; the shadows were inconsistent with the stated time of day and direction. The case was referred back to the investigator without, at that stage, comment on the alleged UFO.

Another case about which I was asked for my opinion involved an 8mm movie film of the London skyline taken from a high-rise block of flats. The view showed a UFO hovering and then moving across the picture and out of the field of view. The witness had stated that the camera had been mounted on a tripod in his living room and while he was looking through the camera's viewfinder he had seen the UFO and commenced to film it. A detailed questionnaire had been completed by him and forwarded to me with the film. A frame by frame study of the film showed, on the left far horizon, a factory chimney. When the object was stationary the chimney was not smoking, but there was a long plume of smoke from it on the frame where the object started to move. As this was supposed to be one, continuous filming, obviously something was wrong. On interviewing the witness, with this in mind, I noticed that in his living room there was a table lamp which resembled the shape of the UFO. It was fairly easy to deduce that he had photographed the reflection of the lamp in the window glass, turned off the camera, presumably to rig a remote shutter release, and then filmed the skyline while he moved the lamp, reflecting its image in the glass. Unfortunately for him, in this period of time, the factory had gone into production and gave me the clue I needed to determine this case to be a hoax.

Photographs and movies will not on their own confirm the existence of 'flying saucers', but add weight to the mass of evidence building up around the world. Of the fact that people see UFOs, there is no doubt. Of the fact that people photograph UFOs, there is also no doubt. But what the objective reality is that they see and photograph and whether collectively it represents one or many things we do not as yet understand. Often, we can say what an object is not, but as the list of possibilities runs out, then the evidence for that object being something unknown, possibly extraterrestrial, becomes stronger. Let us now examine one case that has withstood the tests to date, although controversy will still surround it until the UFO enigma is solved.

On 11 May 1950, on a small farm near McMinnville in Oregon, Mrs Trent was outside giving the rabbits their early evening feed when she noticed a huge disc-shaped object approaching from the north east. She called her husband, who quickly found their camera, and Mrs Trent took two black and white photographs of the object as it passed silently across the sky towards the north west. The Trents did not attach importance to their sighting or to the photographs, and, as there were a few frames on the film to be used up, it was a few days before the film was processed. Even then, they ignored what the photographs showed, but by chance, a local newspaper heard about them. Eventually, they caused a sensation and were featured in *Life* magazine. They became the only photographs not to be dismissed by the Condon Committee, and their investigator, William Hartmann, in his findings, concluded that the evidence presented was consistent with the Trent's testimony 'that an extraordinary flying object, silvery, metallic, disc shaped, tens of metres in diameter, and evidently artificial, flew within sight of two witnesses'. He also said, however, that the evidence did not rule out the possibility of a hoax though it must be remembered that the Condon Committee was highly sceptical and in most cases scathing in their findings on the mass of evidence presented to them.

Much later, GSW applied the technique of colour-contouring, which replaces all shades of grey in a photograph with different colours thereby making the patterns of light and dark areas easier to see. They also compared the ratio of light on the upper and lower parts of the disc, and then compared that with the light and shadows falling on the garage that also appeared in the photographs. As the disc turned out to be much lighter, they concluded that atmospheric haze was the cause, suggesting that the object was in the far distance, around one to one point three kilometres. Additionally, they searched for wires or supports that would confirm the disc as a model; edge enhancement can detect wire a quarter of a millimeter thick at a distance of three metres. GSW could find no such evidence and concluded that the photographs showed a flying disc, twenty to thirty metres in diameter and consistent with being made of polished metal. Many experts have looked at the evidence and none have been able to conclusively prove or disprove this case. It remains one of the most thought provoking to date.

Just outside Thame, England, around nine on the morning of 11 January 1973, Peter Day, a surveyor, was driving along when he noticed a large, glowing, pulsating ball of light moving across the sky. Stopping his car, he shot approximately twenty-five seconds of Super 8mm film of the object before it disappeared. The resulting 400 frames of film clearly shows the object moving from left to right behind some distant trees and into open sky just above the horizon line. An interesting feature of the single frame on which the object disappears is that all the trees in the picture are shown bent over in the direction in which the UFO was travelling. This may or may not be a camera-generated effect, no one to date has clarified this point. Coincidentally, an F1-11 fighter plane crashed that afternoon near Newport Pagnell and some UFO researchers have attributed the film to this event. However, the timing is wrong, and the RAF were not interested in the film in relation to the crashed jet. Other eye-witnesses to the object are in no doubt that it was not a stricken aircraft. Others have dismissed the film as showing an aircraft's afterburner in action, but the film indicates that the aircraft would have to be flying *sideways* to have this effect. In my opinion this film remains one of the most significant UFO cases the UK has ever had.

Probably the most widely publicized case ever was that of the film taken by a professional film crew from an Argosy transport aircraft flying from Christchurch to Wellington, New Zealand on the night of 30 December 1978. Following reports of strange lights in the area ten days earlier, a film crew and news reporter made the trip too. On the return northbound flight at 15,000 feet and thirty-five miles out, the pilot, Captain Bill Startup, and his crew saw bright lights on the horizon and turned towards them. The objects seen were confirmed by air traffic control radar. Many feet of film was shot apparently showing lights in the sky dancing around both near to and far from the aircraft. Some detail appeared visible in the objects when the camera-man zoomed in on them, but this could have been caused by being slightly out of focus. The camera-man was working under considerable difficulty – at night in a vibrating, bouncing aircraft and with a heavy camera. One frame of the film shows the object making a figure of eight movement and no one has yet offered an explanation for that. Dr Bruce Maccabee, an optical physicist, has analyzed the film and stated that it is probably impossible to prove conclusively what the New Zealand film shows.

I have been asked many times 'What is the best way to take a photograph of a UFO?' You have to be in the right place at the right time of course, and no one has yet been able to predict UFO sightings. You will need a camera, but one that is either very simple to operate or one that you are very familiar with. UFO sightings tend to be of very short duration and you cannot waste time fiddling with the camera – you will need to just point and shoot. Most modern films are of high definition and medium to high speed and allow fast shutter speeds that will reduce the likelihood of camera shake. Take as many photographs of the object as you can, note also the time that you started taking them. Include in the frame of the picture some reference points: trees, lamp posts etc, to help fix the object spatially. Make a note of the names and addresses of anybody else who also saw the object and as soon as you can, after the event, write down the details of your sighting, including details of the camera and film used. Get other witnesses to do the same. Include as much information as you can, even the seemingly most trivial thing can assist in analysis of the photographs. Finally, before processing the film, contact the British UFO Research Association, who will wish to have the film processed by a professional laboratory to minimize the risk of loss or damage.

The more photographs that are available for the scientific community to study, the greater the weight of evidence and the sooner the UFO mystery may be solved. One day, a certain picture may not say a thousand words. It may say it all.

HARNESSING THE COMPUTER

COMPILED AND EDITED FROM SEVERAL
ARTICLES SUBMITTED BY STEPHEN GAMBLE,
MICHAEL WOOTTEN, J. DANBY, DR WILLY
SMITH AND BERTIL KUHLEMANN

The use of computers in ufology is growing, but, to quote Peter Hill, 'poor data will merely produce the wrong answer more quickly on a computer. No technology or technique will compensate for deficient data'.[1] The well-known phrase 'garbage in, garbage out' applies equally well to ufology.

In 1973 the International Committee for UFO Research was formed. The major aims of this group were to promote international co-operation and to introduce worldwide standards. The importance of computing was recognized, and a sub-committee was created to deal with this. At that first meeting it was proposed that a standard for transfer of data between all the different computers used by different groups would need to be developed: the International UFO Data Standard.[2]

The recent innovations in computer technology have put computers within the range of UFO research groups, which have always been supported largely by the personal contributions of their members. There are projects being undertaken by groups and individuals in many countries of the world, but the following examples of BUFORA's own applications are typical of these.

BUFORA CASE REPORT DATABASE

This project, headed by Michael Wootten, was started in 1984 with the objective of making identification and extraction of cases for research projects possible. As time goes on it is intended that supplementary databases will be created; for example, collecting additional data on photographic cases.

The database is used to identify groups of cases for further study. The careful sorting of data allows properly conducted statistical evaluation, and some work has already been done on descriptive statistics.

BUFORA BIBLIOGRAPHIC DATABASE

It is common to start off a scientific project by a search of the relevant literature; by building on the knowledge of others one can expect to move forward. BUFORA has been working on such a bibliographical database as a method of supporting researchers in the field.

BUFORA'S MEMBERSHIP RECORDS

In 1986 J. Danby undertook to overhaul and maintain the membership records of the Association using a microcomputer. Apart from the membership and subscription applications BUFORA can now instruct the computer to find, for example, all subscribing members living in the north of England who may be contacted by telephone and who have offered assistance in investigating incidents, supplying equipment etc, etc. The possibilities are wide.

OTHER USES

Computers have been used by a number of organizations for photographic image analysis (see the chapters of this book on 'photographic analysis').

Computers have also been used extensively for statistical work, for example, Project URD,[3] also

Wootten and Gamble, Digby and Phillips.[4] Statistical work is becoming more important in ufology. Scientific disciplines deal with groups of cases rather than individual cases to eliminate spurious results. Unfortunately, ufology has traditionally looked at individual cases and has woken up very late to the advantages of correct experimental design and statistically valid methodology.

USE OF COMPUTERS BY UFO GROUPS OUTSIDE THE UK

There are many worthwhile projects known of at the time of writing. Two are examined here in some detail.

THE UNICAT COMPUTER PROJECT: DR WILLY SMITH

When, in 1984, Dr Hynek and I started the development of UNICAT, one of the objectives was to prove in a manner acceptable to the scientific establishment that the UFO phenomenon is not only real, but also deserving of serious consideration. Consequently, the first order of business was to assemble a database of UFO cases, from which IFO and doubtful cases would have been screened. This database, to be satisfactory, was not to be a mere catalogue or listing of cases.

To do this it was necessary not only to establish criteria for the selection of the cases to eliminate IFOs, but also to ensure that the sample was representative and to identify those repeatable characteristics appearing in the UFO reports. This last is difficult as we do not really know which properties are significant, but we expect that as information is accumulated the answer will emerge from the database itself.

This first selection of the parameters applicable to the UFO phenomenon was done by Dr Hynek on the basis of his experience. As we acquired more experience and the work on the database advanced, new parameters were added. At present we have twenty-five parameters, each identified by a mnemonic two-letter code.

By May, 1987, the number of cases in the database was 606, although many more cases were partially processed. Each case may contain up to 6000 bytes of information, which can be retrieved and correlated in a large number of ways.

The key element in the creation of the database is the report, because, as Dr Hynek used to say, 'We do not have UFOs, we have only UFO reports'.

The essential elements of a UFO report are the witness, the investigator and the investigation. If the investigator is thorough, he will also consider other external elements, like the state of the weather, and the analysis and rejection of conventional explanations.

In practice, we gather all the information existing about a case, which may include an investigation report and one or more reference in the literature. We then proceed to analyze it, identifying which of the parameters apply to the case. This data is finally entered in the computer, or, if the analysis indicates that the information is insufficient, inconsistent, or dubious, the case is listed in an alternative database called MAYBECAT.

The criteria used for the evaluation of the different aspects of a case are not definitive, and are subject to revision. Those who feel they have a positive contribution to offer are urged to write to the UNICAT project. The evaluation process for each entry is five-fold:

(1) The witness is examined. His education, occupation, age, etc. are considered, together with other factors that could have a bearing on his reliability. He is then graded A, B or C. This may seem to be a simplistic scale, but to attempt a finer division is illusory as the information simply is not there.
(2) The investigator/investigation is examined, particularly important factors such as the experience and competence of the investigator and the time elapsed since the incident. This is also graded A, B or C.

(3) The report is considered. While the evaluation of observer and investigator are to some extent subjective, the amount of report information is objective as it is determined by NC, the number of parameters identified for the case. Based on that number, the report is graded A, B or C.

(4) The degree of 'strangeness' (S), is determined by the presence (or absence) of certain parameters.

(5) The final aspect refers to how much confidence one can have in the reality of the events. The name 'weight' (W) is assigned to this parameter; the development of a practical implementation for this is still under way. (Parenthetically, the assessment of UFO cases using S and W was pioneered by Dr Hynek, but we were only halfway through the development of S before he became seriously ill.)

Using the information stored in the database, several studies have been initiated and are at different stages of completion. In what follows, we will describe the results of one of those analyses, centred around only one of the 225 parameters taken into account by UNICAT.

One of the characteristics of the UFO phenomenon that appears in the database with a high incidence is that represented by the parameter LR (Lonely Road); thirty-eight per cent of the cases show that parameter. It has become clear that the key word is *lonely*: and the parameter is used now to represent a *lonely road* or *place*, typifying an isolated situation that could equally well be rural or urban.

This study is based on the information in the data base as of August, 1986, and extracts information for only 606 cases. The bulk of the work has been carried out by Robert D. Boyd. To simplify the notation, let's divide the cases into two groups: Class A – those containing LR (230 cases); and Class B – those NOT containing LR (376 cases).

One would expect any other independent parameter to be uniformly distributed regardless of the presence or absence of LR, and thus it should appear in Classes A and B in the same ratio, i.e: $f = 230/376 = 0.612$

Thus, any parameter whose distribution between the two classes is above this number shows a better than chance incidence for class A.

From the frequency distribution information for all the parameters, we consider the fifty most frequent. Some features come to light:

a) The majority of the first fifty most frequent parameters have an incidence value higher than expected for cases showing the parameter LR.

b) Ten of the parameters have a value larger than TWICE the cutoff value of 0.612, i.e., their incidence is more than twice what would be expected. Those parameters are called 'leading parameters'.

c) The parameters related to the number of witnesses are of a different nature, since SW (single witness) and MW (multiple witnesses) are mutually exclusive, and must be considered separately. For the LR situation MW is numerically larger than SW. Instead of MW, it will be better to use the equivalent, but not identical parameter AW (All Witnesses see).

THE SCENARIOS

The procedure to examine the possible scenarios is to combine LR with each of the leading parameters, as for instance LR and DR; then, taking each one of the remaining parameters, we consider different combinations of three. The analysis will have two steps:

i) calculation of the expected number of cases simultaneously having each of the combinations of three parameters. This is done assuming that the three parameters under consideration are independent. By way of example, take the following parameters: LR (lonely road), DR (driving) and EM (electromagnetic problems). Since we have 230 incidents with LR in a total of 606, the probability for finding LR for a given case is simply: $230/606$. Likewise, for DR we have

205/606, and for EM: 115/606. If the parameters are truly independent the probability of the three occurring simultaneously is the product of the three probabilities – (230/606) × (205/606) × (115/606) = 14·76/606 – i.e., due to chance alone, we expect to find 14·76 cases containing the three parameters.

(ii) the second step is to obtain from the database the actual number of cases simultaneously showing the three parameters. For the example above, we find fifty-eight cases, which is 3.93 times the expected value.

This indicates that the individual parameters are *not* independent as assumed, but strongly correlated. To express the strength of that correlation, we define a coefficient relating those two values:

R = actual number of cases/expected number of cases

Tentatively, we will use R to judge the relevance of the correlation among parameters, until a better statistical analysis can be developed.

For the particular example listed above (LR, DR, EM), one must be careful as it could be argued that there is a connection between the fact of driving and the lonely road or place situation. But it is not so, driving is a very common activity, and people drive most of the time on roads that are not particularly lonely. It seems as if the UFO presence occurs only when the driving takes place in isolated circumstances. In addition, of the 230 LR cases, only 142 correspond to a driving situation, which means that for the other eighty-eight the witness used other means to reach the lonely road or place. And, of course, it cannot be argued that EM is related in any way to the other two.

We have examined many different combinations of LR and two other leading parameters. Each triad defines a 'scenario' that can be developed by considering, one after another, the remaining parameters having f larger than the cutoff value. A great deal of work in this direction has been done by Robert Boyd, and I have repeated and completed his calculations.

The selection of the three-parameter scenario on which it is appropriate to proceed with the analysis has been based on two considerations: a) the value of R is high; and b) the actual number of cases involving the three parameters is high enough to allow a reasonably significant numerical analysis. Since the scope of this paper is of necessity limited, we will concentrate on those two scenarios that are most promising. The first is Having Electromagnetic Problems while DRiving in an Isolated Location, (HEPDRIL for short), which encompasses cases having simultaneously the parameters LR, DR and EM. The second is Craft Landed IN lonely Road Or Place, (CLINROP for short), which considers those cases having simultaneously the parameters LR (lonely road), LG (landed) and CR (craft).

For each of those three-parameter scenarios the expected values for all relevant four-parameter combinations are computed; these are then compared with the actual values obtained from the database. For all the combinations analyzed, without exception, the actual values exceed the expected values, sometimes by a large factor.

All the numbers shown result from exclusive use of information stored in the UNICAT database. Each line refers to cases simultaneously having four parameters that were assumed to be independent for the calculation of the expected values. However, the actual value is always a much larger number, indicating a strong correlation among the parameters.

More significantly, this occurs with all of the four-parameter correlations. Pending a more detailed and in-depth statistical analysis, the strong numerical correlations seem to point to the existence of a common underlying structure linking all those parameters, the observed characteristics of the UFO phenomenon. This suggests a strong reality and well-defined properties, and becomes a legitimate object of scientific study. To quote Lord Kelvin, 'When one can measure what we are speaking about, and express it in numbers, you know something about it. But when you cannot – your knowledge is of a meagre and unsatisfactory kind.'

The above work has been centered around the parameter LR and has resulted in the development of two models of UFO encounter. Perhaps they are not new, but what is important is that we have arrived at them independently, and that they are strongly supported by mathematical evidence provided by a high-quality database.

We first notice that the two models seem to be mutually exclusive, that is, those parameters which are important for one of the situations are irrelevant for the other one. For instance, the first four most significant parameters for HEPDRIL – UC: UFO over car or overhead; HE: health effects; FL: floodlighting effects; FR: fear and/or terror – appear near the bottom of the list for CLINROP. Conversely, the four more significant parameters for CLINROP – EC: entities in craft or emerge; EP: entities (plural); PT: physical traces; WN: windows, openings – appear in HEPDRIL in the middle and lower range of significance.

The two parameters that define HEPDRIL (i.e., DR and EM) are irrelevant in CLINROP, while the parameters LG and CR that characterize CLINROP figure at the bottom of the list for HEPDRIL. This was to be expected, but to find out that the overlap between the two models is very small was surprising. Only seven cases are included in both HEPDRIL and CLINROP, and thus, of the 230 cases associated with LR, a total of 108 (47%) have been considered by this study.

As stated above, the witness circumstances require special attention as the parameters SW and MW (or AW) are mutually exclusive. For HEPDRIL, the cases with a single witness are fewer than those with multiple witnesses, while for CLINROP the numbers are practically the same. However, for both scenarios the coefficient R for SW is nearly twice that for AW, indicating that for both models SW is more significant.

The next stage is to examine the UFO types for each of the models, and an unexpected discovery is made. Of the HEPDRIL cases, only 9% are nocturnal lights (NL); the rest (91%) are close encounters. The majority of the cases (58.6%) are close encounters of the second kind (C2). In addition, seven of the cases (12%) are close encounters of the fourth kind (C4), which constitute the majority of the abductions contained in the database. With respect to CLINROP, all of the cases are close encounters, with a majority (59.6%) of close encounters of the third kind (C3) incidents. Only 3.5% of the cases are C4.

The time distribution of the two scenarios is also essentially different. For HEPDRIL the majority of the observations took place during nighttime, and all the C4 cases without exception occurred at night. For CLINROP, the time distribution is rather erratic, and shows no clear pattern.

Other characteristics associated with HEPDRIL are the presence of a craft (43% of instances), usually overhead (38%) and/or at treetop level (41%), frightening the witnesses (44%) and sometimes affecting their health (31%). Floodlighting effects (26%) and intense lights (34%) are often reported.

Parameters appearing less frequently in HEPDRIL are physical traces (19%), entities in the craft or emerging (17%), or the reporting of a landing (21%).

CLINROP is characterized by an enhanced chance of observing two or more entities (51%) near or inside the craft (58%), and observing details of such craft, such as windows or openings (40%). The nearness of the UFO is emphasized by the fact that in most instances (65%), the witnesses are able to provide a sketch of the craft, in spite of their fear (44%) during the event. In almost half the cases (49%), corrobarative physical traces were observed.

Parameters appearing less frequently in CLINROP are: UFO overhead (9%), or at treetop level (18%); electromagnetic effects (16%) and floodlighting effects (16%). Health effects (18%) are not as common as in the previous model.

The weather conditions are taken into account in UNICAT by three parameters; clear weather (21% of all cases), severe weather conditions (2.8%) and 'other' weather (1.5%). The high incidence of clear weather for the two scenarios described is not surprising, since apparently a majority of all UFO sightings occur in fair weather.

To conclude, one could venture some speculations to be affirmed or denied by further studies. The two scenarios dovetail extremely well, complementing each other in numerous details. It seems that the HEPDRIL situations were the result of intent on the part of intelligence controlling the UFOs to isolate and exploit witnesses, leading to circumstances favourable to an abduction. In the CLINROP scenario, on the contrary, the witnesses seem to have come upon the UFO unexpectedly and unwelcomed, resulting in most cases in the prompt departure of the landed craft instead of the development of an abduction scenario.

PROJECT URD: BERTIL KUHLEMANN

The late Dr Allen Hynek, in his letter to the Editor of the journal 'Science' (Oct, 1967), pleaded for a serious scientific study of the UFO phenomenon and a deep engagement of the scientific community in the matter.

Ufology cannot become a research field in its own right until scientific methodology and principles are applied.

PROJECT URD

Project URD is a project (not an organization) owned

and run by The International Project URD Foundation, Stockholm, Sweden. It has emerged out of the activities of The Working Group for UFO Identification. It has three well defined components:
— a specific goal
— a time set for the fulfilment of its goal
— a defined methodology (to make the achievement of the goal possible); this includes a detailed plan for developing the resources needed during the span of the project.

The goal of Project URD is to give a clear-cut answer to the question: 'Is there really something?' (which is well worth allocating resources to).

The work has to be carried out on a scientifically sound basis to give a statistically verified answer. In order to do this in a way acceptable to the scientific community it was important to first have input from the scientists as to what criteria they considered important before commencing the research, partly to demonstrate the neutrality of the results. A number of scientists and researchers were therefore approached and presented with a list of several thousand types of characteristics connected to UFO observations. Out of this data they chose those they thought would give the most significant results and which they would be willing to support when the results were examined. They also defined those characteristics they thought should not be included if they were to support the findings. Thus it was possible to assemble those characteristics chosen by these people into a database structure. From this point the report data had to be assembled:

COLLECTING THE DATA

The report is divided into two parts;
a) fairly fixed characteristics pertaining to the observation
b) characteristics of the phenomenon observed (very

often of a dynamic nature)

In Form A the features of the surroundings at the observation site are described as well as climatic conditions. Some characteristics regarding the observer are given as well as observations of immediate as well as remaining respectively after-effects of the phenomenon. The report form also has space for extraordinary observations.

In Form B the dimensional form of the object is noted with its size – true or approximate.

REPORTING CONSISTENCY

To allow for a methodological approach the data reported must have equal quality throughout a number of cases – this calls for training of field investigators. The first priority in the work is to try to screen out IFOs. Next, the details of the remaining reports are studied and characteristics defined; this may include laboratory tests and hypnotic regression (carried out by professional hypnotists) of the observer. When a case is finally 'cleared' it is incorporated in the database to make the data available to the UFO researcher for statistical analysis.

A group of dedicated people grew who were able to scrutinize 1000 UFO reports in detail (after appropriate IFO screening) and the pertinent data extracted was put into the database. A first run was carried out in June 1983 covering 518 cases and a second run in March 1985 covering 1000 cases.

There are currently three types of statistical analysis which are of interest:
— the statistical distribution of one chosen characteristic e.g. distribution of the cases over the years, months, days, or hours; or with regard to sizes; or distance to the object etc.
— the cross-tabulation of one of the characteristics against another e.g. size of the object against distance
— a third type of analysis is the statistical occurrence

pattern in relation to a normal distributive curve/along which the occurrence should appear; in statistics there is a figure for significance: if the actual occurrence-distribution differs dramatically from the normal curve there is a high level of anticipation for something unusual in the material studied.

These statistical analyses, run over the years by Project URD, confirm, to an acceptable scientific level, that UFO phenomena does exist and enables further research to proceed from a foundation that is both solid, and evolving.

GOVERNMENT COVER-UP AND CONSPIRACY

Jenny Randles

In July 1987 I took part in a debate on BBC television with astronomer Patrick Moore. We had surprisingly agreed on many things (the surprise being his, not mine, as I am well aware how most so-called sceptics are ignorant of what real ufologists think). But when we came to the question of the withholding of documentation by official sources on the UFO mystery the celebrated English eccentric let out an exasperated cry 'Cover-ups, that's the veritable hallmark of a crank!' So long as I argued 'safe' areas like lights-in-the-sky or weather phenomena all was well, but to venture that a cover-up may exist is equivalent to joining the ranks of the 'Flat Earth' society.

I could see Patrick's point. But I had an answer; I was not *claiming* that there is a cover-up; Government *documents* of several nations *prove* beyond any shadow of a doubt that they are hiding something.

'Have you got any of those documents?' Patrick Moore yelped. 'Of course, I have thousands,' I explained, and I was delighted to point out that the BBC had used one on their captions and during the introduction to the programme.

Of course it sounds extreme to claim a cover-up. But no investigator who pretends to be objective can ignore the governmental record of the world's leading nations. They provide a whole new angle on the UFO subject which we must take seriously, if only because these various defence agencies and institutes take the matter seriously themselves.

Moore's alarm is the result of the overenthusiasm displayed for cover-ups and conspiracies by certain researchers who speak glibly of phone taps and intercepted mail, and swallow every document and story fed to them.

Evidence there is for some kind of conspiracy. But what kind of conspiracy? Is it a cover-up of amazing secret knowledge, even including bits of crashed UFO and dead alien bodies? Or is it ignorance and confusion that is being hidden? Are the authorities as puzzled as the rest of us about what is really going on?

When modern UFO sighting waves began (in 1947) World War II had just ended. The Americans had been caught with their pants down at Pearl Harbour and they had no intention of being duped again. So it was inevitable that this new phenomenon should be subjected to a covert investigation by the US Army-Air Force. What if they were Soviet secret weapons? Naturally this had to be kept secret. Other nations, especially those in the West, tended to follow the American example. The Soviets, learning of the US interest, probably decided that it was worth keeping an eye on (and they do *everything* in secret). A few small nations might have had the freedom to take ufology out of the age of secrecy, but they probably either thought the subject too vague or disregarded it as of no concern.

Recent revelations have come with more enlightened attitudes. The 'Freedom of Information' (FOI) Acts in America and Australia allow access to papers demonstrating attitudes towards UFOs. For them *not* to be released a justification would be necessary under these laws. To plead 'security' as a reason to withhold thousands of files would imply that UFOs were a security threat. So the authorities really had little choice but to release all material except items regarded as too sensitive for public dissemination.

So we do now have a picture of what occurred in the genesis of UFO investigation at an official level. We know that from the very start the authorities *knew* that UFOs were a legitimate field of study. On 23 September 1947, less than three months after the Kenneth Arnold sighting, Lieutenant General Nathan F Twining reviewed early studies for the Pentagon and told them in no uncertain terms that 'the phenomenon reported is something real and not visionary or fictitious'. Many similar official statements from clearly puzzled military and intelligence officers are to be found among the released documents. 'Something is really flying around' one top secret memo insists.

Security agencies quickly got in on the act – the FBI, to check out the communist sympathies of witnesses, and the CIA (to determine methods of manipulating public attitudes towards UFOs for its own dark reasons). In 1950 the FBI put surveillance onto a leading civilian UFO investigator. In 1952 and 1953 the CIA considered employing cartoonists and magicians to help destroy the credibility of witnesses they knew were telling the truth. These things alone (proved by the documents that *have* been released) constitute at best a breach of civil liberties and in my estimation justify my use of the words 'cover-up' and 'conspiracy' sufficiently to challenge Patrick Moore's accusation of crankiness.

But there is much more to it than this. By 1948 Project SIGN (the Air Force intelligence unit set up to collate UFO data for the US Government) had totally ruled out earth-based secret weapons. Since theories at that time were not sophisticated enough to view UFOs as anything but *machines*, if they were not Soviet machines then they had to be extraterrestrial machines. They were space ships.

SIGN concluded by mid-1948 that UFOs *were* space ships and submitted an 'Estimate of Situation'. Captain

Edward Ruppelt, in his remarkably frank 1955 book *The Report on UFOs*, recounts how Project SIGN's estimate was refuted, and the project shut down. All its members were transferred elsewhere and a new project (called GRUDGE) put in its place to debunk UFOs.

This remarkable switch in attitude is odd. SIGN's reasons for concluding as they did were sincere. There *were* unexplained cases. Contrary to expectation the cases that were unresolved had the *best* data and often involved the *most credible* witnesses, making it very improbable that they were unexplained because of insufficient evidence. This strongly implied that what these people consistently reported was real, and (so SIGN believed) therefore space ships.

Even if the Pentagon and the White House did not buy this solution they must have recognized the problem. Their actions at this time only make sense in one way. The importance of the UFO subject (already top secret) was upgraded and put in the hands of a limited group of intelligence men and scientists with a strict brief to find out what was going on and report at the very highest of levels. The people who acted as data collectors in the Air Force UFO projects were merely being used as a public façade and had no 'need-to-know'; Ruppelt admits in his book 'maybe I was just playing the front man to a big cover-up.'

Almost everything we have on official UFO investigation in America after Ruppelt relates to this 'shop window' project, which was itself closed down in 1969 as being a waste of time (after a project sponsored by the US government to the tune of half a million dollars had investigated sixty cases, failed to explain a third of them and concluded that UFOs therefore do not exist!)

However, the memo closing down Project Blue Book (its third name) states something quite extraordinary. Dated 20 October 1969 it was signed by the USAF deputy director of development, Brigadier General

C H Bolender, and explains 'reports of unidentified flying objects which could affect national security are made in accordance with JANAP 146 or Air Force Manual 55–11 and are not part of the Blue Book system ... [they] should continue to be handled through the standard Air Force procedure designed for this purpose.'

Do we see here a slip of the censor's pen? It clearly shows that there was a *covert* procedure for reporting sensitive UFO cases, and explains something that has long puzzled UFO researchers; why the released Blue Book archives of 15,000 cases do *not* contain some of the best sightings (eg jet chases by military pilots, radar intercepts etc) which we know of from other sources.

Another clue comes from CIA memos dated between April and July 1976, which talk of how the agency research and development unit have been receiving 'UFO related material from many of our science and technology sources who are presently conducting related research' and also talk of 'propulsion systems' being based on this work.

NSA (National Security Agency), are more secret still and when UFO files were appealed for from them only one memo, entitled 'UFO hypotheses and survival questions' was released. It showed how this satellite surveillance and electronic interception body (with a vast budget) was taking extraterrestrial UFOs seriously, arguing darkly 'if "they" discover you, it is an old but hardly invalid rule of thumb, "they" are your technological superiors.'

Following such a revelation more NSA files were appealed for. After denials some were 'found'. By the time they reached the highest court of appeal in 1982 the number so traced had risen to 239! Every single one was denied on the grounds of national security. A top security cleared judge at the hearing did not get to see them. He saw a twenty-one page memo explaining why the NSA couldn't release them. He agreed, saying that their release would 'seriously jeopardize the work of the agency and the security of the United States ... public interest and disclosure is far outweighed by the sensitive nature of the material.'

Fair enough, you might think. Even if the UFO data is bunk the means of obtaining it (eg satellite monitoring) had to be kept secret. So why not release only the data, not how it was obtained? To check on the reasons the twenty-one page memo was appealed for using FoI. On 27 April 1982 a 'sanitized' version was made public. Eleven of the four pages were totally censored out and all bar four others almost totally! If that is the sensitive nature of the explanations for the refusal, one can guess at the content of the documents themselves.

Of the parts of the refusal memo we *can* read we see that one file is an account of an NSA agent 'on duty' by attending a UFO conference. Other material 'advances a novel theory [which] could have the effect of stifling [necessary] candour by the risk of diminution of professional standing the employee runs if subsequently found wrong.' And yet other documents are considered irrelevant because they discuss 'the ability of the agency employees to deal with unusual phenomena'. And so on. Clearly at least *some* of these 239 papers are *not* being released precisely *because* of their UFO content. Yet, according to one of the highest judges in the land, this content would 'seriously jeopardize' the 'security of the United States' if it was released. Why?

Although I have only scratched the surface of official documentation from the USA, there can be little doubt that this material constitutes some sort of undercover covert operation. The position elsewhere is reflected in the same sort of light. For instance, the French have a team of scientists investigating close encounters at government expense.

So far as Britain is concerned we are much more in the dark, but it is hard to believe that something similar is not happening. We know that the Ministry of

Defence collate sightings and that since 1967 (when they were ordered to retain case files by Parliament) a large collection has accrued in Whitehall.

In October 1982 they informed me they were now working to open up these records to public scrutiny. In January 1983, I actually received some scraps of paper which they assured me were their 'case reports' on half a dozen incidents. I appealed for specific releases on major cases (not lights-in-the-sky, as all these released 'files' appeared to be). The MoD answered my request with the usual silence and evasion.

Using the FoI act in the USA I did get (with the help of Barry Greenwood, an American ufologist) a copy of one of these MoD files, a report sent by an American Colonel at a NATO base in Suffolk, endorsed by the British Squadron Leader, reporting an incident in which a triangular UFO had been seen, had damaged pine trees, and had left holes in the ground and excess radiation traces. (This was in fact later supplemented by an amazing 'live' tape recording made in the forest by senior base officers, recording the damage and the taking of samples and photographs – interrupted by the sighting of a second UFO as described in the memo!)

Armed with incredible material like this I *went* to Whitehall and told the MoD that I now had evidence they had denied me for some time (I had known about the case for over two years, since a few days after it had happened, when a radar operator had told me of its tracking). As I was forced to enquire, was I now in breach of the Official Secrets Act by possessing this highly sensitive and astonishing material? The MoD confirmed that the material was *bona fide*, that since it came via legitimate FoI sources in the USA they supposed it was okay for us to have it, and added one more staggering piece of news. It was all they had on record about the case!

This was an incident on British soil less than three years before that August 1983 'interview'. It was supported by numerous senior Air Force men, had been witnessed by Air Force personnel and involved a structured device that had reportedly done damage to a forest half a mile outside a strategic NATO base, leaving radiation traces. Perhaps the airmen at the base were out of their minds, or the UFO had been something finally explicable. Despite numerous letters, public statements, questions in the house from Conservative MP Sir Patrick Wall and letters exchanged on my behalf between Defence Minister Lord Trefgarne and Alliance MP David Alton, no explanation has ever been offered by the UK government. Even so it is surely impossible to believe that our security forces – the same forces that seek to ban publication of MI5 memoirs already published in the USA, or who prosecute civil servants such as Clive Ponting – would be so disinterested as to do *nothing*!

Cases such as this demonstrate beyond question that *something* is being hidden. And they make us ponder if this case is just one that slipped through the net and so represents many others that do not.

That view is upheld by the response its revelation generated from the MoD. Their decision to release files was revoked. In April 1984 they chickened out and in a letter to me explained that they did not have the time to do it!

To return to the question that I set at the beginning. What *is* being hidden? It is tempting to believe in some major conspiracy of 'cosmic Watergate' proportions. There are researchers, such as William Moore and Stanton Friedman in the USA and Timothy Good in the UK, who claim to have been given secret papers by 'deep throat' sources which demonstrate the existence of a body called MJ (or Majestic)-12 – supposedly the team of scientists set up in the late 1940s to handle the *real* UFO work.

Is this credible? At least one of these documents *has* since been released via the FoI act, although rather worried clerks at the records office in Washington DC were at pains to point out that they have no idea what MJ-12 is! But does this mean all the other incredible papers are also genuine?

If so they prove that the US government has not merely been involved in a cover-up. It has successfully hidden crashed UFOs and dead alien beings for over forty years. That would be the greatest covert operation in history. I am reluctant to accept the existence of secret papers. There is always the risk of deliberate disinformation. I have myself faced this situation on several occasions, being approached by 'deep throats' with wares they consider sensational. Twice in 1985–6 I was offered 'hot' papers on secret American research into UFOs. In both instances, I reacted in what I consider a prudent fashion, and the story subsequently crumbled.

My experience in these and similar situations causes me to be suspicious about deep throat contacts and wonder if there are not moves to 'set up' ufologists.

If you have been forced into releasing some documents that imply more knowledge of UFOs than you are ready to reveal, how do you prevent an incessant cry for such release? One way might be to trap less careful investigators into accepting material so bizarre that it makes serious and respectable sources wish to distance themselves from the UFO subject. A few carefully placed 'deep throats', luring investigators on, would cast doubt on the documents which *are bona fide* and highly suggestive, by virtue of a sort of overkill. It is easy to lose credibility in the UFO field by claiming too much.

Of course, the alternative (which has been seriously proposed by a number of people – some of high rank in government circles and at least one direct to me when I gave an address to a select group at the House of Lords in 1980) is: some in the know are determined to end the cover-up by a gradual 'education process', slowly conditioning us to accept the awesome truth of alien UFOs through a bit by bit revelation.

Whilst it would be foolish to say this is impossible, I feel it wise to err on the side of caution at this stage, especially as we know how disinformation is a favourite parlour game of the defence authorities and *has* been used in the UFO context on a number of provable occasions in the past.

If UFOs were known to be *just* strange natural phenomena no cover-up would make any sense. But there clearly *is* a cover-up. So what does it hide? I have just given reasons why I doubt it is the presence of aliens from another planet. Although if it is and we have failed to come to grips with their technology then there would be sound reasons for maintaining a conspiracy.

So what else remains? After more than a decade of research I find myself coming more and more to the realization that the truth about UFOs is probably more bizarre than we ever dreamt of.

I feel that the continuation of official UFO study and the maintenance of a cover-up argues strongly that those responsible for gathering UFO information at a governmental level are as thoroughly bemused by what is going on as the UFO community.

They don't know. But they want to know, especially if there is some military technology that might be garnered from its eventual unravelling. That could be as true if UFOs are some kind of rare energy phenomenon, as it would be if they were space ships. The rational course of action any government could adopt in such a situation would be to watch, wait and wonder.

Watch, wait and wonder is precisely what I believe lies behind the UFO conspiracy. It is a cover-up not of what is *known*, but of what is *not* known.

WORKING WITH THE GOVERNMENT

Bill Chalker

While the majority of UFO research and investigation in Australia is undertaken by civilians, either as groups or individuals, official investigations have and are being carried out.

Prior to 1982 civilian UFO researchers had only a confused and vague picture of official Australian research. Since 1982 this writer was able to undertake the first officially sanctioned direct review of the Australian government's UFO files. I was able to:

(i) examine the majority of the extant UFO files held by the Royal Australian Air Force (RAAF).
(ii) examine the entirety of the extant UFO files held by the Department of Aviation.

The extent of file access was unprecedented.[1]

The official files do not confirm activity before 1950, although involvement by the military dates as far back as 1920. In the search for a missing schooner, the *Amelia J*, in Bass Strait, lights, thought at the time to be 'evidently rockets', were observed. Two aircraft were sent out to investigate, one piloted by Major Anderson and the other by Captain W J Stutt. Stutt and his mechanic, Sergeant Dalzell, were last seen by Major Anderson flying into a large cloud. Their plane and the schooner were never found. Fifty-eight years later the Bass Strait became the centre of another extraordinary plane/pilot disappearance, the Valentich affair of 1978.[2]

In 1930 RAAF Squadron Leader George Jones was sent to Warrnambool, Victoria, to investigate mystery aircraft flying over the coast. No explanation was found in this first official RAAF UFO investigation.[3] Further 'mystery aircraft' reports were made in the near Pacific and Papua New Guinea area in 1930. In 1931 the RAAF was denying that any of her planes were the explanation for 'mystery planes' reported widely in Tasmania.[4]

The crew of a RAAF Beaufort bomber, flying at 235mph, 4500 feet over Bass Strait, at about two thirty am during February, 1944, bore witness to what may have been Australia's earliest reported 'electromagnetic' (EM) case. A 'dark shadow' appeared alongside the plane and kept pace with it, at a distance of only some 100–150 feet. The object appeared to have a flickering light and flame belching from its rear end. Only about fifteen feet of the rear end of the UFO was visible to the bomber crew, apparently due to 'reflection of light from the exhaust'. The strange object stayed with the bomber for some eighteen to twenty minutes, during which time all radio and direction finding instruments refused to function. It finally accelerated away from the plane, at approximately three times the speed of the bomber. Beauforts figured heavily in the official Royal Australian Air Force (RAAF) list of planes that went 'missing without trace' during World War II in the Bass Strait area – an area that was not linked to any significant enemy activity.[5]

There was extensive official interest in the movie footage taken by the Deputy Director – DCA at Port Moresby, Tom Drury, in 1953, of an extraordinary unidentified 'missile'. The Drury UFO film became a controversial and famous mainstay of the 'cover-up' argument. It became all the more controversial when it was learned that the UFO section of the film was no longer available and the RAAF were denying any knowledge of its whereabouts. The files I examined clearly indicate that indeed, at least in recent years, the RAAF did not know of the UFO film's whereabouts. Tom Drury himself indicated to me that he felt the Australian Security Intelligence Organisation (ASIO) (which is responsible for internal security in Australia, including counter-espionage) was involved. There is at least cursory evidence for this. A previously confidential RAAF document written in 1966 concluded 'the upshot is that the "excised" frames are either still in DAFI archives, have been destroyed or (perish the thought) have been lost.' At the time the Department of Air advised the Victorian UFO Research Society that the file and film had been destroyed. A 1955 file indicated that DAFI had at that time sold prints of the pictures 'at 4s 9d a pop' to civilian researchers. The RAAF managed to copy one of the civilian sets, and these third generation copies now reside in the RAAF files due to a loan from UFO researcher, Fred Stone.[6]

A classified DAFI file minute dated 2 November 1955, somewhat tellingly revealed: 'A Ministerial statement in the House [Australian parliament] on 19 November 1953 to the effect that the RAAF make detailed investigations of every report received, (which in truth we are not yet doing).'

In 1978 the Victorian UFO Research Society (VUFORS) produced an excellent study of the 1954 flap.[7] The classic report of the period was the Dandenong close encounter of 5 June, 1954. A nuclear physicist who studied the case stated '... the light available and duration of observation were sufficient to discern details of structure that could not possibly be confused with any phenomena other than a machine that is capable of hovering, rotating, and moving in virtual silence without any obvious method of propulsion.'[8] The same physicist concluded in a previously secret report to the Directorate of Air Force

Intelligence that 'this particular sighting has an extremely high probability of being a UFO without any provisos'.[9]

DAFI asked Melbourne University Professor O H Turner to undertake a classified 'scientific appreciation' of the official reports held on file. Turner recommended greater official interest, specific interest in radar visual reports and also that 'the evidence presented by the reports held by RAAF tend to support the ... conclusion ... that certain strange aircraft have been observed to behave in a manner suggestive of extraterrestrial origin'. Turner also utilized Donald Keyhoe's USAF reports and suggested the RAAF seek official USAF confirmation of the legitimacy of Keyhoe's data. The Director of Air Force Intelligence did so, and the Australian Joint Service Staff (intelligence) in Washington replied:

'I have discussed with the USAF the status of Major Keyhoe. I understand that his book is written in such a way as to convey the impression that his statements are based on official documents, and there is some suggestion that he has made improper use of information to which he had access while he was serving with the Marine Corps. He has, however, no official status whatsoever and a dim view is taken officially of both him and his works.'

Turner's findings, in the light of the 'discrediting' of Keyhoe's data, were found to be impractical and unjustified.

The big problem with all this was that it was based on an act of conscious or unconscious misrepresentation on the part of the US Air Force. While Keyhoe may have slightly 'beat up' his USAF data, the USAF Intelligence reports, quoted by Keyhoe and used by Turner to support his conclusions to DAFI, were authentic! Eventually the USAF themselves also admitted that the material Keyhoe used was indeed from official Air Force reports. Political myopia from both the US and Australian military effectively scuttled Australia's first serious flirtation with scientific investigation of UFOs.

The RAAF continued their ad hoc approach to UFOs, pausing only in a cursory attempt in 1966 to rationalize their policy and procedures. However, during that same year separate directorates within the RAAF, namely the Directorates of Air Force Intelligence (DAFI) and Public Relations (DPR) were in conflict over how to handle the UFO problem. DAFI were 'keen to soft pedal the UFO business' because of 'the undesirability of whetting the interest of the public in UFOs'. DPR wanted to utilize a 'Summary of Unidentified Aerial Sightings Reported to Department of Air From 1960' that grew out of 'a requirement for certain statistical UFO information to provide material for a ministerial reply to a parliamentary question as a primary PR handout to answer public UFO enquiries. DPR argued that 'any attempt by us to suppress public interest (however misguided we may think that interest to be) only helps to support the general impression that we are sitting on fat files of information, vital to our security. Further 'it seems self-evident that we should, in our own defence, devise some simple piece of administrative machinery to cope with that steady flow of UFO enquiries, anti-authority press innuendos and statements verging on public accusations of duplicity which we will never be able to dodge, as long as we continue to play our unclassified UFO cards too close to our chests.' By continuing this 'old' policy, DPR argued that the RAAF would 'only foster the incorrect (but nevertheless widely held) belief that we have much vital information to hide'. These quotes come from a restricted Minute Paper, which concluded 'that we are handling this whole business in an unnecessarily rigid and unimaginative way'. The upshot of the DAFI-DPR conflict was that the 'annual Summaries' did become the public front of the RAAF involvement in the

Australian UFO controversy. The RAAF had become locked into a bureaucratically orchestrated formula for handling the 'UFO problem'!

By 1968, Turner was working in the Directorate of Scientific and Technical Intelligence (DSTI) of the Joint Intelligence Bureau (JIB). Turner functioned as a JIB liaison with DAFI and requested access to the latter's UFO reports, which was granted. In May 1969, at Turner's suggestion, a new RAAF UFO report form was devised which was intended to make the reports more scientific. At this time Turner was working with other scientists to set up a 'rapid intervention' team to scientifically investigate cases of UFO physical evidence. A firm proposal was developed with the team to operate within the Defence Science and Technical Organisation (DSTO). The team was to consist of four or five scientists, with its mainstay to be rapid intervention into UFO 'landing' events, for which an aircraft was to be on standby. By early 1969, the plans for the scientific team had been almost completed and authorization to proceed appeared imminent. However, fate intervened.

In the middle of 1969 a major flap broke out in Western Australia, centred in Perth. One of the reports included an impressive radar visual event at Cloverdale and tracked on Kalamunda radar on 23 May.

The Director of Air Force Intelligence felt that things had got out of control and made an appeal for the Defence 'intervention' group to assist. Unfortunately the group had not been finalized, and Harry Turner was seconded to help out. His subsequent report in part criticized the DAFI system for handling UFO reports. The Air Force did not take kindly to criticism from an 'outsider', and the upshot was that Turner's access to the DAFI UFO files was withdrawn. Soon after the plan for the 'rapid intervention' team was dropped. The scientific investigation of UFOs at an official level had all but disappeared, with the primary goal being the resolution of any defence and/or political implications.

The political and military myopia towards UFOs plunged headlong into a potential crisis on 25 October 1973. The restricted and acutely sensitive USN Communications Station at North West Cape in Western Australia was, on that day, used to communicate the general US alert to both conventional and nuclear forces in the region, during the Middle East crisis. On that same day something showed a 'clear intent' for the North West Cape installation. A startling UFO sighting was made by base personnel. A 'large black, airborne object' was observed hovering due west of Area B (the location of High Frequency Transmitters). The UFO was seen to 'accelerate at unbelievable speed and disappeared to the north!' As the National Security Agency (NSA) operated at the base and was responsible for Signals Intelligence (SIGINT) it is possible that it is the 'intrusion' at North West Cape on 25 October 1973 that is contained in the reference to 'a 1973 report' amongst classified SIGINT documents in the Top Secret and heavily censored in-camera NSA court affidavit of 1980 that led to the continuing suppression of NSA UFO documents.[10]

The quality of RAAF investigations has drawn criticism from many sources, perhaps none more pointed though than that of Dr Claude Poher, who led France's first major official UFO research group GEPAN. After the Australian Department of Defence sent him some of their Annual Summaries of UFO information, Dr Poher wrote: 'May I suggest, for transmission to personnel responsible for this work, that some of the "possible causes" mentioned in these summaries are not acceptable ....' Dr Poher gave an example of an innocuous observation at Wickham, New South Wales, on 4 April 1975, of a 'silver object about the size of a cricket ball', which the 'Summary' lists as Venus for the 'possible cause'. Poher concluded 'for the 4 April 1975, the planet was under the horizon so the cause "Venus" is ridiculous. There are many other impossibilities like this in the papers you sent me. I think one should avoid publication of these documents without a careful check by specialists of the different scientific disciplines involved, so as not to have, one day, a journalist or a scientist holding the Services of the Australian Department of Defence up to ridicule.'

The source of such 'impossibilities' is the subject of some speculation. While unconfirmed, I was told the 'inside story' by someone working in Defence:

'While America had an official attitude – the Condon Report etc – our Air Force simply has no expectations of getting any other verdict. Their attitude is to try to quieten everything down. Be bland as possible and hope that everything goes away. At times they were actually rather rude to witnesses, tending to ridicule where possible. Generally speaking the men that are handling it wish they weren't. But in the Air Force it is essential to look as though you're good at your job to get promotion. The attitude is to look as though they are solving all the cases, while looking for an excuse to write it all off.'

Nineteen seventy-eight was a memorable year for UFO activity in Australia. The year got off to a spectacular start with a vivid and prolonged close encounter at Bakers Creek Falls, near Armidale, NSW.[11] In Queensland there was a multiple witness 'shoot-out' with a UFO near St George, confirming the long-term fascination UFOs seemed to have for that district and there was the extraordinary disappearance of pilot Frederick Valentich on 21 October 1978.[12] The year ended with the controversial Kaikoura UFO affair in New Zealand on 31 December 1978.[13] The Valentich and Kaikoura events were given international prominence.

The RAAF were not prepared for 1978. When the year had ended some thirty incidences remained classified as 'unknowns' giving a percentage unknown of 25.4%. The year before, although based on fewer reports, also yielded a similar figure, namely 24.0%. Previous years had been as low as 2.1%. The department of Defence ceased publishing annual Summaries with the appearance of Summary No 9, 1977.

The official files for 1978 include the following highlights: a phenomenon seen in a cane field east of Mandurana, Queensland, for three hours on 6 December; a UFO sighting by the crew of HMAS *Adroit* on 11 April; an apparent 'electromagnetic' case north of Goulburn, New South Wales, on 22 October; a 'daylight disc' seen near Laverton Air Force base on 27 December; a very close encounter between a 'minibus'-like UFO and a taxi driver in Wavell Heights, Queensland, on 10 October 1978; and a large disc-shaped UFO with 'portholes' at Heathcote Road, near Menai, NSW, on 29 October.

It appears that the RAAF's enthusiasm for the UFO controversy diminished sharply after 1977 and 1978. The whole problem was getting unwieldy and unmanageable. Controversy rather than resolution was at every turn. At this time getting any sort of information out of the RAAF was difficult. Letters were either not answered or replies skirted the substance of enquiries. Behind the scenes the frustration was evident.

This was one annotation to a letter in the RAAF files:

'FLO,
   I know it's a P in the A but please respond.
         30 Aug 79 DAFI

That letter went unanswered anyway.

A subsequent letter I wrote in April 1980 drew the following internal exchanges:

'11/4 A/ADRR –
Re reply, I believe there is a policy of not providing
information on UFOs – Is this true?'

'A/ADPR (Press):
Could you please get a policy sorted out with DAFI in
(sic? – B C) whether we should continue to answer such
enquiries? I think we are obliged to, particularly when
FoI comes in (a reference to the Australian Freedom of
Information Act – B C), but I think, you were going to
discuss the matter with (unclear – B C) at one stage.'

DAFI:
I still presume we are still in the UFO business. If so,
could I have a suitable reply to pass on to Mr Chalker,
please (14.4.80).

As it turned out a reply was not forthcoming for a
further five months.

In the face of this lethargy I stepped up my efforts at
diplomatically trying to get direct access to the RAAF
UFO files. It probably surprised me more than
anybody else when the RAAF finally agreed to permit
me to examine their files. The extent of access was
unprecedented in the history of the Australian UFO
controversy. From the first of my visits to the Russell
Offices of the Department of Defence, in Canberra, on
11 January 1982, to my last in June 1984, I was able to
scrutinize the extent of official UFO investigations in
Australia. For the first time a detailed 'inside' picture
was revealed of RAAF investigations. From the
RAAF's point of view, they have been, as Australia's
'official governmental examiner' of UFO reports,
locked into a bureaucratically orchestrated responsibility, which for a long time they have seen as a waste of
their time. They may have allayed possible fear and
alarm in the general public and satisfied the
government that there is no apparent defence
implication. However, the RAAF appear to be as
confused and uncertain as many civilian groups on
what to do about provocative UFO sightings.

It was not long before the RAAF changed their UFO policy. The Defence News Release of 2 May 1984:

'WEDNESDAY, 2 MAY, 1984   No 80/84

**UNUSUAL AERIAL SIGHTINGS –
RAAF CHANGE IN POLICY**

The RAAF in future will investigate fully only those Unusual Aerial Sightings (UAS) which suggest a defence or national security implication.

The Minister for Defence, Mr Gordon Scholes, said today that while the RAAF would continue to be the first point of contact, UAS reports considered not to have a defence or security implication would not be further investigated. Instead they would be recorded and the UAS observer would be given the address of civilian UAS research organizations if the observer wished to pursue the matter further.

Mr Scholes said that in the past the RAAF's investigation of all UAS reports had often proved time consuming, unproductive and had led to many man-hours of follow-up action by the RAAF and other agencies such as the Department of Aviation and the Bureau of Meteorology.

He said that procedures for investigating UAS reports had remained unchanged for many years. The vast majority of reports submitted by the public had proved not to have a national security significance.'

The end of September 1984 saw an embarrassing incident for the government's 'new' UFO policy. Having 'downgraded' their interest, due to an alleged lack of 'national security' impact, a delta-winged aircraft which startled golfers and trail bike riders, at Cunnamulla, in south-west Queensland, put the RAAF into a flap. The UFO was described as having no tail, no windows and no apparent sound. One witness reported it had 'beautiful rainbow colours' and 'seemed to zigzag like it was out of control' for a short time before disappearing. The object ostensibly remained unidentified. The RAAF denied ownership.

The matter was raised in the Senate of Australia's parliament, leading the Senator representing the Defence Minister in the Senate, to confirm that the RAAF advised there had been no 'known' delta-winged aircraft operating in the area at that time. 'Beryl flying off course' was supplied as the only suggestion — a flippant reference to Queensland's premier pilot, Beryl Young.

Since then the RAAF have taken a relatively low profile in the UFO controversy but civilian groups have benefited in that further cases are being reported and passed on to them by the RAAF. Even an abduction case located at an area near Jindabyne, NSW, was referred to UFO Research (NSW) by the RAAF. Clearly advantages are coming through to civilian groups but the official attitude remains unchanged.

We have seen that the Australian experience is a potent microcosm of the world-wide controversy. It is my contention that had a well-supported programme of scientific enquiry replaced the myopic military ethic that had prevailed, then the course of the UFO controversy would have been considerably different and certainly more progressive. Perhaps by now there would not have been an ongoing UFO controversy and indeed no UFO mystery. The wisest counsel we can gain from the contemporary world-wide UFO controversy is that a world-wide *open* multi-disciplined approach is required.

PART IV
EXPLAINING UFOs

EXPLAINING UFOs – INTRODUCTION

The quest for an explanation to the UFO phenomenon has been a long and difficult one and, without being unduly pessimistic, it seems reasonable to say that we know little more about what lies at the heart of the phenomenon now than we did forty years ago. That is not to say that progress has not been made – it has. But when the first UFOs were reported in the 'modern era', just after the second World War, it seemed as if the solution would be a relatively simple one; there are things in the sky, therefore identify them/catch one/unambiguously photograph one and you have your answer. Who could have imagined that we would have to face a journey not only through the skies, but through the mind of man as well?

In short, we thought the journey was to be but a few steps and we would complete it. Now we have made those few steps but we know the journey is to be a very long one. Confucius' belief that 'in a journey of a thousand miles there has to be a first step' is not very comforting when we look back from our position on the thousand mile trek to find we are still close to the starting point.

However, let us not forget that important steps *have* been taken by serious ufologists in the last few decades:

— The study of ufology to date has forever destroyed the myth that there will be one solution to the UFO phenomenon. We know now that the 'solution' is likely to lie in many areas ranging from the identification of previously unknown atmospheric phenomena through to an understanding of the way our own minds work.

— It has enabled us to solve some aspects of the phenomena, particularly the sightings related to atmospheric phenomena.

— We have learned to understand more about the methods and motivations of hoaxers.

— We have managed, at least to some extent, to isolate the field of ufology into legitimate scientific research and divorce this from the worship and cult groups that the press have previously included in their assessments of our subject. It must be admitted, however, that there is still a long way to go in this respect.

— We have begun a divorce from that most suspect of hypotheses, the extraterrestrial theory. This is not to say that we have dismissed it, but that we are beginning to get it firmly in its place. Dr Tough in his article suggests that rather than dismiss or accept it we give it an acceptance level based on our appreciation of the evidence. No more sensible suggestion could be made for any of the hypotheses offered, from the mundane to the exotic and extraordinary.

What have we not done?

— We have failed as yet to attract the respect of the conventional scientific community. We will need to do this in order to progress in a meaningful way. However, there have been many advances in this respect and projects such as UNICAT and URD, described in this book, and a host of other projects not represented here, are beginning to break the ground of structured scientific analysis.

— We have failed to represent ourselves properly in the media. To some extent this is not our fault; the tabloid press has certainly been attracted to the more exotic extraterrestrial theories and have ignored our attempts to prevent that. However, press coverage of ufology at the local level is generally very good and national media is beginning to realize that the public finds 'serious' ufology and the alternatives to ET of sufficient interest for them to begin to present a more balanced view in the future.

In the 1940s and 1950s we would have said that the UFO phenomenon was about objects seen flying in the skies about which we had uncertainties. At least we have come a long way from this and we begin to perceive that the UFO phenomenon is a 'human' one. That does not preclude extraterrestrial intelligences but we know that the phenomenon we are examining is about how we humans perceive whatever it is we are being exposed to and why we misperceive and fail to understand so much. The core phenomenon to which we are addressing ourselves is why do millions of level-headed, ordinary people see things that they cannot understand, and, even more importantly, *why do they feel so moved by these events that they seek to report them?*

So have we recognized the UFO phenomenon for what it is? The answer for this is – we don't know. If we know that no one answer will suffice and we accept that our earlier premises were simplistic to say the least then we cannot be sure that we do not face further complexities in the future. Even now, were we to subdivide the UFO phenomenon into two 'sets', lights and objects in the skies on the one hand and the abduction phenomenon on the other hand, we would possibly be oversimplifying the situation. Could there be other dimensions/other realities? Without any data on which to theorize, to discuss this in any depth would be to head for the realms of science fiction. But the possibilities, though fantastic, are real: time travel; an alternative life from our own earth; a form of terrestrial intelligence that we have not previously appreciated; a link between the entities of UFOs and the myths of folklore; other 'earths' in parallel to our own.

It is pointless to consider such concepts without data or reasonable evidence but we should be aware that one day we may have to consider these possibilities seriously, just as we now face psychological possibilities that we did not previously conceive of.

Is anything certain? Only one 'negative' certainty, as Shakespeare's Hamlet said:

> *There are more things in heaven and earth*
> *... than are dreamt of in your philosophy ...*

EXTRATERRESTRIAL UFOs –
YES OR NO?

Dr Allen Tough

During the past forty years or so, has anyone actually seen an extraterrestrial being or space craft?

A 'yes' answer to this question has been called the Extraterrestrial Hypothesis (ETH) for explaining various reports, claims, experiences, and phenomena in the UFO field.

What is the current status of this hypothesis? We will look at compelling reasons for both a 'yes' and 'no' answer. The conflict between these two indicates the need for fresh projects. Five suggested projects are now high priority in order to settle the question one way or the other.

In favour of a YES answer:

(i) Highly advanced beings and civilizations· have probably evolved elsewhere in our galaxy. Among the scientists interested in discussing and searching for extraterrestrial intelligence, there is general consensus that advanced civilizations would have developed at least a few times among the billions of stars in our Milky Way galaxy. Any extraterrestrial civilizations that are still flourishing today could be 10,000 or even 500,000 years ahead of us. They would therefore possess various capacities far in advance of ours, including the capacity to travel to this Solar System if they so choose.

(ii) Some or all of these extraterrestrial civilizations are probably motivated to observe and study other civilizations, for their own protection if nothing else. They may also be motivated to provide various sorts of help to humankind. In short, advanced extraterrestrials may possess the motivation as well as the capacity to visit our civilization.

(iii) Thousands of reliable, sensible, sober people in many parts of the world have reported seeing unidentified flying craft that execute advanced manoeuvres, such as very rapid acceleration and right-angle turns, and have sometimes reported seeing alien occupants as well. The emotional responses of many witnesses indicate that their experience continues to feel very real to them. Some sightings are reported by several witnesses. Animal reactions, electromagnetic interference with vehicles, radar images, photographs, and physical traces at the site (imprints, residues, damaged trees) often confirm the interpretation that the visual sighting involves a real physical object, apparently a highly advanced space craft.

(iv) Stories of abduction and sometimes medical procedures by extraterrestrials have been recounted by well over a hundred people, often under hypnosis. Some aspects and details in the stories told by unrelated individuals have been remarkably similar, even before these details appeared in print.

(v) James McCampbell has demonstrated that pulsed microwave radiation may well explain a variety of phenomena that are reported in some UFO sightings, such as low-pitched humming sounds, high-pitched whistles, certain smells and tastes, radios going dead or tuning to a different station, and vehicles stalling and sometimes spontaneously restarting. Microwaves could conceivably be emitted by the propulsion or anti-gravity system of an advanced spacecraft. If McCampbell's work turns out to be correct, it supports the notion that some UFOs are advanced spacecraft.

(vi) Documents purportedly from US government and military files suggest that the US government continues to study UFOs seriously and classifies them as 'top secret' or higher. Additional evidence suggests that the British and Canadian governments may be doing the same thing.

(vii) Various individuals have claimed firsthand or secondhand knowledge of US military retrievals of crashed extraterrestrial vehicles and bodies. Prominent scientist Robert Sarbacher recalls his secondhand knowledge of retrievals in Bletchman.

(viii) A variety of individuals receive messages, supposedly from extraterrestrial beings, while in a trance state. The term 'channelling' is commonly applied to this.

In favour of a NO answer:

(i) Although some advanced extraterrestrials probably do have the capacity and motivation for observing us, they might reject a long space ship trip and choose a cheaper or quicker method, such as a robot probe or radio messages. They might even have developed some quick and easy method of distant surveillance that we have not yet achieved: they may be able to observe us somehow without approaching the Solar System.

(ii) People often perceive reality incorrectly. Indeed, the amount of misperception, distortion, optical illusion, fantasy, and wishful thinking among human beings is astounding. Hendry repeatedly found these phenomena, such as a very strong tendency to perceive domed spacecraft when actually viewing an advertizing airplane or a natural phenomenon. One part of our brain may be capable of creating lifelike experiences for us at certain times. Perhaps we do not recognize that the experiences during a daydream or semi-awake fantasy are manufactured by our brain, just as night dreams are. People sometimes have vividly dramatic psychological experiences that do not jibe with outer reality; some psychological mechanism seems capable of producing similar experiences in various unconnected individuals. Given our knowledge of bizarre mental and psychological phenomena, in any given year we might *expect* one person in a million to 'experience' a realistic close-up encounter with an alien being or spacecraft: this source alone translates into 3000 UFO 'encounters' per year.

(iii) Several UFO reports, photographs, and documents have turned out to be hoaxes. People have a fascinating diversity of conscious and subconscious reasons for wanting to fool others.

(iv) Because of this high incidence of distorted perception and deliberate hoaxes, a 'yes' answer to our question would require very convincing evidence of an extraterrestrial visitor or spacecraft. In fact, no single (thoroughly studied) UFO case is highly convincing to most of the people who study it carefully. I cannot think of any single case that I would want to defend vigorously in front of a group of well-informed sceptics.

(v) Civilian researchers who study UFO claims are poorly funded and sometimes insufficiently trained. Usually only one or two individuals investigate a case, rather than a highly trained team with a wide variety of skills ranging from penetrating interview techniques to sophisticated soil sampling. Consequently one worries about the validity of most UFO data.

(vi) Too many UFO researchers have a closed mind about the ETH. For them it should be called a belief or faith rather than a hypothesis. Several times I have seen UFO 'researchers' pass up an excellent and easy opportunity to collect data that might disconfirm the ETH: they fervently believe in an extraterrestrial explanation and therefore have no desire to check out whether they are right or wrong. In a praiseworthy attempt to improve the objectivity and validity of future interviews, one prominent UFO leader has pointed out the weaknesses of past interviews:

'Far too many of us simply have an attitude problem: To find a meteor in what at first appeared to be an anomalous event is viewed as somehow a failure, a disappointment and waste of time ... An appalling lack of commonsense has pervaded the [interview] process, thereby distorting thousands of cases and rendering them useless ... Because of investigator bias and sloppiness, inadequate preparation is made before the interview; improper settings are selected; exaggerated body language by the *interviewer* elicits hyperbole in the retelling; ineffective listening causes important points to be missed or misconstrued; ... leading witnesses with either-or questions and references to the "craft" or the "UFO" affirms a preconception.'

Vigorous investigation by an informed sceptic sometimes finds that earlier investigators overlooked some natural explanation, some hidden motive in a witness, or even an outright hoax. Illuminating examples have been exposed by Philip Klass and Robert Sheaffer.

(vii) There are no photographs of UFO occupants. A UFO has never been clearly photographed by two persons independently. There are extremely few *close-up* photos of an alien craft, and I do not know of one that has passed rigorous laboratory scrutiny of the negative. Angelo has pointed out that we lack irrefutable *physical* evidence of alien visitors and space ships; we have only 'soft' human testimony (eye-witness reports) rather than 'hard' technical and scientific data.

Has any human being actually seen and reported an alien being or space craft? Is the extraterrestrial hypothesis correct for at least one person's experience or report?

Few people who have examined a large portion of the serious UFO literature with a reasonably open mind would estimate the 'yes' probability as less than ten or fifteen per cent. A more appropriate estimate might fall somewhere between twenty and seventy per cent. The evidence is convincing enough that one cannot reject all of it with an extremely high level of certainty and confidence.

At the same time, however, the evidence for extraterrestrial sightings and encounters is not highly convincing. It certainly does not support an eighty or ninety per cent probability that the ETH is correct. It would not convince a knowledgeable hard-headed sceptic nor does it add up to extraordinarily convincing evidence to support an extraordinary claim.

The established facts do not yet permit us to either accept or reject the extraterrestrial hypothesis for UFO reports, concluded Greenwell in *The Encyclopedia of UFOs*. He also commented that 'much emotion has predominated these debates since the 1940s ... The emotional commitment on the part of those speculating on the ETH, positively or negatively, is not likely to diminish as long as UFOs continue to be reported.'

In passing, let us note that if the ETH is rejected, two mutually exclusive possibilities remain concerning the past forty years. One possibility is that no extraterrestrials have visited Earth nor otherwise observed us during that period, perhaps because they do not exist in our galaxy or because they are not interested in us. The other possibility is that some advanced extraterrestrials have observed us but have remained highly inconspicuous; no one has glimpsed them or their craft. Civilizations advanced 10,000 years beyond ours may have developed a variety of unobtrusive methods for close-up or distant surveillance; some of our current espionage techniques would have seemed miraculous just one hundred years ago! The ETH applies, then, only to whether someone has *seen* and *reported* a genuine extraterrestrial being or space craft; it does not deal one way or the other with the possibility of completely inconspicuous observation by extraterrestrials.

If at least one person during the past forty years has glimpsed an alien space craft or interacted with a being from another part of the galaxy, a stunningly important event has occurred. Surely anyone interested in the broad sweep of human history and the human future, anyone interested in our potential interaction with alien civilizations, would agree with the significance of such an event. Yet we simply do not know whether such a fundamental event has occurred or not.

How can we try to permanently settle the extraterrestrial hypothesis, one way or the other?

Clearly we need new approaches and fresh projects. Let me suggest five projects that could be especially crucial for achieving this goal:

(1) Form a small working committee composed of UFO writers, researchers, critics, sceptics, and enthusiasts along with one neutral social scientist and one neutral physical scientist. Encourage a thoughtful, open-minded dialogue among all members. The committee's task: decide what sorts of evidence would be highly convincing to *everyone* for a genuine sighting of an extraterrestrial spacecraft or occupant. Then modify the UFO field investigators' training and instructions or take other steps to increase the chances of collecting such evidence. Either this committee or a separate one should perform the same task for abduction cases.

(2) Select the seven or ten most promising recent and current cases (including at least one or two abduction cases) that might support the ETH. For each case, mount a thorough broad-gauge investigation by a small but varied team of one or two sceptics and two or three other UFO researchers, each of whom is dedicated to discovering the truth about that particular case, no matter what the truth turns out to be.

(3) In several key countries, insist on full and honest disclosure from the armed forces, security agencies,

and national government about any past or present
UFO evidence. Insist on an ironclad promise of
immunity from all consequences for any employee or
former employee who talks freely, reveals documents,
or produces other evidence. (Today's major military
secrets could not be revealed, of course, nor espionage
methods that have not already been described in
print). An ironclad amnesty would soon settle once and
for all whether any government knows more about
alien visitors than the rest of us know.

(4) Encourage two or three sympathetic scientists
and two or three knowledgeable sceptics to independently pursue the McCampbell line of thought and
experimentation. Again, it should not take long to
achieve a conclusive outcome, one way or the other.

(5) Psychological explanations are a key foundation
in the sceptic's refusal to accept the ETH. We need
sophisticated psychological studies of misperception,
distortion, fantasy, archetypes, and perinatal symbols
in order to test whether the sceptic's reliance on
psychological explanations is well founded. (For
example, to be truly scientific, researchers would
conduct a whole *series* of experiments to compare the
detailed stories of mock abductees and witnesses with
those which are 'real'). In fact, even a thorough and
sophisticated review of the relevant existing psychological literature would be useful.

THE COSMIC PERSPECTIVE

John Prytz

Almost immediately following the flowering of the 'flying saucer' phenomenon in the late 1940s, extraterrestrial intelligence (ETI) was suggested as at least a partial explanation by some military, government, and scientific officials, and some of the public too. The argument ran; UFOs therefore ETI.

I propose to reverse the proposition and argue ETI therefore UFOs!

ETI must be aware of mankind! Strong words, but supported by the plausibility that ETI has discovered Earth's existence, and the evidence that ETI has been physically present within the near-Earth environment.

Before one can conclude that ETI is aware of our existence, we must be convinced that ETI themselves exist.

A strong, statistical, case can be made for the existence of life as-we-know-it on many worlds within our own Milky Way Galaxy, and evolutionary biologists are of the opinion that as chemical evolution must give rise to biology, so must biology give rise to intelligence. But intelligence is not enough; it must evolve a *technology*. Again, given the principles behind evolutionary theory, coupled with the proper environmental conditions (dry land, abundant metallic ores, etc), and enough time, there would statistically be still a good million or so technological civilizations currently present within our own galaxy. And, given the sheer age of our galaxy, and the brief time that we ourselves have been a technological civilization, 99.99% of the galaxy's technological civilizations must be in advance of our own. We are the new boy on the block!

Premise one: It is improbable that we are alone as a technological intelligent life form. The question remains, however, how would extraterrestrial technological civilizations know about us?

Our radio signals have been expanding away from Earth for the past seventy or more years, travelling at the speed of light, and could be detected by any suitable ETI within that radius. However, the mathematics of ETI distribution suggest that the nearest technological civilization would be over 1000 light years away, so won't be able to detect our radio/TV/radar waves for another 930 terrestrial years (give or take a century or so).

Of greater likelihood is that ETI has ventured out into the cosmos, and in the course of such voyages, discovered Earth and its life forms.

One reason for such a venture is exploration; a basic scientific curiosity about what is out there, including the potential discovery of alien life forms.

Another is the exploitation of the abundant natural resources to be had in space, far greater than those available on any finite planetary surface.

Further, the combination of population growth with the demands for food, energy, goods, etc by that population, suggest positive reasons for the colonization of space, either on uninhabited planetary surfaces, or (and far easier) in artificially constructed, ecologically self-contained, abodes – which could be the size of small planets. With respect to artificial space colonies, the advantages are many. A controlled environment for one – no nasty weather, volcanoes, earthquakes, etc. A controlled gravity (actually centrifugal force). If you get a bit crowded, add on an extension – better yet, construct a new colony – there's light years of room to expand in. Experience relative freedom from resource limitations – there are plenty of materials to be had from the uninhabited planets, asteroids, moons and other debris. There would also be relative freedom from territorial disputes in self-contained space colonies; colonists could experiment with a wide variety of social structures and political systems. And if things get a bit crowded, even in the size of an entire planetary system, there is all of interstellar space to head for. Which brings up perhaps the major rationalization for interplanetary, hence interstellar, exploration, exploitation and colonization. Species survival.

Consider how vulnerable our race is to extinction if we remain confined to this planet. Daily news reports and environmental experts keep pointing this out. But if mankind were to spread itself throughout even 'nearby' interstellar space, nothing short of the end of the Universe, the destruction of our galaxy, or a massive supernova would wipe us out. Expand throughout the entire galaxy and even the supernova threat is removed.

Further, there is nothing physically impossible about interplanetary, or interstellar space flight. The major problems are economic and having the collective will and desire to do it.

Despite the vast times and distances involved, interstellar travel is technically feasible according to known physical laws. One does not have to stretch the imagination very far to visualize a space-faring race either with very long lifespans (relatives to ourselves) or who employ multi-generation star ships or suspended animation. An extrasolar civilization might employ robots as scouts; self-reproducing machines to which time and distance would have no significance, would radio back any discoveries of interest.

But regardless of how any extraterrestrial civilization chooses to explore and colonize outer space, the two key points are that: a) even at velocities which we can achieve today, the elapsed time between the first interstellar journey and the total colonization/ exploration of the Milky Way Galaxy would be a small fraction of the age of the galaxy, and b) it only takes *one* such extrasolar civilization, in the entire vastness of our galaxy, to do it.

Premise Two: Space travel is both desirable and feasible, and if not quite yet, will shortly be within the capabilities of our own civilization, more so one further advanced than ourselves.

The galaxy may be big, but it has also been around for a very long time, and time can turn the statistically improbable into the inevitable. If ETI is as abundant as we think it is our solar system should have received an exploring visit roughly once every 100,000 years.

No doubt such probes radioed back 'nothing interesting' when scanning Earth on a flyby mission for some considerable period of time, until several hundreds of thousands to millions of years ago. Earth showed the first signs of interest to another intelligence; either the development of life itself, or intelligent life. Even if the Earth had not already been visited in person by such an alien race before that point, the impetus to do so after receiving their probe's radio message of 'interesting developments' would have been strong.

Premise Three: The knowledge of the existence of planet Earth resides in the databank of at least one nonterrestrial civilization. Indeed, it has been suggested that we should be confining our search for ETI to detection of *their* unmanned probes currently in orbit around the sun, maybe even around the Earth itself.

It is one thing to suggest that there exist unmanned and artificially intelligent space probes roaming our solar system, quite another to suggest the follow up, flesh and blood in person visit by the owners of those probes. But a million years could elapse between the probe's initial radio message, and the aliens' arrival. Such aliens could have relatively lengthy life spans, making a journey to Earth of no greater significance to them than were our terrestrial explorations several centuries ago, or our projected flights to Mars in the Twenty-first Century. Further, genetic engineering could create an alien race suitable for space flight and living conditions. Intelligence can direct its own evolution.

Another possibility is the space colony ark; though the first generation start the journey it would be the tenth, hundredth, even thousandth generation that will eventually arrive at their destination.

Perhaps relativistic velocities approaching the speed of light are feasible to super technological societies. Perhaps superluminary 'warp drive' velocities and/or alternative hyperspace pathways through space, such as travel through black holes, really are possible.

Finally, the possibility always exists that UFO phenomena are the product of a completely artificially intelligent society which has superseded its biological creators, or that the organic beings stay at home and obtain all their data via unmanned probes.

All such logical concepts allow ETI visitations. But, given the number of sightings, the ETI must have a nearby base of operations, probably external, such as in interplanetary space or on some surface, such as the moon. Some have postulated that the moon itself is an artificially constructed space (ark) ship, covered with rock debris for protection from radiation and meteors, as well as camouflage from terrestrial eyes.

Premise Four: There is nothing impossible, improbable, or even illogical in suggesting that ETI has been and/or is now present within our own near-Earth environment.

Planet Earth may have been visited many times in

the geological past, noted and logged, considered to be of possible future but not current interest, but there must come a time when local developments here warrant a more in-depth, perhaps personal, investigation. Whether this was ten, a hundred, or a thousand years ago is neither here nor there.

Myths and legends from around the world suggest the presence of superbeings. Archaeological mysteries have been suggested by some as showing the influence of 'ancient astronauts'. Most such evidence and speculation is clearly wrong but beneath the covering of fertilizer could lie a sprout of truth.

If extraterrestrials were around in our recent past, then it is not illogical to assume they wouldn't have gone away. After all, we are more interesting today than we were four thousand and more generations ago.

References to strange lights and alien beings go back to the dawn of historical records. However, it is the post-World War II period that really sees the UFO phenomenon come into its own, whether as the product of incredible observers reporting relatively credible things, or credible observers reporting relatively incredible things. The data suggest the latter, but the question remains unsolved. As long as the human being is the interface between what is seen and what the UFOs *are* we have to accept that the intelligence associated with the behaviour of UFOs could as easily be a product of the human observer as of any alien intelligence.

However, we do have motion pictures, radar trackings, physical trace/ground markings, uncharacteristic animal reactions and electro-magnetic effects. All in addition to eye-witness reports of close encounters, sometimes coupled with accounts of humanoids, and on occasions even reports of human beings being briefly abducted and studied by non-human life forms.

Finally, apart from UFO and 'ancient astronaut'

evidence, one can point to historical and recent records of astronomical phenomena, not always easily dismissed as natural, such as spots traversing the sun where no spots should be; transient lunar phenomena (TLP); flashes of light on Mars; and some curious shapes (artefacts?) photographed on both the lunar and Martian surfaces.

There have been astronautical phenomena such as off-again, on-again satellites; satellites detecting what have been glossed over as 'zoo animals' and satellites which have vanished without trace or explanation (such as Satcom III and Ayame 2).

Geophysical phenomena could be taken as suggestive. For example, the Tunguska, Siberia explosion of 30 June 1908; or the series of mysterious sonic booms off the American east coast in late 1977/early 1978.

Historical mysteries too play a suggestive role, the most obvious of which are disappearances of aircraft, ships, and human beings. Then, too, are the biological mysteries, such as sightings of weird creatures, for example, Mothman in West Virginia, in 1967.

All this is only suggestive. It does not prove that extraterrestrials are sharing our environment with us.

However, it reinforces the scientists' belief that extraterrestrial civilizations, with an advanced state of technology, not only must exist, but must be aware of our existence. We can state, with a fair degree of confidence, that we are known, not alone, in the Universe.

EXTRATERRESTRIAL UFOs –
WHAT THEY MAY BE

Kenneth W Behrendt

To understand the advanced physics utilized by an airborne extraterrestrial UFO as it appears to move about without any apparent means of propulsion requires an intensive analysis of the shapes, motions and associated effects. Along, too, with a complete re-evaluation of our current theories of gravity, dynamics, quantum physics, and relativity, to see how they might be used in their current forms or with slight modification to rationalize a real UFO phenomenon.

A new 'anti-mass field theory' has proven highly successful in rationalizing the bulk of the anomalous behaviours displayed by the UFOs. Originally developed to account for UFOs' gravity-free, inertia-less flight in our atmosphere it also explains: how UFOs produce visible glows ('haloes') near their hull surfaces, (the chief observable feature of nocturnal UFOs); the burning of the eyes and skin of witnesses; how UFOs affect compasses and cause automobiles to malfunction; how UFOs operate underwater; and how they so easily and conveniently traverse the vast distances between star systems and galaxies. Further-more, 'AMF theory' has, unlike previously unsuccess-ful hypotheses, proven to be mathematically rigorous, and has given us the first indications of what the crew of a UFO experiences, the structures and placement of the propulsion equipment aboard their craft, and how the external Universe appears from their craft.

The gravitational and inertial forces objects experience are produced by the bending of their own mass field radiations.

There are only two ways in which to eliminate the gravitational and inertial properties of an object. We could somehow prevent the mass field radiations the objects emit from having their outward paths bent by the mass fields of other objects or the object's own motion, or we could prevent the object from emitting any mass field radiation which could then have its paths bent.

According to AMF theory, UFOs utilize the second option. Figure 1(e) shows how this may be achieved by combining a second field of the appropriate symmetry over the mass field normally surrounding an object. This second field will have a 'polarity' opposite to that of the mass field so that when the two fields are superimposed, the second field will cancel out and thereby weaken the object's normal mass field. This second field is the 'anti-mass field', from which AMF theory receives its name.

In Figure 1(e) the object's mass field is completely cancelled out by the anti-mass field. If located in a planet's atmosphere, such an object would rise like a helium filled balloon and, if the means could be found to eliminate aerodynamic drag it could then be rapidly moved about by the application of propulsive forces to its structure.

The anti-mass field needed to render an object massless must be provided artificially; every UFO must contain one or more 'AMF generator'.

AMF assumes that one can imagine all of the subatomic particles which compose the atoms and molecules of a piece of matter to be continuously radiating a form of non-electromagnetic radiation in all directions. This radiation is referred to as 'mass field radiation' and as it radiates away from an object, it

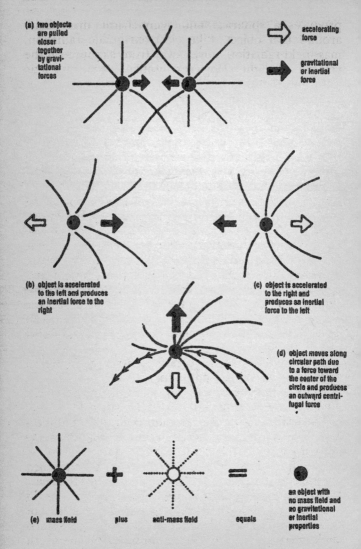

Figure 1 – Distortions of the Mass Fields
Surrounding Objects

produces a spherical and symmetrical 'mass field' around that object. Like electromagnetic radiation, mass field radiation moves away from its source at the velocity of light. However, unlike electromagnetic radiation, the emission of mass field radiation carries no energy away from the object.

Figure 1 (a two-dimensional representation) shows how distortions in the mass fields produce 'gravity' and 'inertia'. In the figure, the gravitational and inertial forces experienced by the objects are represented by solid black arrows while the forces applied to the objects to acclerate them are represented by white arrows. The mass field about an object created by its mass field radiations can be represented by solid radial lines which are each imagined to be extending away from the object at the velocity of light.

Figure 1(a) shows what happens when two objects emitting mass field radiation are brought into proximity.

Figures 1(b) and 1(c) show what happens to an object's mass field when that object has a force applied to it that causes it to accelerate.

Figure 1(d) shows what happens when an object moves along a circular trajectory.

Varying the amount of anti-mass produced would allow a UFO's pilot to vary the craft's remaining uncancelled mass. As the amount of anti-mass produced is gradually increased in quantity, the UFO and crew would gradually lose mass. At some point the UFO and crew would become light enough to float in a planetary atmosphere. When the amount of anti-mass equals the mass of the UFO and its crew, they would become massless. If, at this point, the amount of anti-mass then exceeds the craft and crew's combined mass, the 'excess' may even reduce the masses of nearby objects.

For example, there have been many cases in which the human driver of a vehicle has found that the

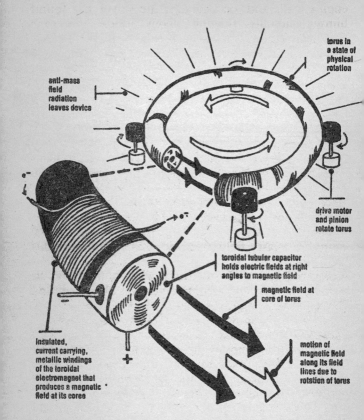

torus in
a state of
physical
rotation

anti-mass
field
radiation
leaves device

drive motor
and pinion
rotate torus

toroidal tubular capacitor
holds electric fields at right
angles to magnetic field

magnetic field at
core of torus

motion of
magnetic field
along its field
lines due to
rotation of torus

insulated,
current carrying,
metallic windings
of the toroidal
electromagnet that
produces a magnetic
field at its core

Figure 2 – A Rotating Anti-Mass Field Generator
with Section Removed

proximity of a large hovering UFO, directly overhead, causes the vehicle's ignition system to fail so that the engine stalls and, occasionally, the driver has found himself literally floating about inside the car's passenger compartment. As the UFO leaves, vehicle and driver regain their normal masses and weights.

Next we must consider the physical principles and equipment used by our extraterrestrial visitors to generate these artificial anti-mass fields.

Figure 2 illustrates the configuration of a typical 'rotating' anti-mass field generator with a section removed to reveal its internal structural details. It consists of a conventional toroidal electromagnet whose current-carrying, insulated metallic windings can produce a toroidal magnetic field at the core. Also located at the core is a toroidal tubular capacitor. This capacitor consists of a large number of concentric metallic layers separated by thin layers of an electrical insulator capable of resisting current flows caused by high voltages. When alternating layers of the metallic film are oppositely electrically charged, the entire volume of the capacitor will hold electric fields that are everywhere at right angles to the magnetic field at the core of the toroidal electromagnet. To cause the device to produce an anti-mass field about itself requires that the entire structure of the anti-mass generator be physically rotated. This action then causes the toroidal magnetic field to move along its field lines at right angles to the electric fields so that the anti-mass field radiation will be radiated from the generator's core to produce an anti-mass field.

For most disc-shaped UFOs, several toroidal AMF generators will be used. In order for such a craft to take off from the Earth, when at its normal mass and weight, all the toroidal tubular capacitors must be activated and all the toroidal electromagnets of its AMF generators energized. This will establish the electric and magnetic fields at right angles to each other in all of the cores of its AMF generators, but the craft will still emit no anti-mass field radiation and will still possess its normal mass and weight.

Next the drive motors are activated, to rotate the energized AMF generator tori around the central crew section inside the craft's hull. As the speed of rotation of the tori increases, the intensity of the anti-mass field radiation will increase and the UFO's mass will slowly dwindle.

When the craft has lost a sufficient amount of mass and weight, it will become buoyant and may gently begin to rise. To gain altitude rapidly, even if the craft is not yet quite buoyant, the UFO may fire a rocket engine, in order to overcome aerodynamic drag.

It is critical when using large radius rotating AMF generators that they be used in sets of two tori, each of which rotates in the opposite direction to the other member of the pair. This guarantees that, when landed and just starting up its AMF generators to become massless, the reactional torques transmitted to the UFO's hull and crew section through the drive motors rotating the tori will cancel each other out so that the hull will receive no net torque that might make it rotate.

So far, we only have a metallic craft with no more manoeuverability than a hot air balloon and, like such a craft, it would go wherever the wind took it.

To allow the massless UFO to undergo horizontal motion in our atmosphere, it is necessary that the craft apply driving forces to its hull. Many UFOs solve this problem by being equipped with either rocket or jet engines or even, on rare occasions, sets of propellers. It will usually not be able to attain a velocity of more than a few thousands of miles per hour in our atmosphere due to aerodynamic drag and frictional surface heating.

To attain far higher atmospheric velocities eg tens or hundreds of thousands of miles per hour, the UFO must be able to force the air near its leading surfaces to rapidly flow around its hull to its trailing side without touching the hull of the massless craft. Furthermore, in order to control its motion and undergo various aerobatic manoeuvres, the pilots of the UFO must be able to control the direction of air flow around their craft's hull. The quicker the UFO pilot can change the direction of air flow relative to the craft's hull, the quicker the craft can change direction. Even if the craft should execute a right angle turn within a turn radius of only a few feet while moving at tens of thousands of miles per hour, the crew of the vehicle will feel no inertial forces acting on their bodies because they are massless and any mass field radiation emitted by their bodies has been neutralized by the craft's AMF generators.

There are a variety of ways to move the air surrounding a massless UFO around the craft's hull, but they all require that the layer of air immediately surrounding the hull first be converted to a rich plasma or mixture of negatively electrically charged electrons and the positively electrically charged atmospheric gas ions from which the electrons were removed. Once this is done, the nearby boundary layer of plasma surrounding the UFO can, in one form of propulsion known as the 'plasmadynamic mode of propulsion', be exposed to crossed or perpendicular electric and magnetic fields that are projected into it from special pieces of equipment mounted on the inside of the vehicle's hull which are known as 'drive units'.

These drive units project the necessary crossed electric and magnetic fields into the surrounding plasma to move it around the craft's hull. By controlling the strength of the electric fields the UFO can vary the velocity with which the plasma will flow over the drive unit. If the electric field is extinguished so that only the magnetic field is left, then plasma flow ceases. If the polarity of the electrically charged regions induced on the hull is reversed then the direction of plasma flow can be reversed. As the

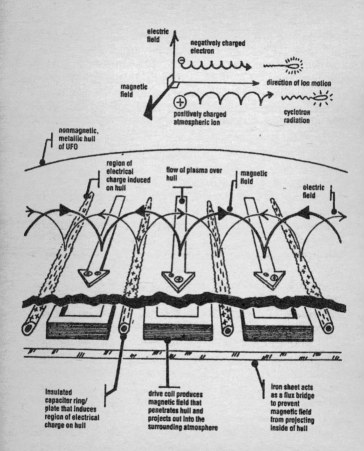

Figure 3 – The Plasmadynamic Mode of Propulsion

strength of the electric field is increased, the velocity of plasma flow will also increase. Conservative calculations show that a plasmadynamically propelled UFO can force the plasma which envelopes its hull to flow around the hull with a maximum velocity that can be hundreds of thousands of miles per hour.[1] Since the plasma is made to flow tangentially around the craft's hull without touching the hull, and the craft is itself massless, the UFO will then find itself moving forward at hundreds of thousands of miles per hour as the plasma is made to flow from the craft's leading to trailing surface and encounters stationary air near the trailing end of the craft.

Figure 3 shows a cross-sectional view of a portion of a plasmadynamically propelled UFO's hull.

In a real, extraterrestrial UFO using the plasmadynamic mode of propulsion, the hull will be underlaid with several drive units which can be independently activated and controlled so that plasma can be made to flow in a variety of directions with respect to the craft's hull.

The drive units will require sources of low and high voltage electrical current. The low voltage will energize the drive coils and the toroidal electromagnets of the craft's AMF generators while the high voltage will be used to charge the capacitor ring/plates. The low voltage current can be derived from batteries or from fuel cells reacting gaseous hydrogen and oxygen to obtain electricity and water. The high voltage current will have to be provided by motor driven, rotatory electrostatic generators.

It has long been suspected that most UFO's used the above plasmadynamic mode of propulsion, but the exact means by which the crossed electric and magnetic fields would be projected into the plasma layer surrounding the UFO's hull was not precisely understood.[2] It was also a mystery as to just how the UFO could heavily ionize the air immediately surrounding its hull so that plasmadynamic propulsion could be used. Now, however, in light of AMF theory, we know how the UFO creates the highly ionized boundary layer that envelopes its hull.

Apparently, it is the combined action of the UFO's anti-mass field and the magnetic fields emanating from its drive units that induces the ionization of the boundary layer near the craft's nonmagnetic metallic hull.[3] Energy that is necessary for the removal of the electrons from the atmospheric particles will come from the thermal energy of the air that is being affected by the craft's anti-mass field and magnetic fields and, as the air is converted to plasma near the UFO's hull, it will experience a drop in temperature.

If the energy output of the plasmadynamically propelled UFO's plasma boundary layer at microwave frequencies is high enough, then a nearby witness may experience headaches or, at very high intensity levels,[4] a state of temporary blindness, which effects are possible even if the craft emits no visible cyclotron radiation[5] (however, as pointed out by the American ufologist, James M McCampbell, intense microwave radiation might cause a secondary emission of visible light from the air surrounding the UFO). Such microwave radiation may also account for some of the radio and television interference these UFOs cause.[6]

Often when an automobile approaches an extraterrestrial craft, its headlights may dim, its engine may stall, and its starter motor may become inoperative although, once the UFO has departed, the starter may mysteriously activate itself without the ignition key having to be turned. All of these malfunctions are of a temporary nature and disappear soon after the UFO departs.

AMF theory allows all of these automotive malfunctions to be rationalized.[7] For each of the malfunctions cited, it is a combination of the anti-mass field radiation from the UFO and *local* magnetic fields in the automobile that produces an ionization of either metal or air atoms in the automobile that then causes the malfunction.

To explain automobile engine stalling, we can assume that the UFO's anti-mass field can similarly ionize air in the magnetic fields that exist around the wiring and ignition coil inside of the car's engine compartment. Once ionized to form a plasma, air loses its normal insulating properties and will conduct electricity at lower voltages. Thus, the automobile's high voltage electrical current will follow the path of least electrical resistance to jump directly from the grounded engine block through the ionized air surrounding ignition wiring, to enter any cracks in the wiring's insulation to make its way back to the positive pole of the car's battery rather than jump across the still non-ionized air between the spark plugs. The current may also return to the battery through an ionized coating of grime on the ignition wires or, if there is extensive ionization of most of the air in the engine compartment, directly through this ionized air. When this happens, the spark plugs will not fire properly, the engine will miss, and eventually stall as its idle speed drops. Ionization near the ignition coil's external magnetic field may also allow high voltage short-circuiting here that can stall the engine. Again, as the UFO departs, the plasma that causes this malfunction deionizes and the ignition system can function normally again because its high voltage components are again properly insulated by air with its normally high resistance to high voltage electrical current.

Automobiles with diesel engines seem to be immune to being stalled by the proximity of a UFO, the reason being that diesel engines do not utilize a high voltage ignition system.

Once the car is stalled, the motorist may, upon seeing the UFO, desperately try to start his or her engine. Upon turning the ignition key to the 'start' position, a heavy electrical current will flow through the starter motor field and armature windings which are usually wired together in series. As battery current flows through the starter's field windings, it produces a powerful magnetic field that projects out of the starter's die-cast aluminium housing. This magnetic field then combines with the UFO's anti-mass field radiation penetrating the engine compartment and the air around the starter becomes highly ionized. The resulting ions will now orbit around the magnetic field of the field windings to form an 'ionic vortex' of moving atmospheric ions. This vortex then generates its own magnetic field of the field windings. The two opposed magnetic fields then cancel each other out and, for all practical purposes, it is as though the starter had no field windings which, of course, means that the starter cannot turn the pinion gear attached to its armature to crank the engine. After the UFO leaves the scene, the ionic vortex will dissipate and its collapsing magnetic field will cut across the starter's field windings to induce a powerful current flow in them. It is this current that activates the starter and often will restart the again functional engine without any effort on the driver's part as long as the ignition key is still in the 'on' position.

This process of ionic vortex build up to neutralize local magnetic fields is also the reason that compass needles will deflect or even spin when a UFO is near. In these cases, the ionic vortex applies torques to the needle to move it out of alignment with the Earth's natural magnetic field.[8]

The same process which is responsible for the failure of high voltage ignition systems in automobiles is also responsible for the heavy current drains that cause brownouts and blackouts when UFOs hover over high voltage electrical transmission towers.

Figure 4 illustrates a typical plasmadynamic UFO with some of its internal propulsion equipment exposed. The entire mass of the craft and its crew is negated via

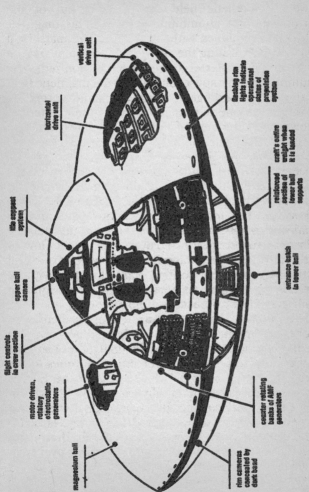

Figure 4 – A Plasmadynamically Propelled, Discoidal UFO that is 32 feet in diameter

the action of two banks of counter-rotating AMF generators (with six separate units per bank) that rotate about the crew section. The AMF generators are attached by ball-bearing assemblies to circular tracks in the upper and lower hull sections and are counter-rotated by eight drive motors whose rubber pinions are sandwiched between the upper and lower banks of AMF generators. This vehicle is not designed for travel in space and must be carried from one planetary atmosphere to another by a larger mother ship.

Conditions aboard a UFO: With the advent of AMF theory it is possible to picture what life aboard is like for craft both in a planet's atmosphere and engaged in space travel at hyperlight velocities.

The state of masslessness could pose a problem for ufonauts wishing to move around in their craft while airborne. While massless they cannot float from one location to another because air drag would immediately slow them to a stop. To overcome this effect, one of the ufonaut's 'feet' must remain in contact with the craft's interior surface (ceiling, walls, floor) at all times, perhaps by the use of plastic suction cups on the ufonaut's 'shoes'. Thus the ufonaut could easily walk about the craft's interior regardless of how violently the vehicle might be manoeuvering about a planet's skies. To make this method of ambulation work, the interior surfaces of the UFO must be smooth and clean.

Hovering plasmadynamically propelled UFOs often emit a variety of sounds with the humming and higher pitched whining sounds predominating; bearing-carried motions will create vibrations in the craft's interior structures.

There is now considerable evidence that some UFOs are able to become invisible. There are many cases in which an observed hovering UFO fades away or alternates between visibility and transparency. Very occasionally, one finds a case wherein the UFO is detected on radar, but cannot be observed visually. There are also some photographs of strange glows in the sky that are UFO shaped and which may or may not have been visible to the photographer. AMF theory can explain the UFOs' capability of becoming invisible in the optical or visible region of the electromagnetic spectrum.[9] This fascinating effect occurs when the UFO's AFM generators alter the 'character' of the craft's emitted anti-mass field radiation. The ufonauts of such a craft will increase the intensity of the electric fields inside the toroidal tubular capacitors at the cores of their craft's AMF generators while simultaneously lowering the intensity of the moving magnetic fields at the cores of the devices' toroidal electromagnets. The vehicle's anti-mass field then retains its original quantity of anti-mass and still negates the mass of the craft and crew as it previously did, but the anti-mass field is now said to possess 'E-rich character'. This type of anti-mass field has the additional property of being able to slightly reduce the electrostatic attractions between unlike electrically charged subatomic particles in matter.

Thus, as the UFO's anti-mass field is made more and more E-rich in character, the electrons in its atoms will orbit at slightly farther and farther distances from their nuclei. The energy differences between the atomic electron orbits determines the energies and frequencies of the photons of light that can be absorbed or emitted as electrons move between these orbits. As the E-rich anti-mass field of the UFO alters the electronic structures of the atoms of the UFO and its crew by expanding their electron orbits and lowering the energy differences between these orbits, these atoms will reach a point at which they no longer can absorb, refract, or reflect photons of electromagnetic energy with visible frequencies. The UFO and its crew will then slowly fade from view, although the vehicle is still physically present and propulsively active. The craft's atoms may now absorb, refract, or reflect photons at lower energies and frequencies and, though optically invisible, can show up on film as a dark shape when they block background infrared radiation or on radar when they reflect microwave radiation.

As long as the craft emits no visible cyclotron radiation or exhaust trails and flies below radar beams, it will be completely undetectable. Of course, there is always the danger that an Earth aircraft may accidentally fly into an invisible UFO, and such accidents would account for the few cases on record wherein airplanes have mysteriously broken up in the air, as though they had struck something solid before crashing.

The ufonauts aboard an invisible UFO, however, do not have any trouble seeing themselves or the scenery outside of their UFO! The atoms in the retinas of the ufonaut crew are also electronically altered so that they can now be stimulated by the lower frequency photons emitted by the craft's lighting system when the UFO is invisible. However, the invisible photons that an invisible ufonaut's eyes are now supplied with aboard the invisible UFO still stimulate the same rods and cones in the ufonaut's eyes that they stimulated before they had their frequencies lowered by the craft's E-rich anti-mass field as the UFO became invisible: the craft and its crew are only invisible to outside observers not affected by the craft's E-rich anti-mass field, while the interior of the craft as well as their own bodies appear completely visible and normal to the ufonauts. When they view the exterior world through a window, however, the situation changes somewhat. The invisible ufonauts can still view the scenery external to their craft, but they may see it by the infrared radiation it emits rather than any visible light.

The vast majority of the smaller UFOs (ie those under about sixty-four feet in one dimension) are plasmadynamically propelled and must be carried from one planet to another aboard a mother ship.

Craft in the intermediate size range (ie about 64-128 feet in at least one dimension) may use plasmadynamic or thruster propulsion for atmospheric operation and then use thruster propulsion for interplanetary and interstellar voyages. Any craft over about 128 feet in at least one dimension is incapable of directly landing on a planet's surface and turning off its AMF generators to achieve its full normal mass (it would then be crushed by its own weight) and must carry smaller craft to convey crew members to and from a planet's surface.

A UFO cannot use plasmadynamic propulsion in space because the thermal energies of the gas atoms found in interstellar and intergalactic space are too low to ionize these atoms if they are simultaneously affected by the anti-mass and magnetic fields near a UFO's hull.[10]

For interplanetary or limited interstellar voyages, the energy needed to vaporize propellant for ejection or ionize it for acceleration through external electric fields can come from conventional energy sources such as fuel cells that react gaseous hydrogen and oxygen to produce the needed energy in the form of electricity and water molecules to serve as propellant material. However, for long-range interstellar and all intergalactic voyages, the vessel must use nuclear reactors for electricity and carry supplies of ejectable propellant.

Regardless of how powerful the propulsion system of such a massive spacecraft is, it will never reach the velocity of light in practice so that round trip voyages between even the nearest star systems will take years as far as the inhabitants of those star systems are concerned. But there is an even more severe problem that would make it impossible for a conventional space craft to achieve a velocity that was only a thousandth that of light. At even this small sublight velocity the space craft would be totally destroyed if it was to impact a particle of solid material only the size of a grain of sand that laid along its trajectory! Space contains large quantities of such solid matter in the form of dust.

The only thing that allows the real, extraterrestrial UFOs to overcome these limitations is the fact that they can maintain a state of masslessness throughout the entire space voyage; that is, while massless, the UFOs can exceed the velocity of light and not be destroyed by impacts with particulate matter in space regardless of their velocity relative to such matter.

A massless craft can survive such impacts because, as the piece of space debris contacts the vessel's massless hull, it will become massless like the UFO and be instantly deflected or moved along by the hull.

We can see that travel aboard a massless UFO moving at hyperlight velocity is an ideal way (and perhaps the only way) to traverse the vast distances of the Universe in conveniently short time periods.

With the recent development of AMF theory, we now have a fairly detailed understanding of the extraterrestrial science and technology that allow UFOs to visit the Earth and display the performance capabilities and secondary effects that they do. Only a minimal amount of experimental work still needs to be done before humanity produces its own first crude AMF generators.

GEOPHYSICAL ALTERNATIVES

Chris A Rutkowski

This theory deals with UFO reports using geophysical principles by relating UFO sightings with energies produced inside the Earth itself. The Earth is constantly being subjected to a number of forces, including heating from its interior and tidal effects from the sun and moon. Mountain ranges are evidence of the slow but constant movement of the Earth's crust; the Himalayas, as geologists now know, were formed by the continental collision of India with Asia, many millions of years ago, as huge land masses moved.

It should not be surprising, then, that these movements can generate energy. This is especially obvious from the catastrophic results of the final release of pressure from continental plates moving against each other; earthquakes. Such seismic events are caused when rock under pressure or stress suddenly gives way, sending tremendous shock waves through the Earth. But in addition to shock waves, electromagnetic radiation (EMR) can be generated.

Scientists have been able to show that rock, under pressure deep beneath the surface of the Earth, can give off radio waves.[1] Some of these results are from tests done deep in mines with electrodes attached to the rock, picking up the radiated signals when the mines were being blasted.

For a long time, seismologists have been trying to develop ways to predict earthquakes. Along the San Andreas Fault in California, for example, they have been carefully monitoring each slight movement with ultrasensitive sensors and sampling the air to detect any release of gas.[2] Some attention has also been given to the observation of animals in the area, as it has often been noted that some creatures seem to 'know' when an earthquake is about to happen, becoming agitated several minutes, hours or possibly even days before a major seismic event.[3]

For this reason, some scientists are looking at the evidence that suggests EMR is released in advance of, or during, seismic events. Several Russian studies seem to suggest that this is so.[4]

This release of energy is the basis for the Tectonic Strain Theory (TST). A number of years ago, Canadian psychologist, Michael Persinger found that when he compared the times and locations of UFO sightings with those of seismic events or earthquakes, there was a relationship. The relationship is not a direct one, but points to the existence of something called a strain field.

When underground rock is subjected to strain, the rock material is forced to deform. A good analogy is walking upon thin river ice. Your weight forces the ice to deform or bend until eventually some combination of your transfer of weight and weakness in the ice causes the ice to 'give way'. Similarly, weaknesses in underground rock can support tremendous weight or pressure until a 'breaking point' is reached, but between the time the pressure is first applied and the time the rock actually breaks, there is a period of time when the pressure can build up or decline.

Underground rock exists in three-dimensional space. Stress builds up in a roughly spherical area around the point that the pressure is exerted, and may travel to a weak point some distance away. This area is known as the 'strain field'. In an area prone to earthquakes, strain fields build up with stress from moving rock plates.[5]

It has also been said that stressed rock gives off radiation. It would seem logical that this radiation is related to the strain field and should tell us something about the state of the rock; but what if this radiation was visible?

The TST postulates that UFOs are the visible radiation caused by stressed rock within strain fields. Persinger plotted the locations of reported UFO sightings and locations of seismic events on the same map, and produced interesting coincidences. An increase in UFO sightings seemed to coincide with an increase in seismic activity.[6]

In Britain, Paul Devereux has a similar theory. [Discussed in this book – Ed]

Both Persinger and Devereux have offered theories that the Earth gives off some kind of energy at certain locations and at certain times, caused by geological or geophysical processes. These theories acknowledge both that UFOs exist and may have an explanation based on known science.

If UFOs are representative of energy emanating from inside the Earth, this energy could, Persinger reasons, affect people in other ways besides merely becoming visible. If UFOs were some form of radiated energy, then there could be, say, X-ray UFOs as well as visible UFOs, as has already been suggested by the number of radar UFOs detected.

Persinger has pointed out that if such energy were being radiated, its intensity would make a difference to the observer, perhaps producing physiological effects. Even if no visible UFO were seen, something might be there to cause harm. The victim might experience headaches or nausea. Persinger has cautioned that in the event that a person were to be standing too close to an intense outburst of such energy, then severe effects such as the induction of epileptic fits or even death by electrocution might be the result.[7]

However, there is no evidence that this energy really exists.

Scientists have only just found that some radiation is given off by rock under stress, they have not developed a consistent explanation for its production. We know that some radiation can be produced under certain conditions, but whether this means that UFOs can be created is still open to debate.

There are other problems with TST: If the energy is released or created underground, there are difficulties in explaining how the energy travels to the surface and then into the air to be seen as a UFO. Earthquakes occur many kilometres underground, and if the strain field is that deep, how does the energy travel to the surface? This is of special concern since rock generally deadens electrical energy passing through it.

Allan Hendry, formerly of the Centre for UFO Studies, published *The UFO Handbook*, which contained some highly critical analyses of UFO investigation and research.[8] In the book, he discussed UFOCAT, a listing of UFO cases compiled by David Saunders for CUFOS. UFOCAT was used by Persinger in his statistical studies with the TST to produce the correlations between UFO cases and earthquakes. But Hendry pointed out what many other researchers knew: UFOCAT is a listing not of UFO sightings, but of *sources of information* about UFO sightings. It was produced from newspaper clippings, magazine files and some investigators' files, and was never designed for stastistical studies. UFOCAT cannot distinguish between IFOs and UFOs, for example.

There do exist some UFO files upon which analyses can be done, among them UNICAT, a project undertaken by Dr Willy Smith, containing many elements very different from UFOCAT.

But Persinger claims that the correlations are correct, even with the data problem. What his positive correlations of IFOs and earthquakes means is not clear, though it is difficult to imagine how a misperceived balloon might be related to a seismic event. His rebuttal is that the IFOs are the statistical 'noise' within which the real UFOs are embedded and produce the postulated results.

An additional statistical quirk is the suggestion that proximity is not required for the TST. Studies showed that the TST could be verified if a large distance factor was incorporated into the analyses. For example, one study found the UFO sightings were correlated with seismic events several hundreds of kilometres away, in addition to occurring months earlier or later.

The appeal of the TST lies partly with its use of accepted scientific phenomena to explain UFOs, but the extent to which these scientific phenomena are understood has in some cases been misrepresented. The Royal Astronomical Society held a special meeting to discuss electromagnetic radiation from earthquakes in 1985.[9] Papers were given by researchers in fields such as physics, geology and chemistry. The meeting showed that there was no consensus among the scientists on the mechanisms which produced radiation and the meeting concluded that 'earthquake lights may originate from a number of different processes ... under different physical conditions'. John Darr, an American geophysicist who is considered by some to be the leading authority on earthquake lights has suggested that whereas earthquake lights are pro-duced during generally strong seismic events, UFOs could be scaled-down versions resulting from less substantial and energetic seismic events.[10] This is especially curious since the energy required to produce a luminous, aerial UFO could be quite significant, and may require a much stronger seismic event. This debate is at the heart of the TST problem, and it may take many years before the issue is satisfactorily resolved.

The strain field itself is not well understood, either. While it is generally agreed that the field probably does exist, its dimensions and actual effect on surrounding rock is not known with any certainty, and while the energy contained in such a field may be substantial, measurements are difficult. Although seismologists can calculate the amount of energy released during an earthquake, the calculations of stored underground energy are another matter entirely.[11]

Jenny Randles, BUFORA's Director of Investigations, has pointed out that the only experimental results to support the TST are those claimed by Brian Brady of the US Geophysical Survey, who has offered evidence in the form of minute lights produced by the fracture of core samples under pressure in a laboratory, and Paul Devereux,[12] who with a team of associates has met with basically similar results in Britain.[13] Another American group, Vestigia, has offered some field evidence and observations of 'ground lights'. Their observations of several particular recurring lights suggested that the phenomena appear to be related to piezoelectricity, which is a form of radiation given off by certain types of rock, particularly crystals, under stress.[14] However, the laboratory results of Brady and his team showed that rock will give off visible radiation only during fracture, not just stress. Many TST studies, though, suggest luminous bodies were created by strain fields without accompanying fractures. Whether stress alone could emanate natural and luminous objects has not been satisfactorily demonstrated.

Philip Klass has offered evidence that many UFOs can be explained as electromagnetic plasmas, such as ball-lightning, produced under certain atmospheric conditions.[15] Ball lightning is so rare that some scientists still will not acknowledge its existence, though there is a wealth of eye-witness reports. Like UFOs, however, there does not appear to be a consistent theory for its production, though many have been proposed.[16]

In its path through space, the Earth is being affected by a number of external forces that greatly affect life on its surface. The Sun sends out many radiations besides life-giving light and heat; solar wind is a deadly barrage of energy that constantly bombards the Earth and only the Earth's own magnetic field shields us from this. Because the Sun's radiation output fluctuates, scientists carefully measure this output for signs of solar flares, which can interrupt communications and radio transmissions. It has been suggested that earthquakes are somehow triggered by changes in the Earth's magnetic field, possibly by changes in the solar wind. Such changes are related to the number of sunspots visible on the surface of the Sun, and these numbers are carefully recorded. Numbers of sunspots have also been added to correlational studies with the TST on the assumption that UFOs might ultimately be related to solar effects.

The vast majority of UFOs are misidentifications of ordinary objects and phenomena. A very small fraction of UFOs may have some sort of geophysical explanation. Researchers such as Steuart Campbell and Jenny Randles have shown that some UFO cases may have been generated by atmospheric plasmas of some sort, and Paul Devereux and Michael Persinger have put forth theories which link UFOs to geophysical processes. However, the link between theory and observation is still quite weak, and requires a great deal more research and substantiation before it can be widely accepted.

SPOOKLIGHTS

David W Clarke

Weird lights in the night sky have puzzled and fascinated mankind since the beginning of recorded history. Their comings and goings have become woven into the legends and folklore of cultures throughout the world, and since the year 1947 a new element – belief in visitors from outer space – has become attached to the lights, which previous generations regarded as ghosts and mischievous elementals.

Few people in Britain today will have heard of the once common phenomenon known as 'Will o' the wisp' or 'jack o' lantern'. Prior to the end of the nineteenth century these mysterious lights were a terror familiar to night travellers, especially in the marshy undrained areas which still remained in many parts of the country.

Will o'the wisp was known to the ancients by its Latin name 'ignis fatuus' (foolish fire) and was described as a strong, flame-like light seen hovering over marshland just after sunset on summer evenings. Although these marsh lights have been explained inconclusively as mere pockets of methane or 'phosphoretted hydrogen', this can hardly account for brilliant will o'the wisps dancing over hedgerows, rising high into the air and describing complicated movements – advancing, retiring and combining. They are often seen to move against the prevailing wind, and appear to display signs of intelligence – the light is said to recede from an observer who approaches it, and follows him if he retires from it. This alludes to the most durable part of the legend, ie that the lights deliberately lead people to their deaths by enticing them to follow across bogs and fens:

> '... of purpose to deceive us,
> And, leading us make us stray
> Long winter nights out of the way,
> And when we stick in mire or clay
> He doth with laughter leave us'
> (Drayton's *Nymphibia*)

These lights are as much a mystery in our present technological age as they were in Shakespeare's time, but anyone seeing lights in the sky nowadays would report what they had seen as a UFO, rather than the 'corpse candles' or evil spirits of past ages.

Virtually every country district of Britain had its own vernacular name for its peculiar lights – Joan in the wad (Devon and Cornwall), Jenny Burntail (Warwickshire), Peggy wi't lantern (South Yorkshire), Kitty wi' the wisp (Northumberland), and many others. Similar names can be found in other countries – the German *Irrlichtern* (wandering light), the French *feux-follets*, Italian *fuoco fatuo*, and the Swedish *lyktgubbe* (lantern-bearer) – suggesting a world-wide occurrence of similar phenomena. Other names have been given, or related, to will o' the wisp. Countryfolk and folklore collectors connect him with Puck, Friar Rush and Robin Goodfellow, as well as other pagan nature spirits, known as mischievous sprites, and the natural enemies of mankind. These beliefs are unknowingly continued today on Hallowe'en when children place a candle inside a hollowed-out turnip to represent the evil spirit or jack o'lantern.

However, will o'the wisp and his friends do not

appear to have died out entirely with the draining of marshes and fens during the early nineteenth century, for newspapers and popular science journals of the period are a treasure trove of accounts describing the phenomenon. Many locations throughout the British Isles have legends attached to them describing the appearances of strange lights – often spanning several centuries, around particular spots – more often than not ancient churches, old burial mounds, moorland and stretches of water, especially lakes and lochs.

In 1912 the Earl of Erne of Crom Castle, County Fermanagh, Northern Ireland, wrote to the London *Daily Mail* to describe the appearance of a strange light over Loch Erne, nearby. 'This light has been seen at intervals several times within the last six or seven years', he wrote 'by all sorts and conditions of men, and women too. It is of a yellow colour, and in size and shape very much the same as a motor-car lamp. It travels at a considerable pace along the top of the water – sometimes against the wind, at other times with it. It lights up all objects within a certain radius and disappears as quickly as it appears.'

One fascinating sighting occurred earlier this century, when two walkers returning to Keswick from an ascent of Helvellyn, in the Lake District, saw a number of bright white lights moving around over Castlerigg stone circle. One of these lights separated from the others and approached the two witnesses, but before it reached them it went out 'as if the matter producing the light had become exhausted'.

Near the village of West Witton, in Wensleydale, North Yorkshire, appears from time to time the 'Pennine light' which has been seen by motorists on a particular stretch of the A684 road between Leyburn and Swinithwaite, usually near Christmas. This light is so brilliant that it first appears to be the headlights of an approaching motor car, but then disappears into thin air. However, some lights are always in constant motion, as in the case of the 'Cammeringham light'

(Lincolnshire), a brilliant yellow light which spends its time speeding along country lanes, materializing and dematerializing when pursued.

Other lights follow particular routes across the countryside. The 'green light of Halton' (Merseyside) haunts the route of an underground passage between Norton Priory and Halton Castle. The folklore of the Scottish Highlands is particularly rich with stories concerning strange lights, which the ancient peoples regarded as omens or forewarnings of death or disaster (hence the name 'corpse candle' given to lights seen hovering in churchyards and burial grounds). The Gaelic language has several names for the different kinds of spooklights: *solus bais* (death light), *solus taisg* (spectre light), and *teine biorach* (fire floating in the air like a bird).

The lights reported to haunt the hamlets of Fenny Compton and Burton Dassett, in South Warwickshire, are supposed to have been seen on and off since the middle of the nineteenth century. In 1923 and 1924 many local residents and visiting journalists testified to having seen this particular light, which one witness, Mr George White, described as 'a strong and dazzling light like a motor-car headlight ... a perfectly lovely sight, it floated about and passed through bushes and over fences at a great speed; then with a final flash it disappeared.' At least three visiting journalists actually caught a glimpse of this phenomenon, which one described in the *Birmingham Gazette* (23 February 1923) as 'well defined and spherical, it moved across our field of vision with its peculiar switchback motion from left to right, disappearing as quick as it had come ... like a dull yellow eye, it was glowering at us apparently from beneath a nearby tree.'

The Burton Dassett ghostlight appeared to centre its attentions around the pre-Norman All Saints Church, and the ancient beacon tower on the highest point of the hills nearby. Many theories were given at the time (and since) in order to explain these lights – some possible others downright silly — including hoaxers with torches or candles, ignited marsh-gas, stars seen on the horizon, overheated imaginations, car head-lights and even 'luminous owls'.

The longest surviving and most pervasive of all the theories to account for the lights seen over bogs and marshland is that they are caused by the ignited flames of marsh-gas or methane ($CH4$), evolved from rotting organic matter. It was suggested that some form of phospine ($PH3$) or a higher hydride could produce the natural ignition for the flame, even though recent research has proven that will o'the wisp-type luminosi-ties are not produced in swamps recreated under controlled conditions in the laboratory.

Furthermore, phosphorous is never found in its pure state in nature, and vapour-phase chromatogra-phy has failed to detect even parts per million traces of phosphorus in marsh gases analyzed in the laboratory.

At face value the marsh-gas theory appears to be the most convincing, but it does not stand up to scientific investigation. However, the natural generation of some kind of luminous bio-gas should not be ruled out as a possible explanation for some sightings.

Certainly, the unusual lights which are seen from time to time over Dartmoor, especially around Ashburton, appear to lend themselves to the above theory. Although will o'the wisps are now rarely if ever seen over Dartmoor (and if they are seen today they will be reported as UFOs), they were once a commonplace occurrence there.

At the outbreak of World War I military intelligence officers were chasing will o'the wisps (or being 'pixie-led' according to the folklore of Dartmoor) over the south-east edges of the moors in the belief that the lights were being used as signals by German spies.

At nine thirty pm on 4 September 1915, Lieutenant Colonel W P Drury, sent to track down the spies to their lair, saw 'a bright white light considerably larger than a planet, steadily ascend from a meadow to an approximate height of fifty or sixty feet', whilst observing Dartmoor from a spot near Dartington Point. 'Its course was clearly visible against the dark background of wood and hill', said Drury in his official report to the War Office '... we were within a mile of the light and saw its ascension and transit distinctly.'

The most recent explanation put forward to account for the comings and goings of these unexplained aerial lights is the earthlight theory proposed by the Canadian scientist Dr Michael Persinger and by British writer Paul Devereux. [For details of this theory see 'Earthlights' in this book – Ed]

A recently founded research venture, Project Pennine, has been set up to correlate and document the earthlights material and to compare it against other variables, especially geological faulting and earth-tremor epicentres. An example of the phenomena observed in the Pennines are the 'Longdendale lights', which appear on the remote and craggy heights of Shining Clough and Bramah Edge on Bleaklow, above the Torside Reservoir in the High Peak of North Derbyshire. They often appear as a string of moving, elusive and eventually fading luminosities which have been mistaken by rescue teams for the torches of ramblers lost on the mountainside.

Although sightings of strange aerial lights since the year 1947 have become distorted by the present cultural belief in visitors from outer space, the underlying objective phenomena remain the same. In 1967 American UFO investigator John A Keel realized that behind the illusory space craft there lurked 'the real phenomenon', what he termed the 'soft objects', ie 'sightings of transparent or translucent objects seemingly capable of altering their size and shape dramatically'. He added that 'most of these objects are temporary manipulations of matter and energy'.

Several 'trigger' events, which may help to initiate the production of these lights in areas of geological strain, have been identified by Persinger and

Devereux. The theory also proposes a connection between the witnesses' minds and the objective phenomenon. As these lights may be surrounded by strong electromagnetic fields it has been suggested that they are capable of stimulating the production of hallucinatory imagery within the electrical circuitry of the human brain.

In each individual case witnesses will superimpose, or manipulate what they see, to produce images of alien spaceships, religious symbolism, or denizens of fairyland, depending upon the predominant cultural perception of the unknown. An example of this is the 'Cammeringham light' of Lincolnshire, mentioned earlier, which has been 'seen' by some observers as a vision of the ghost of Queen Boadicea, riding out of the mists on a chariot drawn by two white horses!

Enough evidence has now been collected to enable us to prove the existence of these luminous phenomena. They have several notable characteristics, being predominantly ball shaped, with diameters varying from ten centimetres to five metres, though are more probably amorphous or gaseous in composition. Many reports describe them as passing through fences and hedgerows, and this may have given rise to many apparition reports, such as the 'White Lady of Castle Hill', which haunts an ancient mound near Newton-le-Willows in Lancashire. One witness who has reported seeing this particular 'white lady', angling journalist John Weedon, has described it as 'a white mass of apparently malevolent energy'.

Religious visions, such as those of the apparition of the Virgin Mary, should perhaps also be reassessed in the light of the above. Belgian Ufologist Marc Hallet, who has studied this phenomenon, makes the following remarks:

[Many] of the visions of the Virgin Mary are based on strange lights seen in strange conditions ... At Lourdes and Banneux the young girls saw a pale white light. It was cold and misty. They were questioned again and again, and finally they spoke of a young woman dressed in white. But at the beginning they spoke only of a white light which had a human form and disappeared as a light that is turned off. At Beauraing several children saw a white light which moved slowly along a railway ...

Sometimes these lights appear to resemble giant human eyes, or brilliant car headlights, and pulsate internally. Close observers often see two lights above each other, one a kind of reflection of the brighter light. Others are composed of numerous small lights, which may split up into smaller combinations and then rejoin the main areas. They always display inquisitive or elusive behaviour, and seemingly have an awareness of the observer's movements and thoughts – reacting especially to intense enthusiasm and emotional excitement (eg the Virgin Mary apparitions, and the phenomena accompanying the Welsh revival in 1905), in a way similar to poltergeist manifestations.

It is sometimes hard to avoid the suggestion that the lights are living beings possessed of some kind of rudimentary intelligence, or more likely it could be that they are simply reacting to changes in the environment which merely give the *impression* of intelligent control.

Although in recent years reports of these phenomena have become distorted by the modern obsession with visitors from outer space, underlying the thousands of case reports lurks evidence for an unknown natural phenomenon with inherent potential to revolutionize our current conception of time and space.

EARTHLIGHTS

Paul Devereux

The link between tectonic activity and anomalous lights in the sky has been slow to dawn in both scientific and ufological circles, though the appearance of mysterious lights in association with earthquake activity has been popular knowledge in certain parts of the world for generations. The first serious attention to the association seems to have been provided by Italian scientist I Galli who, in 1910, published a report on 148 observations of light phenomena during earthquakes in the United States. That reporter of the anomalous, Charles Fort, also made connections between unusual aerial lights and earthquakes in his books on phenomena, excluded from the scientific consensus of his day. Probably the first association between UFOs considered as such and geological factors was in a 1968 *Flying Saucer Review* article by F Lagarde,[1] who noted that a substantial percentage of low-level or landed alleged UFO events during the 1954 French UFO 'flap' occurred on or close to surface fault lines.

I kept Lagarde's findings in mind when, between 1972 and 1976, Andrew York and I conducted a multi-disciplinary study of the central English county of Leicestershire, in which we looked at the recorded strange phenomena over four centuries, the ancient sites, the traditional gatherings, the geology, the ghost accounts and traditions, and so on, of the area. One pattern that was particularly interesting was that the highest incidence of reported UFO activity occurred over the surface faulting in the county, regions where the greatest number of abnormal meteorological events had also been recorded down the centuries.

In 1977 *Space-Time Transients and Unusual Events*[2] by Canadians Michael Persinger and Gyslaine Lafreniere, was the first book, (though not the first research) to associate UFO phenomena with geology. The authors studied large data bases of reported UFO and other anomalous events, principally from North America, and found some statistical correlations between tectonic factors and the reported appearance of UFOs. They reasoned that the mechanism causing this must be related to the piezoelectrical effect (the production of an electric charge in certain crystals by means of mechanical pressure), occasioned by tectonic stress and strain on faulted rocks containing crystalline elements. They showed that the voltage from such a source could be very high in small areas at the Earth's surface causing ionization in the atmosphere, creating a glowing shape. They suggested that as pressure built up along a fault, a localized 'electric column' would be produced in the atmosphere above the area of stress. Within this column an ionization glow would appear. The column would move along a fault as the stress moved, thus making the light phenomenon seem to an observer to be moving freely through the air. The authors pointed out that relatively subtle stress might produce such an effect – a major earthquake, even a noticeable tremor, would not be necessary.

Helmut Tributsch' book *When the Snakes Awake* (1978) described his investigations into the uneasy behaviour sometimes noted in animals prior to earthquakes.[3] After exhausting other theories as to what mechanisms could cause such sensing in animals, he came to the conclusion that the Earth could produce static electricity prior to a quake and that the atmosphere could change its charge through the presence of aerosol particles suspended in it, creating all manner of light and other phenomena as well as affecting living creatures in a variety of ways.

In 1982 my book *Earth Lights*[4] attempted to put the concept of geologically related light phenomena on the ufological agenda, as all previous work — Lagarde, Persinger and my own — had been largely ignored. With the help of geologist Paul McCartney, I provided a comprehensive summary of most of the known material on the subject to that date, and offered new research and fresh ideas.

Lights in the landscape: Amongst the new research initiated by *Earth Lights* was the study of locations where high UFO incidence had been reported and where a reasonably detailed set of light phenomena reports coexisted with available *detailed* geological information — a balance of data not easily found. We initially studied the famous 'ufocal' of Warminster, in Wiltshire, England, which had produced an upsurge of UFO reports in the 1960s. Our investigations suggested that much of these were misperceptions of mundane aerial objects enhanced by a certain amount of media 'hype', but that a significant percentage might relate to an unknown aerial phenomenon often appearing as an amber light ball. Although Warminster is in chalk country, as a rule tectonically stable, the only two faults on the geological map run by Cley Hill, a key UFO 'window' during the period of high incidence of reported UFO activity, and one of the faults passes on through Warminster itself. This 'coincidence' was impressive.

We also studied the Barmouth-Harlech area of north-west Wales, because of an interesting set of reports dating from 1904-5 recounted by Kevin and Sue McClure in *Stars and Rumours of Stars*. The light phenomena were widely regarded at the time as religious portents, the concept of a UFO not being in existence at that period. Fieldwork, along with detailed geological information, indicated tight correlations between reported light events and faulting. In particular, it was found that Barmouth and Harlech are virtually linked by a major local geological feature, the Mochras fault. The reported lights were placed like pearls on a thread along this fault.

This area of north-west Wales has a history of both seismicity and unusual light phenomena dating back centuries, and I have recently been informed by the Edinburgh Seismic Unit that the Barmouth outbreak occurred in the midst of a period of seismic unrest in Wales as a whole; for over a decade the geology of Wales was under more or less continuous stress. The Barmouth lights are now considered by geologists working in Wales as resulting from seismicity.

In 1977 there was an outbreak of light phenomena in the St Brides Bay area of south-west Wales. This time the lights were conceptualized as UFOs, and the events provided the excuse for some media hype. As with the Barmouth incidents, people across the local social spectrum witnessed lights, and there were multiple witness sightings. Working from sightings where sufficiently accurate geographical information was provided, and over that part of the region for which detailed geological data was available, Paul McCartney was able to produce a histogram that clearly demonstrates that not only were the lights associated with surface faulting, but also that the incidence of reported light phenomena *increased with proximity to* faulting.

These examples provided the first *highly detailed* event-geology correlations to be published. Subsequent similar work has been carried out, most notably the study of the Yakima Indian reservation area in southern Washington State, by J S Derr of the US Geological Survey and Michael Persinger.[5]

McCartney and I have continued to study some

event locations. For example, we were alerted by
researcher Jonathan Mullard to the case of Linley, a
hamlet in Shropshire, western England, scene of odd
light events in 1913. Lightballs were seen clinging to
the tower of the Norman church there as well as
floating freely near Linley Hall and the handful of
local cottages. Strange spirals of both light and dark
'vapours' were seen moving around – columns of this
gaseous-like material are sometimes noted when there
are localized outbreaks of light phenomena, and they
may be responsible for the 'black monk' and 'white
lady' genre of supposed ghost. Two faults cradle
Linley and a drift boundary crosses between the
church and the hall. A UFO flap in North Wales in
1985 has been studied by McCartney, and found to
tightly correlate with local faulting.

In 1986 I was fortunate to obtain an eye-witness
report and photograph of a remarkable light seen near
the Pinnacles Park National Monument, California, in
1973. The witness was physicist Dr David Kubrin who,
with three other observers, saw a bright light streak
across the sky just above nearby tree tops. Kubrin
observed that the light created shock waves in the air
ahead of it, and these streamed down the sides of the
phenomenon. The light then stopped 'without
deceleration', and began to spin on its own axis. At this
point Kubrin managed to photograph it. The matter
comprising the light dissolved into invisibility as it
rotated. The location of the sighting was virtually on
the Pinnacles fault, itself only a few miles from the
great San Andreas fault, the source of so much seismic
and earthquake light activity.

An exciting research programme is just getting
under way in Britain under the co-ordination of David
Clarke, Andy Roberts and Martin Daglass. Project
Pennine aims to look at unexplained light phenomena,
both current and historical, over the wild Pennine
region of central north England, relating them to
faulting and other possible factors. I also hope to

instigate a similar study, Project Preseli, in south Wales.

During the first half of the 1980s there were many unexplained light phenomena at Hessdalen, a Norwegian valley near the Swedish border. Hundreds of photographs have been taken and there are many eye-witness reports. Lights of all sizes and colours have been seen, but a common form is that of an 'inverted pine tree' which can be seen hovering over mountain ridges, slowly rising and falling, growing brighter at times and fading to near transparency at others. A combined Norwegian/Swedish team of ufologists has spent three or four winters observing the lights, under the most difficult conditions. It is one of the very rare occasions where a team of researchers has been in the field to actually witness a light phenomenon outbreak. The detailed geology of the region is either not known or not available at present, but faulting certainly occurs within the vicinity of Hessdalen. Seismographic data suggest that increased light phenomena incidence spans periods of relatively greater crustal movement (not thought to have been caused by local tremors in this instance.)

Dan Mattson and Michael Persinger have studied Swedish UFO reports for the 1963-77 period, and found temporal relationships between reports and seismic activity.[6]

Other lights: It is clear that spooklights [For details of this phenomenon see 'Spooklights' in this book – Ed] and many reported UFO lights are probably the same basic phenomenon. But other natural lights are also known. The most closely related could be 'earthquake lights' (EQLs). These are usually aurora-like effects in the sky, but can also appear as balls of light, sparks and columns, associated with some (though not all) earthquakes.[7] Even small quakes can produce these lights on occasion, sometimes at quite a distance from the epicentre. The 1957 Charnwood quake, England, which I experienced and have investigated, was preceded by widespread sightings of high-flying lines of 'tadpole-shaped lights'. EQLs were not properly accepted by scientists until the Matushiro earthquake swarm of 1965-67 in Japan produced some excellent photographic evidence. No theory satisfactorily explains EQLs.

Mountains are quite often associated with unusual light effects – 'mountain peak discharge' (MPD). In 1937 John Blofield observed soft orange lights parading around the southernmost peak of the Chinese mountain Wu Tai, where a temple had been built in response to the phenomenon.[8] In 1982 I and three other people witnessed a light shoot out of a volcanic wall of rock on the legendary Welsh mountain of Cader Idris, which is situated on the major Bala fault. The light travelled at about 600 mph. Mount Shasta in the Cascade range in northern California is a sacred Indian mountain, and light phenomena have been reported around it. Researcher Andy Collins has investigated a Greek Orthodox monastry at the foot of Mount Athos, Greece:[9] columnar light emerging from the mountain, and other light displays, are invested with religious significance and are a major part of the community's belief system. Greece, of course, is perhaps the most seismically active country in Europe.

Finally, it is of interest to note that the 1950s contactee George Adamski's first 'UFO' experience is said to have been his observation of spheres of light leaping out from the top of Mount Palomar, California. From such experiences, belief systems can grow.

The third type of 'other light' is ball lightning. Again, it is now scientifically accepted that nature can produce stable lightforms in association with electrical storms. These lights sometimes disappear soundlessly, sometimes with explosive force. Theories attempting to explain ball lightning, like those dealing with EQLs, have so far failed to be completely successful.

Laboratory lights: In 1981, Dr Brian Brady of the US Bureau of Mines, Denver, demonstrated that rock under pressure can produce lights in its immediate vicinity. Extreme slow motion film of such rock crushing experiments by Brady showed small light-forms flitting around the rock crusher's chamber. These lights, on analysis, were frequently ovoid in shape, and could also change shape – characteristics shared with the landscape-scale UFOs. Brady noted that electromagnetic fields are created when rock is stressed and he felt these could act like 'magnetic bottles' to contain and give shape to the lights. In 1983 Paul McCartney, John Merron, myself and others carried out similar experiments in London. We witnessed diffuse curtains of light, orange spheres of light and, on one occasion, a delicate, tiny blue light of exquisite inner complexity moving in a geometric flight path around the granite core under pressure. The lights were certainly not 'sparks' (ie incandescent fragments of rock) – they were assumed at the time to be a form of plasma (ionized gas). However, McCartney, Dr G V Robins and I became steadily dissatisfied with the piezoelectrical theory and said so in a 1983 *New Scientist* article.[10] While piezoelectricity might be a component factor, it alone cannot explain the existence of the lights in forms that have been observed. We favoured some form of mechanism which allowed for the discharge of electrons from the matrix of the rock under pressure (exoelectron effect). We offered triboluminescence (friction-created light) as a possible mechanism. Although I doubt this is the answer, homespun experiments by McCartney and myself showed that even modest friction can produce a 'slow', soft light from rock, occuring under water as well as in the air, and enhanced in a negative ion-enriched atmosphere. Our doubts about the piezoelectrical theory were confirmed in 1984 when, after a talk to the Physical Society at the University of Sussex, I was shown slides by a researcher there of light effects produced from *non*-piezo rocks. This has subsequently been further confirmed by the work of Brian Brady and Glen Rowell, published in *Nature* in 1986.[11] They have shown that the lights can be produced in a variety of gases and under water. Spectrascopic analysis of these lights revealed nothing about the type of rock from which they were produced, but only about the medium in which they occurred. A major discovery by Brady and Rowell was that the lights could not be plasmas – they produced no microwaves. As Derr has stated: 'A new, challenging area of geophysics is just opening.'[12]

Brady and Rowell went on to make the startling suggestion that with these lights we could be looking at another possible candidate for the origins of life on Earth: here was an energy mechanism that could have activated the pre-Cambrian soups into producing amino acids just as well as lightning, and just as likely as organic spores reaching Earth on meteorites. Birth from Earth: certainly the most poetically satisfying image for biogenesis!

Lights and ancient sites: Stone circle sites in England and Wales correlate with surface faulting in a dramatic way, and are to be found in the very same landscapes in which light phenomena are reported. The world's greatest megalithic complex in the Carnac area of Brittany is also placed in a faulted and tectonically unstable area. This could be coincidence, but it could also be a reflection of prehistoric response to observed light phenomena which were invested with spiritual significance. Ancient shamanic activity might have related to such light phenomena – instances of this are already being investigated. Megalithic sites are usually remote and thus usually have scant perceptual cover, and what there is is rarely at night. Nevertheless, a list of sites where light phenomena have been reported is beginning to grow, and other sites have associated folklore referring to mystery lights and 'fairy lights'.

The research programme called the Dragon Project has been studying certain megalithic sites, seeking geophysical anomalies which have been indicated by folklore and anecdotal experiences. Some unusual results have been noted. Two of these, anomalous ultrasound and broadband radio signals, have also been suggested with regard to light phenomena by Derr and Persinger.[5] Geomagnetic anomalies have certainly been recorded by the Dragon Project and other researchers at megaliths, and unusual results with infrared and radiation monitoring have also been obtained. These large stones may mark geophysically unusual spots, or it could be that megaliths in the vicinity of faulting may act as conductors or foci for certain electromagnetic effects. Something akin to static electrical discharge from the stones has been widely reported.

Geo-psychic interactions: It became obvious early on in the earthlights research that we may be touching on other areas that at first glance seem unrelated. For example, it could hardly escape notice that the 1904-5 Barmouth area lights coincided with a local outbreak of Revivalism, centred on the figure of Mary Jones, who claimed visions and a religious mission. The 1977 St Brides Bay events included reports of major poltergeist activity at Ripperstone Farm, on the edge of the bay. (Although reports of these poltergeist events have probably been exaggerated, it would be unwise to dismiss them completely). The 1913 Linley events were accompanied by poltergeist manifestations: metal door latches moving by themselves, furniture and clothing being flung across rooms. I asked members of the Hessdalen team if examples of psychism had occurred there too. Although the area has a thin population, I was told that a few homesteads had reportedly experienced poltergeist and other psychic effects. I think it fair to pose the question: can the range of conditions that conspire to create strange luminous

aerial phenomena in particular regions at particular
times also affect brain functioning in certain susceptible individuals residing in those regions, resulting in
visionary and ESP episodes concurrent with the
appearance of light phenomena? Is there a common
denominator?

Certainly electromagnetic effects have been noted at
times of UFO appearance, eg electrical failure in cars.
(This has happened alongside stone circles, too).[14] We
know that electromagnetic disturbance, even of a low
order, can produce marked effects in the waking
consciousness of individuals. Recent research by
Michael Persinger and Robert Cameron[15] showed that
two unusually intense electromagnetic events lasting
for about ten seconds each were recorded during the
last stages of a possible poltergeist episode in Sudbury,
Ontario. Witnesses had reported an odd light,
shadowy forms and strange noises. In other
research,[16] Persinger has analyzed 109 ESP cases
studied at the end of last century by Gurney, Myers
and Podmore in relation to recorded geomagnetic
activity for the period. The seventy-eight cases that
contained no 'temporal inaccuracies' all occurred on
days when geomagnetic activity was significantly lower
than on the days preceding or following the
experience.

There are indications that the type of unusual
energy forming earthlight events may be sensitive to
consciousness; that the interaction between witness and
light might be truly two-way. In *Project Identification*,[17]
Dr Harley D Rutledge, investigating lights in a
mountainous area of southern Missouri in the 1970s,
notes that there were cases in which lights 'may have
reacted' to the thoughts or subtle actions of team
members, including himself. Hessdalen researchers
told me they too had experienced instances when the
lights seemed to respond to their thoughts or subtle
actions. Allied aircrew who experienced 'foo fighters' in
World War II (light forms seen near aircraft in flight)

also sometimes complained that the lights seemed to respond to their thoughts. There have been occasional similar feelings on the part of witnesses of apparent ball lightning events.

While it is easy to read apparent intelligence into random or automatic movement, it would be desirable to test the possibility of consciousness interaction. It might be testable, if the lights produced in laboratories are essentially of the same nature as earthlights. I have designed an experiment I am prepared to discuss with anyone who can provide rock-crushing and slow motion filming resources.

How place, time and geophysical conditions can create experiences in certain individuals similar to those of a visionary, out-of-the-body or near-death (NDE) nature has hardly been looked at by modern science and culture, though it seems to have been more important to earlier peoples, to judge by the concern some of them expressed through systems of *geomancy* — the optimal placing of human artefacts and activity within the landscape.[18,19,20] Even celebrated 'abductee' events may relate to such mechanisms. For example, Whitley Strieber, author of *Communion*,[21] has stated that his experience, far from being an encounter with extraterrestrials, may have been triggered by subtle geophysical rhythms of Earth itself. Two other contactees with whom I have spoken, Gaynor Sunderland and John Day, likewise are not convinced that their encounters were necessarily to do with extraterrestrial visitation. There may be a symbiosis between geophysical fields and consciousness as yet undreamt of by our science.

Nature of the lights: The lights seem to be at least partially electromagnetic, though it must be a form of electromagnetism very unfamiliar to us at present. We are entering a new field of geophysics: the implications are that we will have to encompass hitherto unknown aspects of known energies, and perhaps even have to identify intermeshed energies as yet unperceived by science. Certainly the apparent longevity of some of the lights begs questions, as also does the way a light can display the qualities of an object both with and without mass, as in the Kubrin case. We seem to be seeing an energy form on the very margin of physical existence. It is this aspect which, I believe, makes it sensitive to consciousness. Earthlights reveal a primordial energy base only tomorrow's civilization will be able to get the measure of.

IS THERE A UFO STATE OF MIND?

Mark Moravec

Is there such a thing as a 'UFO state of mind'? An 'altered state of consciousness' (ASC) is a mental state, induced physiologically, psychologically or pharmacologically, which represents a significant deviation from the individual's normal, waking consciousness. It may involve a greater preoccupation than usual with internal sensations or mental processes; changes in the formal characteristics of thought; and/or some impairment of reality testing.

Also common to most altered states are changes in time sense (eg timelessness), emotional expression (eg ecstasy), body image (eg oneness), perception (eg hallucinations), meaning or significance (eg illumination, sense of the ineffable), feelings of rejuvenation (rebirth), and hypersuggestibility (fantasies accepted as objectively true).

Hypnopompic and hypnagogic imagery: The intermediate state between wakefulness and sleep is referred to as 'hypnagogic'; the state preceding full wakefulness after sleep is termed 'hypnopompic'. Psychologists have found that during these states, many people experience sudden, involuntary sounds and images such as hearing one's name called and seeing 'faces in the dark'. Very often the images are

vivid and realistic, although their content may be
bizarre.

In their study of hypnagogic imagery, Vogel and his
colleagues found 'that loss of volitional control over
mentation [thinking] tended to occur first; then loss of
awareness of surroundings; and finally, loss of reality
testing (hallucination) occurred'. There are several
instances of bizarre, inappropriate or distorted images
(eg the image of tiny, hairy people sitting inside the
chest cavity) and magical, omnipotent thinking (one
subject reported that he was a giant waving his hand
over an entire town, and with each wave of his hand
the lights of the town became dimmer). Note the
resemblances between these examples and reports of
UFO entities and 'electromagnetic effects'.

A number of close encounter UFO reports could be
instances of imagery. This includes both UFO
experiences where the subject is in bed and is
'awakened' only to observe a vivid light or exotic entity;
and UFO experiences reported by solitary motorists
who are tired, lose concentration and enter a
hypnagogic state. The content of the imagery –
spaceships and entities – are a result of a cultural belief
in extraterrestrial life and its possible visitation of
Earth.

Amnesias: A number of altered states can be
considered as examples of the psychological defence
strategy of 'dissociation'. Dissociative amnesia is not a
mere forgetting, but an active process whereby
unpleasant features are blotted out of awareness
following a traumatic experience.

Fugues: A fugue state consists of:

'... transitory abnormal behaviour characterized by
aimless wandering and more or less alteration of
consciousness, usually, but not necessarily followed by
amnesia. A desire for escape from some intolerable
situation is usually the immediately precipitating factor

in the production of the fugue ... In fugues of short duration, the patient wanders aimlessly, is highly emotional and when found is agitated and confused. In long fugues, he travels far, appears self-possessed, and lives in every way like a normal person except that he is not where he should be.'

(Kolb)

A fugue differs from simple amnesia in that there is an actual physical flight from the individual's current environment. Also, the amnesia may extend to the individual blocking out memory of his own identity.

Possessions:

'A trance is usually defined as a temporary change in the person when he seems to be a very different person from his usual self, familiar before the episode and found again when the trance is ended ... In possession trance, as different from nonpossession trance, the person is believed to be invaded by a spirit or a new sense of power for good or ill.'

(Hilgard)

Thus possession is an ASC with a specific, superimposed, supernatural belief.

Multiple personalities: 'Multiple personality' is a 'condition in which the integrated personality fragments into two or more personalities each of which manifests a relatively complete integration of its own and which is relatively independent of the other personalities.' (Chaplin)

One view of the origin of multiple personality is that where there is an active incompatibility between repressed elements and the rest of the personality, the former may separate from the usual consciousness and organize a personality of its own. This new secondary personality has its own consciousness which often has no recollection of the usual primary personality and carries out acts independent of it. The disposition and character of the secondary personality usually differs from that of the primary personality since it is made up of thoughts and feelings rejected by the primary personality.

The main difference between possession and multiple personality is that the latter consists of fully developed personalities with their own individual identities.

Whilst the multiple personality has commonly been considered a rare occurrence in the psychiatric context, a case can be made for its existence in the non-psychopathological, transient context of the UFO and the psychic mediums.

Automatic writing: Like fugues and multiple personalities, automatic writing is an example of an automatism or dissociation of personality 'in which unconscious factors temporarily gain control, act independently and dictate behaviour.' (Kolb) Amnesia may or may not be associated with the experience.

Automatic writing has been with us for a long time. Many messages have been attributed to spirits of the dead. As UFO experiences have become more common, a proportion of messages have been attributed to UFO entities.

Autohypnosis: In contrast with artificially induced hypnotic states, autohypnosis is a hypnosis which is self-induced. Features suggestive of a hypnotic state include: the entrancement by the fascinating colours of the phenomenon; the effect of relaxation and elimination of tension; the feeling of happiness; the complete distraction from everyday worries.

Hypnosis: The classic 'interrupted journey' of Betty and Barney Hill paved the way for a new type of UFO report – the 'abduction' experience – and the use of hypnosis in UFO investigations. Hypnosis has been used to both relax the subject after a traumatic experience and as a technique for retrieving information from subjects who have experienced a period of amnesia.

Hypnosis, as traditionally conceptualized, is an artificially induced ASC brought about through certain 'induction' techniques. The basic characteristics include passivity, redistribution of attention, increased fantasy and role behaviour, reduction in reality testing with increased tolerance for reality distortion, and hypersuggestibility. (Hilgard)

The exact nature of hypnosis remains a matter of debate. Some researchers suggest that it is a specific altered state whilst others suggest it is a conscious roleplay featuring a heightened suggestibility. Similarly, there has been extensive debate as to the reliability of information gained during hypnotic age regression; research suggests that the hypnotic subject creates a hallucinated environment appropriate to the suggestion, combined random memories from both past and present, and contributes a certain amount of confabulation.

Could hypnosis actually *promote* abduction fantasies, given the right social context and the now readily available abduction lore? Lawson compared the narratives of 'real' UFO abductees and 'imaginary' abductees who were hypnotized and directed to imagine that they had such an experience. The narratives of both groups revealed many parallels, including many presumed obscure patterns from the UFO literature. He suggested several sources for the data: the imagination; general UFO information within the culture at large; extrasensory perception of UFO information from ufologists present or from other sources; and the incorporation of memories, such as past real-life surgery incorporated in a fantasized medical examination by UFO entities.

One suggested explanation for the Betty and Barney Hill abduction case is that Barney became entranced by staring at the star-like object he initially observed, and consistent with the increased fantasy and reduced reality-testing typical of hypnotic states, then fantasized an entity contact experience. Following the UFO sighting, Betty Hill had nightmares of being abducted by UFO entities. The Hills were regressed independently but not before Betty had communicated details of her abduction dreams to Barney. These dreams contained details similar to what the couple were later to relate when hypnotized, and could therefore be the ultimate source of the abduction story.

A number of UFO experiences appear to have involved subjective perceptions during altered states of consciousness. There is scope for much future research into the methods of induction and the personality and situational characteristics necessary to produce an ASC-mediated UFO experience. One important point requiring clarification is whether the ASC is responsible for the entire reported experience or whether a physical phenomenon is also involved. A number of cases exist where alleged physical damage has been done to the vehicles involved in the UFO incidents. So a purely psychological hypothesis may be insufficient to cover all the aspects of some UFO reports.

A critical question is whether close encounter UFO percipients are more likely to be prone to experience dissociated states of consciousness. The Bloecher et al study of UFO abductees found no evidence of psychopathology or personalities prone to fugue states or multiple personality shifts. Yet it also found that, under stressful conditions, six of the nine subjects showed a potential for transient psychotic experiences involving a loss of reality testing along with confused and disordered thinking that can be bizarre, peculiar or very primitive and emotionally charged.

Other anomalous experiences may also occur during ASCs. The image of an intense white light, a feeling of paralysis, movement through a tunnel, an encounter with strange, non-human entities, have all been reported in UFO abductions, but also in lucid dreams, out-of-body experiences, near-death experiences, drug-induced hallucinations and mystical experiences. The difference consists not so much in the *content* of the experience as in the *interpretation*, and this varies according to the situational context in which the experience occurs and the socially-conditioned beliefs held by the percipient.

Three hypotheses might account for these constant images: social conditioning (where people incorporate generally circulated knowledge of 'mysterious phenomena' into their hallucinated experiences); archetypes (Jung's notion of unconscious images originating from a hypothesized 'collective unconscious' common to all mankind); and neurophysiology (Siegel's conception that because of the common neurophysiological makeup of human beings, there is a finite number of images which the brain consistently hallucinates).

How do people react when they observe an unidentified flying object?: Two studies have been carried out by the author to answer this question. The first study examined a sample of fifty-six unidentified, close encounter cases from the files of UFO Research (New South Wales). Forty-six cases specified a psychological reaction. The second study used data from the Australian UFO Computer File. Out of 1006 coded unidentified cases of all types, ninety (nine per cent) specified a psychological reaction.

Both studies indicate that fear is the most common reaction, and then curiosity. In a number of cases in Study 1, both fear and curiosity were experienced simultaneously, indicating an approach-avoidance conflict where the witness wants to find out more about what he or she is observing but is afraid of the unknown consequences.

Negative feelings predominate, but this is mainly determined by the large proportion of cases where fear is experienced. Reactions *subsequent* to a sighting tend to be continuations of reactions *during* the sighting. Even subsequent dreams or nightmares could well be a continuation of the initial fear reaction.

In a number of cases, physiological reactions also accompanied or followed the UFO experience, for example, impaired eyesight and insomnia. It is possible that many of the physiological effects described in the UFO literature are psychosomatic in origin, rather than direct physical effects of the UFO.

Are psychological reactions to *unidentified* flying objects different from reactions to *identified* flying objects? There are case examples which show that it is possible for people to become quite alarmed and upset while watching the apparent motions of the planet Venus distorted by the atmosphere. After a study of 1307 cases, Hendry concluded that: 'The fear elicited by the UFO and IFO sightings is not in direct response to what is being experienced, but rather to what is being anticipated in advance.' People have been socially conditioned to believe in, and fear, 'extraterrestrial spaceships'. Thus, a percipient's dramatic emotional reaction may not necessarily indicate the presence of an 'authentic' UFO, but rather that the percipient believes the event is a genuine unknown.

Hynek has referred to the 'escalation of hypotheses' where a UFO witness may attempt to explain the phenomenon he is observing by a series of increasingly more complex and exotic explanations. For example, a person may observe the approach of an airborne light and interpret it, in turn, as an airplane, helicopter, a man with a torch and, finally, a UFO. In Hynek's view, this reaction adds credibility to the person reporting the UFO and shows that he or she is not automatically jumping to exotic interpretations until forced to by the strangeness of the experience. However, it is possible that sometimes the witness may come to an ultimately erroneous conclusion that he or she is observing a UFO.

A dramatic emotional reaction does not necessarily

make a UFO report more believable; however, the fact that fear is generated in many UFO experiences is, in itself, a powerful reason for continued study.

PHYSICAL TRIGGERS / PSYCHIC RESPONSES

Nigel Watson

Films like *Close Encounters of the Third Kind* give the impression that UFOs are monstrous cathedral-like space ships piloted by effeminate bendy-toys. On a more scientific level UFO research has generated two potentially rewarding approaches: the birth trauma hypothesis and the piezoelectric hypothesis. Proponents of both these hypotheses claim that they can be tested scientifically, and that they go far towards explaining the underlying cause of the UFO phenomenon.

In the early years of UFO research the extraterrestrial hypothesis (ETH) was the most popular since it was easy to believe that advanced civilizations had developed space vehicles that had originated from the same kind of space technology our own super powers were building. Indeed, it can be no coincidence that when the first moon landings were occuring the book *Chariots of the Gods?* by Erich von Däniken, which speculated that we were nothing more than slaves or descendants of a space-travelling race of superior beings, became a bestseller. Even today some UFO investigators and researchers believe that the small percentage of UFO sightings that remain unexplained are of space ships. Less popular theories have embraced the idea that UFOs come from the centre of the Earth through holes in the north and south poles, or that they are time or dimensional travellers. Keel and others have suggested that the intelligence controlling the UFOs is able to manipulate both our minds and our physical environment, leading to the paranoid conclusion that neither yourself nor your world are real but just figments of a UFO operator's whim.

Then in 1977 Dr Alvin Lawson and William McCall took an interest in what are known as abduction cases, which generally occur after a person has reported seeing a strange light or object in the sky – often whilst driving late at night – and discovered that the witnesses could not account for the few minutes or hours that immediately followed the sighting.

Under hypnotic regression they told of abduction by foetus-like entities who, typically, medically examine them in a big brightly lit room.

A case of this type involved Mrs Betty Andreasson, who, in 1967, saw strange lights outside her Massachusetts home. Under hypnosis she said that four beings escorted her to a flying saucer parked in her garden. Inside the saucer Betty was subjected to a frightening examination, during which a long silver needle was pushed into her left nostril and another into her naval. She was seated in a chair, a cover was placed over her body, and tubes were applied to her mouth and nostrils. Then a liquid was pumped into her 'immersion' chair which completely shrouded her body. This womb-like experience was further enhanced when Betty explained how afterwards she and two aliens travelled down a long dark tunnel. Emerging in a weird, alien environment she had what can only be described as a religious experience before she was returned home.

In 1980 Police Constable Alan Godfrey saw something unusual in the road while on duty in Todmorden, Yorkshire. A dome-shaped spinning object, which contained a row of dark windows and projected a beam of fluorescent light, spanned the road, hovering only a few metres from the ground. When he recovered from seeing this vision he found that he could not remember what had happened to him for ten or fifteen minutes.

Under hypnotic regression Godfrey told the investigators what had happened during this period of memory loss. Apparently he was suddenly inside the UFO. Here he saw eight figures in one room who looked like eight-year-old children. As they gathered around him he got the impression that they were robots. On looking down he saw a dog the size of a German Shepherd, and nearby he saw a human-sized figure who wore a skull cap.

The occupants of the UFO spoke to him inside his head, and told him to get up on the table that dominated the centre of the room. His reply to them was 'not bloody likely' but seconds later his scruples were eradicated and he acquiesced. On the table he watched them conduct some form of examination of his body. Other than the fact that he felt a pain in his head when he was asked to describe the machinery in the room, not much else happened inside the UFO.

Some of the hypnotic regression sessions were videotaped. On watching these it is surprising to see how hesitant Godfrey was in answering the investigator's questions. I got the distinct impression that the framing of the questions and their repetition helped sort the witnesses' vague and disordered thoughts into a coherent structure that would satisfy the investigator's own expectations. Godfrey himself seemed genuinely puzzled by the whole affair.

To try to understand this type of story Lawson and McCall hypnotically regressed a group of people who had no intimate knowledge of the UFO subject. The idea was to compare their 'imaginary abduction' stories with those of 'real abductions'. Much to their surprise they found that there was no difference between the two and that there were similarities between the UFO experience and the birth experience. Thus, they postulated that since birth is an experience common to everybody this must be the factor that influences abduction stories. Their theory received additional support when they found that people who have had normal births tend to recall UFO encounters that involve tubes and tunnels (symbols of the birth canal) whilst those given birth by Caesarian section do not seem to remember such details.

A quite different though not necessarily incompatible hypothesis was proposed by Dr Michael Persinger when he claimed that relatively minute seismic activity in the Earth's crust could discharge piezoelectrical energy that would be seen as blobs of light. Paul Devereux, in his book *Earthlights*, supports this, noting that much of the UFO activity in Great Britain can be linked to geophysically unstable regions. To account for more complicated UFO sightings and the abduction cases, Persinger speculates that this piezoelectrical energy can disturb the human brain in such a manner as to cause the person affected to hallucinate them.

Interestingly both theories represent the diametrically opposed extremes of psychology. At one end there is the psychoanalytic approach (which is basically influenced by Freudian concepts). The BTH emerges from this psychological tradition and as a consequence puts a great deal of stress on early experience and its influence on the unconscious. The piezoelectrical hypothesis can be seen as a product of behaviourism, which tends to concentrate on how a given stimulus here-and-now produces a particular response. Slotted between these is the cognitive approach to the study of human behaviour which is dominated by the concepts introduced by Piaget. This approach postulates that our knowledge of the world is constructed by the bi-directional interaction between man and his environment.

Before this degenerates into a survey of contemporary psychology it is worth reflecting on the attitudes underlying the two ufological hypotheses. With regard to the BTH the question is; 'Why consider birth to be traumatic?' It reflects the attitude that life is inherently stressed and painful, a struggle to juggle with internal, external and social forces, whilst the womb or death are the only safe havens. On the other hand the piezoelectrical hypothesis ignores such worries, and regards humans as biological machines – press button A and B will happen!

These developments take Ufologists a long way from simply determining whether someone has seen a space ship or not.

However if we retreat from the fringes of these two hypotheses we can examine the more conventional sociological and psychological factors which might work to produce or influence the generation and reportage of UFO sightings. And there are other psychological theories which can be used to explain individual cases (Jungian psychoanalysis has been a favourite due to his personal interest in the subject).

From what I have written it may appear that the ufologist has stumbled into a hall of mirrors where he is lost in a maze of complexities. However, my view is that we should become aware of the factors which influence our theories and hypotheses which can have a chicken-and-egg relationship with our data collection.

I see it as a healthy sign that ufologists are willing to agree and test the validity of different hypotheses and theories. However, we all require a flexibility of perspective that will take into account the sheer variety and number of UFO reports. As yet no one has discovered the ufological Holy Grail.

PART V
SOCIETY AND UFOs

SOCIETY AND UFOs – INTRODUCTION

UFOs have undoubtedly become a part of our society. There are millions of people who have been directly affected by their existence; from having seen and reported them to merely having read about them.

Also, it would be fair to say that few people in our technological world have been untouched by the mythology of UFOs, principally through film and television stories of alien invasions. Most interestingly, not only have these films been influenced by the UFO myth, but it can clearly be demonstrated that they have influenced the UFO myth *themselves*.

A potentially interesting example of the degree of penetration of the UFO phenomenon into the public's awareness was the transmission of a season's final episode of the soap opera *The Colbys*. Transmitted on 2 September 1987 in the UK, and earlier in the USA, it featured the abduction by UFO of its star. This represents the exposure of an audience – the peak-time, entertainment-slot, viewer – to a subject it wasn't previously regarded receptive to. What effect this will have on public awareness of the subject is not yet clear, but if there are follow-up episodes the reaction of the public may be an interesting sociological study.

The public's perception of extraterrestrial life – that

is whether it would be hostile or friendly – itself varies widely, based on how the subject has been presented and what existing belief structures are. On the one hand we have the astonishing acceptance of Orson Wells' *War of the Worlds* broadcast in the 1930s over American radio and on the other hand the following story:

An army unit doing parachute-training at night made a group drop. In order to see where they were in the air in relation to each other they were fitted with lights on their shoulders and heads. One of the team landed off course, some way from the others, and made his way to a remote farmhouse. On arriving he knocked at the door, which was opened by what can only be described as a 'sweet little old lady'.

'Can you tell me where I am?' asked the visitor.

'Yes my dear,' was the unflustered reply, 'you're on Earth.'

Society's eyes and ears are the media. The perceptions individual people have of almost every subject, including UFOs, is presented to them through television, radio, newspapers, etc. Such presentations have been firmly, if hysterically, biased towards the extraterrestrial hypothesis in the past, and this is an image we still are a long way from correcting. The impression given to the public is that UFOs are believed to be alien spacecraft (but just maybe some of them are not!), and the ufologists who do not lean toward such a belief are, far from being rational, regarded as being sceptical. This leads to a polarization of views that all UFO researchers are either 'ET buffs' or 'disbelievers'. As this book demonstrates, that is not the case: there are many theories to be considered, and exploration of all them is research and not scepticism.

Society has been affected by the existence of UFOs in other ways. Belief systems have grown up not only around the extraterrestrial hypothesis but around the machinations of alien gods in whatever form. In some cases this has led to a direct worship of alien entities, in most cases the creation of cult groups based around a contactee who takes the form of a prophet. These cults and contactees are a legitimate area of study for the ufologist, as they represent an undeniable aspect of the subject, but the people involved in these cults are *not* part of serious UFO research, and the perception that they are must be corrected in the public view and in the view of the scientific community.

For the future, the effects on society are far reaching. If it does become apparent that alien intelligence is no part of the reality behind the myth, then the lessons learnt from our study of ourselves will still have been of much importance. If alien intelligence is at work, and we one day are able to meet with it on an equal level, our society will of course change totally. Our perspective on the universe will change, our religious beliefs may be subjected to severe strain. But if alien intelligence is at work and does not wish to, or cannot, see us as equals, then we will resist being what Charles Fort described as 'someone's property'. And we must be ready for that potential conflict because, as human history tells us, only one culture will survive.

WHAT 'ET' WOULD MEAN FOR MANKIND

James M McCampbell

Because the UFO phenomenon is global in nature and transcends all boundaries of nations, religions, cultures, languages, and educational levels, the questions of how UFOs have influenced the global community, how they are presently interacting with it, and the long-term consequences, are, indeed, a grand challenge.

Individual and public responses: Most UFO witnesses are convinced they saw something unusual and were compelled to tell someone about it. But only ten per cent report the sighting to an official agency or a UFO study group. The person's emotional reaction at the time of the sighting may vary greatly. This scale of reaction is usually related to the proximity of the UFO and particular details such as the presence and behaviour of alien creatures. These emotional responses are usually transitory with little lasting psychological effect although the original emotion may be triggered later by telling the story. Lasting psychological damage may result if the UFO experience is so far removed from the witness's perception of the world that he has no mental compartment where it will fit.

In contrast to people who have simply seen a UFO, those who have been abducted by the aliens frequently experience long-term effects. Long afterward, the abductee may have grave difficulty in adjusting to the facts by experiencing periodic setbacks. Some may require extended theory to learn how to accept their recollection whereas others never do.

Despite these debilitating experiences, a few abductees experience a new psychological growth that elevates them well beyond their previous life. For these rare individuals, the abduction must be judged beneficial.

The Gallup poll has been monitoring public opinion on UFOs for many years. In February 1987, they found that eighty-eight per cent of the population of the US had heard or read about UFOs. Among those aware of the subject, nine per cent affirmed that they had seen something they thought was a UFO. Taking the US population as 241,000,000 and discounting the unaware group, one calculates that an astounding 19,000,000 Americans believe they have seen a UFO! Nearly half of the aware group believe that UFOs are real with men slightly outnumbering women. Belief in the reality of UFOs is significantly higher among college graduates than among highschool graduates and dropouts. Half of the respondents believe that people somewhat like humans live on other planets in the Universe.

Study groups and scientists: A notable social response to UFO sightings has been the formation of numerous, volunteer organizations to investigate important cases, assemble case histories, study the phenomenon as a whole, and distribute information to the public through meetings and publications.

The American Association For The Advancement of Science held a symposium on UFOs in Boston in 1969. The agenda was a balanced presentation of pro-and-con positions. Dr James E McDonald described well-documented cases and faulted the scientific community for inadequately studying the data. Dr

Donald H Menzel, on the other hand, continued his long-term evaluation that UFOs are nothing but a myth. Dr Carl Sagan, who maintained that the extraterrestrial hypothesis is an unlikely explanation, reflected the prevailing attitude of the scientific community.

Another leading scientific society, the American Institute of Aeronautics and Astronautics, established a subcommittee on UFOs. The latter's interest was represented by many technical papers presented at the 13th Aerospace Sciences Meeting in Pasadena, California in January 1975 and subsequent conferences.

With these exceptions, efforts at investigating UFOs by the professional, organized scientists have been pathetic, an attitude that reflects not so much a lack of curiosity as the stigma that has been attached to UFOs by the media and government propaganda.

Government affairs: Nothing has been more confusing than the attitude of government towards UFOs. A keen interest was displayed in the US before 1969 by Project Blue Book and the famous study headed by Dr Edward U Condon. The generally negative tone of the Condon Report allowed the Air Force to disengage from the subject at least as far as the public knew. A review by the National Academy of Sciences endorsed and echoed the conclusions, namely:

a) the subject is not classified,

b) UFO's present no threat to national security,

c) future sightings should be handled in normal surveillance operations,

d) no new agency is needed for that purpose,

e) study of UFOs offers little promise of expanding scientific knowledge,

f) some cases are not easily explained, and

g) specific research proposals of merit should be supported.

The existence of UFOs, it will be noted, was officially accepted although it is commonly believed that their existence was denied.

Requests and lawsuits under the Freedom of Information Act have forced the government to release many thousands of pages of documents that were previously Secret or Top Secret. They confirmed the above assertions and further showed that UFOs have been visiting military installations, nuclear power stations, landing in storage areas for nuclear weapons and a launch site for an Intercontinental Ballistic Missile, whose on-board, targeting computer was deprogrammed. Yet American citizens are expected to believe that UFOs are not a threat to national security nor is the subject classified!

Deception of mankind by the aliens?: Starting in the late 70s, Budd Hopkins located more than one hundred abductee cases of which six were discussed in his book *Missing Time*. After the recent publication of his *Intruders*, he has been contacted by another hundred or so people who think that they may also have been abducted. Similarly, before completing a promotional tour for his book *Communion*, Whitley Strieber has been contacted by more than a hundred people. Last summer, Dr Leo Sprinkle at the University of Wyoming held the eighth annual conference of abductees. Who can guess how many other people have been abducted that recall nothing about it? Or, considering the intense stigma attached to contact with aliens in the early days, balked at telling anyone? Because the UFO phenomenon is homogeneous throughout the world, the total number of abductions on a global basis must be truly shocking.

Cults: One consequence of UFO sightings is the formation of small groups clustered around a charismatic person. The leader frequently claims, perhaps rightly so, that he or she has observed the landing of a UFO at close range, saw a handsome or beautiful person emerge, then engaged in direct communication by voice or telepathy. Typically, the key figure is informed that he has been selected to guide humanity to the ultimate truth and becomes the guru among some dedicated and trusting disciples. The so-called space brothers are interested only in the welfare of mankind and uniformly emphasize the hazards of nuclear weapons. Repeat meetings with the aliens are often claimed but more commonly the communication is reported to take the form of spontaneous ideas and thoughts in the leader's head; he, alone, is the channel through which divine wisdom is transmitted to the less fortunate.

Closer resemblance to a religious organization takes shape when the leaders adopt a unique and colourful dress. Flowing robes or gowns are frequently embellished with massive jewellery, turbans, or other flamboyant headgear. On the other hand, leaders dressed like working-class people on Saturday afternoon still persuade their followers to give them all their earthly possessions. The character of a religion comes into clear focus when the leader receives a message from above that on a particular mountain at midnight one or more UFOs will appear to take the faithful out of this grievous world into paradise. More than once such groups have assembled at the designated place full of hope, faith, and expectation. All they have received thus far has been chills and disappointment.

Lessons from history: In his survey of history Professor Toynbee shows that in encounters between civilizations, the more advanced is uniformly the aggressor, the less developed is invariably destroyed. Would this apply to the encounter between the existing civilizations on Earth and one or more from space? It might if extraterrestrials could sustain an immigration in large numbers. However, it must be emphasized that they have displayed no hostility toward mankind despite their intolerable abductions. Neither has there been any indication that they wish to colonize Earth. On the other hand, it would be foolhardy to ignore the possibilities and fail to make contingency plans.

Cosmic perspective: The concept of space travel has taken root in the US. Prior to 1950 there were on average only seven such science fiction movies per decade. During the 1950s there were eighty-six such films, and during the 1960s the number remained very high at seventy-three. Public interest is illustrated by the popularity of *Star Trek*, *Close Encounters of The Third Kind*, and *ET*.

Nuclear physicist Stanton T Friedman has devoted many years to the lecture circuit, telling audiences in over 500 colleges and universities that some UFOs are extraterrestrial space ships. He believes that UFOs are elevating the perspective of humanity to a cosmic focus in recognizing the existence of other intelligent and sentient beings who may be very far advanced by human standards. That realization should cause people everywhere to consider themselves as Earthlings travelling with brothers on the only space ship we have. The cosmic perspective has much potential for influencing humanity to resolve differences peacefully rather than by warfare.

The long-term objectives of the aliens are not known and cannot be deciphered from the available data. They apparently have not sought to establish a close association with any person or group. Some evidence, however, suggests that they may have contacted government scientists and Air Force officers.

Even if UFOs went away today, they have already made an indelible impact upon society. As we have seen, a) numerous study groups have been formed worldwide; b) technical societies have addressed the subject; c) people carry life-long memories of UFO experiences; d) the US government set up a UFO investigating network, sponsored a sham study, then retreated behind a wall of secrecy; e) the United Nations expressed an interest; f) science fiction shifted its emphasis; and g) films captured the public imagination. The seeds have been planted in these areas, and undoubtedly others, and they will continue to grow. The net effect thus far has been a change in attitudes toward space and extraterrestrial life. The realization that creatures similar to humans are visiting the Earth make our world seem much smaller and emphasizes the unity of mankind. It can contribute mightily to the solution of social and political problems. In the long run, one can foresee an infusion of new science, technology, medicine, transportation and energy sources. Even an external threat to mankind would force co-operation between hostile nations. Ultimately, mankind will find the party line to communication with other civilizations in space.

No one can predict what may happen but it appears that the UFO phenomenon foreshadows many changes for humanity. They may be good or bad as viewed differently by each person. But either way, they are likely to be revolutionary. The sojourn of extraterrestrials upon Earth has to be the most important fact for modern man.

UFOs THROUGH INNOCENT EYES

Cynthia Hind

UFO observations in Africa, taking into account the numerous interpretations over tribal law and superstition, and including white and black reactions to limited belief systems, provide researchers with a unique opportunity to compare experiences in highly technological cultures with those in less developed regions.

My interest leans more to physical trace cases and CE 3s (in particular where several witnesses are involved) and, in the light of recent developments in the United States, the possibility of abduction cases in Africa.

Over the years there have been a number of cases of contactees and physical traces, or one or the other, which illustrate the 'strangeness factor', which invites comparison with other cases in many different parts of the world, establishing, although in a limited way, a UFO pattern.

The Groendal Reserve, bordering on Uitenhage and Despatch in the Cape Province of South Africa, certainly fulfilled the UFO strangeness factor of my research.

Four young boys, Peter Simpson (16), Jannie Bezuidenhout (15), Hugo Ferreira (12) and Joe Perino (13) were out hiking in the Reserve on the weekend of Sunday 1 October 1978. The next day, Monday, was a public holiday and Mrs Simpson, wife of a Despatch doctor, was to pick the boys up at a prearranged rendezvous at mid-day.

The day was overcast and the boys sat quietly waiting for Mrs Simpson. The Reserve is an isolated area of veld containing many of the smaller species of wild African animals, such as rock-rabbits, baboons and leopard.

The time was eleven fifteen when all four boys saw a glistening stone in the distance, about 900 metres away. Almost at the same time, Jannie drew their attention to two men who were to the west of the stone. The boys thought they were poachers but were surprised to see that the men wore silver 'firefighters' suits.

'Their silver suits looked just like aluminium foil' Hugo said later.

The men appeared to come from the direction of the glistening object. They moved across the terrain in a 'gliding' motion, as though they were on trolleys. In the middle of the hill they were joined by a third man carrying a small, square suitcase. The boys could not see the men's arms, although one seemed to be holding the suitcase.

When the men reached a dividing fence and either climbed or glided over, one of them stopped to let the others through and he looked at the boys. They could see that the silver suit covered his forehead, leaving only his face clear. The skin was grey. The men continued on their way, moving up the hill to the summit and then suddenly disappeared.

All the boys noted that during the incident, which apparently took place over sixty seconds, they felt 'peculiar'. Peter Simpson felt disoriented and there was an unusual quietness in the Reserve as though all the birds and animals were silenced.

On checking with Mr Zeelie, the Game Park Warden, he verified that there were no firefighters in the Reserve at the time.

I worked on this case with Sergeant Christopher Powell of the South African Police, who later became very helpful and a useful member of MUFON.

Powell, together with journalist Keith Ross and photographer Evert Smith, a police major, and two trackers, made the journey to where the boys had seen the glistening stone. They were surprised to find that the bush in the area, called *fynbos*, was about two metres high. In the area indicated they found a large oval depression, 7 × 20 metres, with eight or nine indentations on the outside perimeter. There were no marks of burning.

With the assistance of Professor Rust of the Geology Department at the University of Port Elizabeth, two geology lecturers, Russell Shone and Dave Glenister went back with Powell to the depression twenty-nine days after the original sighting. There had been some heavy rain. Shone's comments to me read as follows:

> 'Unfortunately the impressions were not at all clear when we visited the site. However, they were symmetrically distributed and this alone makes them interesting. From the site, I would guess that the object … must have been about six metres high … However, if a hoax is involved, then there can be no doubt that the hoaxer is imbued with … ingenuity and a large resource of energy.'

Shone's official report mentions nine marks, *symmetrically* arranged. Four of the impressions were sub-oval in shape, with four small holes within the impression which could have been made with a tubular prong. There was some evidence of soil compaction. There were no burn marks or radioactivity. The site was in such dense bush that it would be almost impossible to imagine any equipment being taken into the area.

Strangeness factor:

a) The feeling of unreality felt by all four boys during the sixty-second event.

b) The gliding (as opposed to walking) of the men, obviously moving above the bush at a height of two metres or more.

c) As the men moved up the hill, which is fairly steep, they did not bend forward as a normal person would, but remained upright.

The interpretations in these two particular cases are those of average English or Afrikaans-speaking white South Africans; fairly sophisticated and certainly aware of the UFO syndrome, although rarely familiar with its intricate and unpredictable pattern.

It becomes apparent in my investigations that, in the case of the coloured or black people, the interpretation is often one of extreme fear and superstition. Four cases will illustrate this.

Case One: On 26 June 1972 Bennie Smit, owner of the farm Braeside just outside Port Beaufort, South Africa, was alerted by his coloured labourer, Boer de Klerk. He had had a 'terrible fright' while at the farm reservoir when he saw smoke near a *krans* which had erupted into a big ball of fire.

He quickly came to report the *lelike ding* (ugly thing). Later he was joined by other labourers and with the reinforcement of manpower giving them fresh courage, they tried to round up the 'thing' which, apparently, responded to their voices.

Case Two: On 31 July 1975, Danie van Graan of Loxton in South Africa's Cape Province, arose early to inspect his sheep *kraal* (pens). On the way there he saw a caravan parked in the enclosure and assumed it to be from the Government Geological Survey, who were prospecting for uranium. As he approached he realized it was *not* a caravan and that the beings inside were certainly not geologists!

Suddenly, they looked up at him and hit him with a blinding beam of light. Then the 'caravan' rapidly took off, leaving behind several indentations and a circular burned patch where, for some years subsequently, nothing grew. The object was also seen by a young coloured boy who ran to fetch his mother, Meitjie Devenish. When she arrived to see what it was, the object took off rapidly, making no sound.

Van Graan went to the boy's mother and it was obvious she was too frightened to talk to him. He tried to reassure her but it did not help. Both mother and son were terrified of the police and she felt that if she was involved with anything unusual, they might pay her a visit.

I wanted to speak to Meitjie and her son but van Graan told me they had moved to the Cape Town area.

'The boy was about eight or nine at the time' van Graan said 'and his mother and a young man of twenty with her, all saw the object on the ground. While the people were familiar with planes and helicopters, this was something they did not recognize and they were terrified of what they had seen.'

Case Three: On 15 August 1981, twenty labourers returning from work in the fields at six o'clock, saw a fireball rolling across the grounds of La Rochelle, a Forestry Commission station some nine kilometres from Mutare in eastern Zimbabwe. In charge of the group was Clifford Muchena and he was as stunned as the others; they watched the one and a half metre diameter fireball move from one side of the lawns to the other, and then roll up the sloping lawn to an observation tower attached to the main house. 'It walked up the wall of the tower' said Clifford 'and entered the top window – then it burst into flame.'

Clifford rushed to ring the warning bell at the side of the house, to call one of the Game Wardens to come quickly. As he was ringing the bell, the fire 'gathered into a ball again, came down the tower wall' past Clifford, and then burst into flames again when it reached the Fantasy, an outbuilding which used to house the ex-owner's orchids.

Clifford ran to try and douse the flames, when he saw three men standing there with their backs to him. He was sure one of them was Andrew Connolley, a Game Warden and his Supervisor. He called out 'Mr Connolley, Mr Connolley' and slowly the men turned round, whereupon Clifford fell to the ground.

'I couldn't see their faces because there was so much light shining from them that I had to put my hands up to protect my eyes. They were wearing shiny overalls ...'

The power from the light forced Clifford to his knees and he remained there until the light went out. When he looked again, both the fireball and the men were gone.

'All the time I was very frightened' he said. Indeed the women in the compound, witnesses to the sighting, had run off into the bush with their children and were not easily persuaded to return. All the witnesses I spoke to, Naison Sampindi, Clifford Muchena, Eunice Kachiti, were convinced that what they had seen were ghosts, the spirits of their ancestors. Probably a *shave*, a lost spirit who has not found his way home because his descendants have not done their duty by him. There was no question in their minds that the figures were anything else. They had never heard of UFOs nor of men from outer space. In fact, they were openly sceptical about men having landed on the moon!

Case Four: Solomon Kativu and his brother, together with two other men, were on their way home to a village near the Hwange Game Reserve in southern Zimbabwe one evening in 1983 (the exact date could not be recalled). They had arrived on a bus from Harare about eight o'clock and the bus had dropped them off as close to the village as it could. But they still had a few kilometres to go. It was dark and the bush was thick. Suddenly, the men were aware of a very bright light in the sky. They stopped to watch and then realized it was descending towards them. They were sure it was an ancestral spirit and hid behind some trees. The light came lower and lower until at tree-top level it settled nearby. 'We could see it was a machine, dish-shaped. We were terrified but watched to see what would happen' Solomon recounted. A door at the top of the 'machine' opened and two men with light coloured skin got out. They 'floated' down to the ground. This was too much for the four watchers; they took to their heels and ran, never stopping until they reached their village.

I realize the obvious comment is, this is what most people would do, anyway; but in actual fact, perhaps more sophisticated people would be too curious, indeed too intrigued, to run away. They might be cautious, watch whilst hidden, or shout out a greeting, perhaps move forward to see what in heaven's name was happening. To me, it is an interesting aspect of the UFO phenomenon: how people with varying backgrounds react to this fascinating confrontation.

What reality there may be in abduction experiences is difficult to assess; there is so much of the 'ridiculous' or 'unbelievable' in the UFO phenomenon that investigators are not often surprised at the turn of events.

Elizabeth Klarer of Johannesburg, South Africa, presents such a case. She says she was taken aboard a craft in the 1950s. The pilot was a man named Akon, a tall, attractive humanoid from the planet Meton near Alpha Centauri. Elizabeth and Akon fell in love and she eventually found herself pregnant with his child. When she was five months pregnant, Akon came to fetch her to Meton where she claims she gave birth to her son Ayling. The reason why she did not remain in Meton was that she had a great deal of difficulty with her breathing and it affected her heart.

Elizabeth has written a book about her experiences, *Beyond the Light Barrier*. For years she has withstood the ridicule and often cruel barbs of the media, maintaining that her experience was a reality – that it all actually happened.

I am very fond of Elizabeth Klarer. I think she is a gracious lady, intelligent and extremely knowledgeable. I suspect that much of her story has been enhanced by her contact with other UFO witnesses, by her spiritual awareness and certainly by her own knowledge. Nevertheless, despite my logical attitude to UFOs, despite my wariness of this type of experience, I cannot believe that Elizabeth's experience does not arise from some fantastic happening in which she took part. Why now, suddenly, are American ufologists starting to take the abduction stories at face value, stories for instance of women who claim to have had their ova removed and who have been shown resulting children? And what of Dr Walter Bühler of Rio de Janeiro, Brazil, who authored the book on the Mirassol case, where a Brazilian man, forced to have sex with an alien woman, was subsequently shown his strange, red-haired baby some two years after the event? If these reports are accepted, then perhaps ufologists should re-examine Elizabeth Klarer's story.

Apart from Elizabeth, there is 'Edwin' and his acceptance of hundreds of radio broadcasts, collected on tape, from his outer space friend, Valdar. Edwin claims he met Valdar when he was the foreman of a factory where Edwin worked. They became very close and often went fishing together. One night, Valdar showed Edwin a space craft manoeuvering in the sky and explained his alien background to Edwin. Not long after this, he returned to his home planet, Edwin witnessing his departure from a beach at Richard's Bay, in Natal, South Africa.

Some months later, Valdar began a radio contact with Edwin which lasts to this day. If this is a hoax on Edwin's part, it is certainly an expensive one, for the broadcasts and taping have been going on since 1962. The messages are generally of the 'improve yourselves' nature, with promises of Earth's destruction if this advice is ignored, and offers of alternative accommodation for *some*, on a planet similar to Earth, when the disaster occurs.

Some of the messages are almost childish in context and have their 'ridiculous' elements; some are so sophisticated technologically that it seems impossible they could have emanated from Edwin's mind. Edwin's mentor and great friend, Carl von Vlierden, a sincere and dedicated man, has recorded these incidents in the book *UFO Contact from Koldas*, recently published in the USA.

I have come to know Carl and Edwin well. I am friendly with their families and, like Elizabeth Klarer, they are nice, highly likeable people. What psychological yardstick does one use to sift the hoaxers from decent, ordinary people? If hoaxers they be!

There are other cases, some quite simple and yet unexplained as to what they may be. Then there are uncomplicated, ongoing cases with numerous phenomena and weird, frightening connotations. If I did not know how many ufologists in the world continue to investigate, continue to be my friends, and are often of great assistance to me in these rather isolated and lonely investigations I would have given up years ago but now my determination to find the truth becomes stronger each year.

THE UFO CULTS

Kevin McClure

Frequent claims have been made during the past forty years, that individuals and groups have received messages, information and instruction from intelligences and entities that claim to come from the same sources as UFOs.

There are few cultures in the world that do not have as their spiritual centre a belief system based on information from a non-human source. That source can be personalized – the issue of the Ten Commandments by Jehovah to Moses – or it can be found in a body of writing – The Koran, The Talmud. The relationship to the non-human source can vary considerably. Buddhism encourages a striving to become one with that source. Judaism a detailed adherence to its laws, Catholicism promotes a judgemental system of error and forgiveness, where there can be a relationship with the divine. In simpler societies the relationship is managed through a shaman, or witch-doctor figure, chosen by a village or tribe. The more a culture develops sophistication and intellectual achievement, the more likely it is to develop a priesthood and the need to explain and understand its relationship to the rest of creation, and to the time before the birth and after the death of each individual.

Consequently, it is hardly surprising that the most ancient of cultural mysteries – religion – has become deeply involved with the most modern of cultural mysteries – the UFO Experience.

Most of our knowledge of the UFO Experience comes from reports from those who have witnessed UFOs of many kinds, from simple light-in-the-sky, to complex close encounter cases. There is objective evidence for very few of these, but it is important that they were *unexpected* experiences; events that occurred out of the blue, that surprised and mystified the witnesses. Though a few go on to have repeat experiences, and to anticipate and welcome them, a great majority of witnesses shun publicity, and gain little pleasure from their experience. It is clear that a great many decide never even to tell anybody outside their immediate family. The credibility of the UFO experience as a whole rests not on individual reports but on what the ancient Greeks called 'common notion'. Simply, if enough people believed something to be true, then it probably was. The only fair conclusion to be drawn on this basis is that a substantial number of reasonable people have been witnesses to events that cannot be rationally explained. However, the UFO cults, or belief groups, almost entirely avoid the accepted processes of report and investigation, but still play a part in the public understanding of the UFO field. It is proper that we look at their claims.

Claims of communication and instruction from UFO-related intelligences are frequent and persistent. Most groups are short lived and, to judge from material recently received from the USA, we are entering a golden age of UFO belief groups. However, let us look at what a few extraterrestrial intelligences have had to say:

'I *am* one of these Advanced Spiritual Beings. I have come from a very high spiritual world called Aries; I am not an Earth Person. I am now living as an Earth

Person in a physical body. I came to teach the Earth people.' (Uriel, through Ruth E Norman of the Unarius Foundation.)

'Will you agree to be the saviour of the world?' (Ashtar, to American contactee Allen-Michael Noonan.)

'Prepare yourself! You are to become the voice of Interplanetary Parliament!' (Invisible entity to George King, founder of the Aetherius Society.)

'I, Raymere, transmit once more upon this occasion in order to speak with you about the things of the next period of time ... you will find that you are moving into a higher frequency wherein there is a totally new dimension'. (Raymere, a space being, through Alenti Francesca at the Solar Light Retreat.)

'Earth's vortex is about to break because of an excess amount of hatred ...' (The space brothers resident on Io, one of the moons of Jupiter, to 'Gordon', a US contactee from 1967.)

These are typical of a great many more. They purport to be from non-human sources, channelled through a particular human being who then becomes the centre of attention in a belief group. The source claims a knowledge of human and universal affairs superior to any that humanity could hope to achieve. In addition to this display of knowledge, there is almost always an exhortation for members of the belief group to undertake a task, or live in a particular, unusual way, in order to do something about a situation of which the source has made them aware. This task may be as complex as constructing a working flying saucer, or working in prayer with UFO entities to avoid disasters and change the history of the world, or as simple as spreading the word of the reality of Martians or Venusians, or of the civilizations in the centre of the Earth. All too often, a way of life is demanded that immediately sets the group members apart from the friends and neighbours around them.

On such a basis have been founded many UFO-based belief groups. The classic account of the life and death of such a group is in the excellent book *When Prophecy Fails* by Festinger, Reicken, and Schachter, sociologists who joined a group in Utah as observers, and spent many hours within the group. The leader and 'channel' for the group was Marion Keech, who first received messages from her father, then from the 'Elder Brother', and then from entities who said they came from the planets Clarion and Cerus. Her closest contact was Sananda, who had previously been Jesus! In 1954 her group forecast a major and disastrous flood, from which she and her followers would be physically removed by extraterrestrials. The group and its message received considerable publicity, and its members gave up jobs and possessions. During the last few days before the predicted end the messages became wilder and more contradictory, and when the appointed night came there was neither flood nor rescue. Deeply disappointed, the group drifted apart.

A couple of other cases from the USA: I mentioned 'Gordon' whose Institute for Cosmic Research was given the task of building a flying saucer – The Bluebird – by one of the Great White Brothers (who make remarkably frequent appearances among many belief groups). Gordon's followers persisted with their task for seven years before they began to realize that they were getting nowhere, and the group broke up. More rewarding – for its founders at least – was HIM, Human Individual Metamorphosis, which appeared in California in 1975. Run by Bo and Peep – the chosen names of a psychiatric nurse and one of her patients – they procured a substantial following among the post-hippy generation by preaching that they would be assassinated, only to be resurrected after three days. They also promised that once their followers had achieved a lifestyle of sufficient asceticism, UFOs would come for them, and they would be removed to a physical plane above the Earth. Bo and Peep made a good deal of money, but nobody made any exciting journeys!

Perhaps the belief group which has attracted the largest and most consistent following is the Aetherius Society, founded and based in Britain, but with active branches in major cities throughout the world. Following his call to become the 'Voice of Interplanetary Parliament' George King, who had a background in what, in the 1950s, was known as 'the occult', founded the Aetherius Society. Over the past thirty years it has developed a detailed cosmology, in which many flying saucers represent a benign and concerned force, the Interplanetary Parliament. King wrote extensively, and explained how he had travelled to Mars and Venus, stating that Mercury was the only uninhabited planet. He detailed a battle he fought on a massive flying saucer of an interplanetary space fleet, 40,000,000 miles from Earth. In public meetings he gave out – and continues to give – messages from entities such as Mars Sector 6, the Master Aetherius and even the Master Jesus, who is apparently living on or near Venus. The tasks set for members of the Aetherius Society are usually of charging 'spiritual batteries' for the use and protection of suffering humanity, at various sites around the Earth. To quote briefly from the Society's account of Operation Prayer Power, an effort to help invasion-threatened Poland in 1981, as published in the journal *Cosmic Voice*: 'The Los Angeles battery had to be substituted for the inadequate Detroit one, because the Prayer Energies were not being picked up by Adepts 002 and 003 in position in their *invisible* [!] space craft above the central base of operations in Los Angeles … the Great White Brotherhood Retreat in Kilimanjaro, East Africa, had now joined in the release pattern ….' At the end of the operation, Mars Sector 6 informed King that 'there was a heavy resonance of Spiritual Energies over the whole of Poland'.

In the great majority of belief groups the source intelligences do nothing to prove themselves to the world at large, nothing to *prove* themselves even to their own followers: 'Only believe, and thou shalt see.' But what is it that the average group member really believes in? The channel; the person through whom the messages are being transmitted, who runs the group or cult, who asks, and organizes, demands and – of course – promises. Perhaps this is why the group members take so long to become critical and untrusting – it is the charisma of the messenger that holds the group together, not the conviction of the message.

Evidence is problem enough in relation to the mainstream UFO experience, but far more elusive where belief-groups are concerned. Amongst the hundreds of belief-group messages I have come across over the years, I can think of no two that have clearly been in contact with the same entity, giving the same information. And while some of the names – like Ashtar and Uriel – do crop up more than once, they seem to be different from other Ashtars and Uriels, who have never even met each other, and are unaware each of the others' existence.

Historically, most of these groups have collapsed in failure, disappointment and dissent. Promises have not been fulfilled, disasters predicted have not occurred, and nobody has been flown away by the UFOs as so frequently promised. In every case, all we know of the intelligence or entity is what its channel says about it. In no way does that constitute evidence.

The relationship of the communicator's revelations to the developing scientific knowledge of space is an obscure one. While there has been the occasional coincidence, exploration has made a mockery of reports of visits to alien civilizations on the nearby planets. Though the Aetherius Society covers the contradictions with the cloak of invisibility, it is noticeable that as the space programme has extended its reach, so the belief-groups have extended to parts of the galaxy well beyond the reach of scientific knowledge!

It must be clear by now that I am less than convinced that the messages that inspire the UFO belief groups have anything to do with the broader, witness-based UFO experience.

There are a great many more examples of allegedly non-human communicators who claim knowledge outside and ahead of our understanding, and who almost invariably fail; the Theosophical version of the Great White Brotherhood; the magical visitors of Eliphas Levi and Aleister Crowley and Dion Fortune; the Witch of Endor or the Delphic Oracle. We could list hundreds of spirit guides and local deities the world over: Elijah, Mahommed, Joan of Arc, and many appearances of the Blessed Virgin Mary. All have had their messages, their convictions and, inevitably, their followers. But in no case is there any significant evidence to suggest that the communicators had any separate existence from those who said they had been chosen to transmit those communications.

To put my argument in its simplest form, the UFO belief-groups are a contemporary form of a tradition that has been with us for thousands of years, in a guise that is attractive and convincing to followers. I do not think that the channels, the leaders of the groups, intentionally set out to deceive; they are part of a long-established cultural phenomenon, that grows and changes with the fears, wishes and priorities of succeeding generations.

PART VI
THE CHALLENGE OF UFOs

THE CASE FOR SCEPTICISM

Hilary Evans

The question 'Do you believe in UFOs?' is nonsense. Of course objects are seen in the sky which are not identified.

Only when the question is changed to 'Do you believe that these unidentified objects are a phenomenon in their own right, hitherto unknown?' does it become meaningful, and belief and scepticism become meaningful responses.

But it is only when that question is made more specific still, changed perhaps to 'Do you believe that UFOs are extraterrestrial space craft?' or 'Do you believe that UFOs are sent by the Devil?' that belief or scepticism can prove their value.

To be of value, scepticism must be *informed*. Ufology has been challenged by many sceptics during its brief span, but only a very few of them have taken the trouble to make a proper study of the evidence. Most have argued from *a priori* positions – it *can't* be, so it *isn't* – so their comments are valueless. This is why the best criticism has always come from within the ufological community. When Allan Hendry in the United States published *The UFO Handbook*, when Michel Monnerie in France published *And what if UFOs don't exist?*, their comments carried weight, for these were experienced researchers whose own studies had led them to question what they were doing – in Hendry's case, to question much, in Monnerie's case, to question all.

To be of value, scepticism must also be *constructive*. It is not enough for the sceptic to indicate the shortcomings of an explanation; he must be able to offer a better one.

The difference between the *sceptical* approach and the *negative* approach is well illustrated by a 1981 case. Towards the end of that year, BUFORA's Director of Investigations, Jenny Randles, received a report from a Mrs Adams (pseudonym), aged sixty-five, who, while watching a TV film, had felt 'compelled' to go to the window, where she saw a large bright yellow object stationary in the sky. Going outside, she saw it more clearly as 'like two blobs of golden jelly' wobbling and pulsating, which shortly afterwards changed to a cross. Greatly excited, she phoned her son who lived nearby; he and his wife Janette couldn't see it, but Janette came over to her mother-in-law's home and both watched enthralled as the object changed shape repeatedly, seemed to emit smoke as though to camouflage itself, and was approached by aircraft which seemed to be investigating it.

When at one stage the object disappeared, the women expressed a wish that it would return; and when it did, they felt this was in response to their wish. It was now very close, seemingly hovering over a nearby house, and Janette was able to see lights and structured sides on the object. The police were called, and two officers came round and promised to put in a report.

The next day Mrs Adams saw strange figures on her TV screen which she believed were a message directed at her. Both she and Janette suffered from severe and recurrent headaches, and four days after the sighting Mrs Adams had what she believed to be a fourteen hour 'missing time' experience, and speculated that she might have been contacted. She believed she had been chosen and 'called' to look out of the window; that the beings in the UFO were protecting her, despite the headaches; and her overall response was a surge of fresh confidence in coping with the world.

Investigation by Jenny Randles and Philip Taylor, both of BUFORA, established beyond any reasonable doubt that the UFO was simply the moon; that the 'smoke' was passing clouds; and that no aircraft had been sent to investigate the object.

But as Randles herself recognized, the fact that we can explain the stimulus for the witness's response by no means explains the response itself. Clearly there were psychological factors involved which predisposed Mrs Adams to turn a simple observation of a natural phenomenon into a highly specific experience which was directed at her personally. And the fact that the witness obtained positive benefits from the events adds an additional dimension to the matter.

Clearly, the negative view: 'What was said to have happened *hadn't* really happened, so *nothing* really happened', falls far short of the true state of affairs. A *truly* sceptical approach, however, by establishing the fantasy nature of the ostensible event, reveals what was *really* going on – which was clearly some kind of psychological event personal to Mrs Adams alone (though her daughter-in-law participated as a kind of assistant). To know the full significance of the event, we would need to know much more about Mrs Adams' personal life than we are likely to learn from a straightforward UFO investigation.

Much the same would no doubt be true of thousands of other cases involving misinterpretations. In his *UFO Handbook* Hendry quotes many examples of witness reactions:

– to advertizing planes – 'I got so scared I nearly ran off the street' – 'screamed for my husband to get back in car ... had a camera and CB but too scared to use them ... hope I never see it again'; – to meteors seen for *two seconds* – 'Scared ... guy I was with was crying'.

– to stars – 'it's a sign, a premonition' – 'daughter projected thoughts at it to move' – 'Oh my Lord, it's the end of the world! I'd better get down on my knees and pray!'

In all such cases we must suppose that psychological and sociological forces were at work, much like those which made the radio audience of Orson Welles' 1938 dramatization of H G Wells' *War of the Worlds* believe, against all reason, that the events of the drama were really taking place, that Martians were really invading America.

Scepticism, in such cases, does a valuable job by showing that the surface report may be cloaking a powerful and possibly dangerous response fuelled by personal motivation. And that word 'dangerous' is no mere figure of speech. In 1986 another English woman, aged, like Mrs Adams, in her sixties, was inspired to kill her grandchildren because she 'believed a machine like a giant vacuum cleaner threatened to suck them to another planet ... She thought that if she killed the children and herself they would be united in paradise and escape the space men.'

If that is what belief leads to, there is much to be said for scepticism.

Naturally, the question then presents itself: if so many cases can be shown to have a psychosocial rather than a material basis, could this not be true in *every* case?

A comparison is often made between belief in UFOs and belief in witchcraft, and in many respects the comparison is valid. It is now generally recognized that the entire witch persecution, which raged for centuries and led to thousands of deaths, had its basis not in the existence of any sabbat-attending devil-worshipping witchcraft cult, but in a combination of social and psychological forces: there were no witches, there was no witchcraft. What there was, was a monstrous but plausible fantasy created by the Church, which, because its raw materials were popular beliefs cunningly distorted, was accepted by the common people, who responded to the fantasy in accordance with their conscious beliefs and their subconscious motivations.

Could something of the sort be happening in the case of UFOs?

It is easy to underestimate the capabilities of the human mind; yet study the literature of hallucination and hypnosis and you will come to recognize that there are scarcely any limits to the ability of the human mind to delude itself.

In 1949 a Chicago housewife, Mrs Marion Dorothy Martin, began to receive messages from extraterrestrials warning her that a catastrophe involving the destruction of the world was about to take place. However, those who believed in the ETs would be rescued in time. She managed to persuade a handful of others: Charles Laughead of Michigan State University gave up his teaching post and devoted himself to spreading the warning, issuing press releases about the forthcoming event and the possibility of safety by evacuation for the chosen few. Others too gave up their jobs, left their homes, broke family ties, and joined Mrs Martin in waiting hopefully for the great day.

That day never arrived, nor did the flying saucers that would carry the faithful away to safety. For a while the believers clung together hopefully; then gradually they dispersed.

Among them, though incognito, were sociologists who had seized the opportunity to observe the cult from within. Their resulting study (Festinger, Riecken & Schachter, *When Prophecy Fails*, University of Minnesota Press, 1956) is an astonishing insight into how people, driven by hope or fear, override the reality-testing process which prevents most of us, most of the time, from mistaking illusion for reality.

Countless such cults have sprung up in consequence of such supposed 'channelling' from extraterrestrial sources. The very fact that there are so many of them, each emanating from a different set of cosmic brothers, would in itself be grounds for scepticism, apart from the dubious aspects of the messages themselves – the lack of any reliable evidence, the contradiction, the patent feedback of all-too-human preoccupations.

Most communications claiming to originate from the space brothers are so absurd as to convince no one except the individuals involved; but there are some which have a persuasive force. During the 1960s, the proprietor of a rustic inn in the Ardennes and his friend, the narrator, went out to investigate some strange lights, only to find an ET spacecraft parked in the field. A voice came to them from inside it, telling them, among other things:

'We are not the first extraterrestrials to come from a distant galaxy to visit you. Beings like us are among you in all parts of your planet, for our total knowledge of the body enables us to reproduce an individual in multiple starting from his genetic code, and has given us the power to mingle with you in order to know the nature of your development and with a view to eventually establishing a scientific contact.

Alas! Without realizing it, you have committed the error of taking the path which leads inexorably to destruction without the chance of retreat, and the present age is the final phase of that path.

You have not polluted your planet with impunity; radioactive dust impregnates its atmosphere after each insane atomic test explosion. And the least war, be it nuclear, chemical or bacteriological, would lead to the biological end of your generation.

Life will continue for millions of years on Earth, but the way things are going, it is highly unlikely that man will be among the surviving species.

What we say to you now, we have said many times before. We know that nobody will believe you if you dare to report this declaration, just as those we have warned in the past have not been believed.'

Because such a message is very much the sort of thing we would expect a visiting ET to say, it is not difficult to see how it would be accepted at face value by someone who was looking to cosmic guardians to save our Earth from its follies. A sceptic would find it easier to believe that the message was feedback from the witness's own mind, and that the event itself was a fantasy incorporating his expectations. Unless it could be proved beyond doubt that there either was or wasn't a real space ship out there in the field, there's no way of resolving the problem: it is up to the individual to decide which he thinks more probable.

Clearly, a similar explanation could well hold good for Mrs Adams, and for other cases in which the individual seems to be imposing his own private fantasy on a mundane happening. But it can be little more than speculation. The two witnesses who claimed to see an actual, material spacecraft parked in the field outside that inn in the Ardennes may not be able to prove to us it was there, but we for our part are not likely to be able to prove it wasn't.

Unfortunately, this is only too often the case. In report after report, we simply do not possess sufficient information on which to base a convincing conclusion. Instead, it has to be a matter of assessing relative probabilities: is it more likely to have been fact or fantasy? The quality of the evidence, our evaluation of the witness – and sometimes of the investigator, our ability to draw parallels with other fields of research – all these will weigh the balance towards acceptance or rejection. Just as, in English law, an accused person is given the benefit of the doubt and presumed innocent until sufficient evidence is produced to show otherwise, so it may be that we should accept a UFO witness's account unless so many doubts accumulate that scepticism becomes easier than acceptance. Unfortunately, there is hardly a case which does not contain grounds for doubt of one sort or another.

Contradictions: What at first sight appears to be a very clearly reported incident occurred about one am on 6 November 1967, when truck driver Carl Farlow was driving his diesel truck near Fordingbridge in southern England. Approaching a crossroads, his lights faded and extinguished. He pulled up, and saw a large egg-shaped object, seemingly about twenty-five metres in length, move slowly across the road. After a short while it gradually accelerated, and disappeared in a few seconds. Only then did Farlow notice another car, halted on the far side of the stretch of road traversed by the object. Its driver, a veterinary surgeon, came over to Farlow and explained that his engine had failed; they decided to telephone the police. The girl travelling with the vet was taken to hospital for shock, while the two men were taken to Bournemouth police station for questioning by the Ministry of Defence.

If we had only the one account, that would be quite an impressive story. Unfortunately we have several, and they all disagree substantially. Thus *The Daily Express* gives us basically the same story, but tells us that the second motorist didn't want to be involved, and drove away before the police arrived. APRO's Coral Lorenzen, writing in *Fate*, tells a much more exciting tale, in which a porthole opens in the side of the object from which vacuum-cleaner-like tubes emerge and suck up gravel etc from the roadside, but, according to her account, the vet was travelling alone. Other versions have yet other variations.

If reports can't agree on so straightforward a matter as whether the second driver had a passenger, and whether or not he drove away before being questioned, clearly no other item in the account can be trusted, unless of course we could establish for sure that one account was trustworthy and all the others spurious. But which one?

Poor Investigation: In 1979 there was a whole rash of

dramatic sightings near Broadhaven in west Wales. Amazing events were reported, including:

* A UFO reported by schoolchildren on the ground in a field over a period of several hours in full daylight.
* The teleportation of a herd of cattle.
* The use of an offshore island as a base by the UFOs.
* A space man appearing at a cottage window.

All this was seriously reported by the witnesses and just as seriously accepted by the local investigators. Yet a subsequent counter-investigation showed that vital features had been ignored or overlooked, whether through sloppy work or as a result of deliberate selection:

* The grounded UFO had been in a position where it was overlooked by a score of houses, making it inconceivable that it could have spent hours in broad daylight unnoticed by a single one of the residents.
* The fact that the alleged 'teleportation' took the cattle only to a neighbouring farm was itself sufficient to encourage scepticism; in addition, enquiry revealed that the cows were continually escaping from their yard (in this case, the original investigators had not even troubled to question the witness's next-door neighbour and fellow-cattleman!)
* The island did *not* contain a UFO base, as Brynmor Williams of the BBC found when he visited the island to see for himself, something that the investigators who originally made the claim had not bothered to do, though if they had done so, and had found what they so confidently asserted, they would have achieved the scoop of the century!
* The 'space man' at the window was in fact a member of the local Rotarians, dressed in a protective fireman's suit, playing a trick on the witness whose earlier experiences had been reported in the local paper.

The west Wales 'wave' generated three full-length books, over and above countless press articles and radio and TV broadcasts. Yet all were based on the original investigation which was revealed as wholly unreliable. It is not surprising that the investigator who carried out the counter-investigation concluded:

> 'The story of the west Wales flap is a sad revelation of human nature. Some of those involved emerge as simple minded, only too ready to believe what they are told without questioning. Others, though claiming to be objective investigators, have shown themselves to be incompetent or prejudiced. Some who have proffered evidence are to be seen as simply unreliable, others may be considered fraudulent. Just a few people seem to have had genuinely paranormal experiences. But because of the way in which the affair was treated, the truth has been buried beneath every kind of error and evasion, fiction and fraud.'

In the fall of 1954, a vast wave of sightings swept over France. In 1979, when a quarter of a century had elapsed, investigators Barthel and Brucker published a reappraisal of the dramatic events. Checking on more than 200 reports, they found grounds for doubt in every single case. In one comic (but which might well have been tragic) incident, M Faisan, a farmer in northern France, had seen what he took to be a space man repairing his space craft, and fired two shots at him. The truth was that the 'space man' was his neighbour, M Ruant, repairing his car, and who was not at all pleased when bullets slammed into his vehicle just centimetres from his head!

Evry Schatzmann, in his introduction to the book titled, appropriately, *The Great Martian Panic*, writes:

> 'The authors demonstrate that even the most detailed testimonies may be caused by blatant hoaxes, picked up and sensationalized by the press, and accepted without check or control by the ufologists. One finished reading their book with the conviction that none of the witness reports which are the basis of UFO research measure up to scientific standards. The witnesses can't be trusted (whether they acted deliberately or

unwittingly), the press don't give a damn about getting their facts right, and the researchers don't hesitate to fill their catalogues with cases that are unchecked and lacking in precision.' (*La grande peur Martienne*, Nouvelles Editions Rationalistes)

Improbability: Though the old 'contactee' cases were so full of contradictions and absurdities that only the most credulous could accept them, the current spate of abduction cases present a greater challenge. Any one of them, taken on its own, displays a certain plausibility: no one can fail to be impressed by the accounts given in Fowler's *The Andreasson Affair*, Hopkins' *Missing Time* and *Intruders*, Strieber's *Communion* or other such tales.

Doubt sets in, however, when they are set one alongside the other. We then find, among other grounds for doubt:

* Though there are many shared details in the *kind* of events reported, no two space ships are alike, no two crews of abductors are alike, and so forth.
* Though the abductees are taken on board space craft hovering overhead, not one of these spacecraft has ever been convincingly confirmed by an independent witness. Still less has anyone seen the abductee in the process of being abducted.
* Moreover, we find that today's abduction reports have a disconcerting similarity to stories told by folklorists and anthropologists. French researcher Bertrand Méheust has listed numerous parallels between abduction reports on the one hand, and on the other science fiction stories, folk tales and native legends. Thus in Carl Higdon's 1974 experience, he is out hunting when, firing at a deer, his bullet drops to the ground, and 'a sort of man' appears who, after asking him if he is hungry, takes him on board his space ship. Méheust compares this with a native American legend in which a hunter's arrows are stopped in mid-flight by a mysterious spirit who enquires if he is hungry and involves him in strange dreamlike experiences.

Confirmation that incidents of this sort are stereotypes shared by all of us comes from the work of Alvin Lawson and his colleagues in the 'imaginary abductee' experiment. This came about as a consequence of a UFO investigation in which investigator John DeHerrera was puzzled by the ambiguous indications of a witness who refused to admit that any abduction had occurred, yet under hypnosis fabricated an *imaginary* abduction of extraordinary verisimilitude.

The experiment consisted of hypnotizing volunteer subjects – who had no particular interest in the UFO phenomenon – then suggesting to them that they are involved in a UFO abduction. Because they were led through its successive phases by means of guided questions, there is no question of the subjects fabricating the entire story. But what the experiment showed was that the bare bones of the questions, involving a minimum of suggestion, were sufficient to inspire the subjects to create an elaborate, detailed and dramatic story – which was of course entire fiction.

Moreover, the way in which the 'imaginary abductees' developed their story, the details they supplied, were strikingly similar to the claims of the 'true' abductees.

There have been a number of critical comments on this experiment, and any conclusions we draw must be tentative. But it is safe to say that *while the experiments do not prove that the 'true' abductees are making up their stories, they do suggest that anyone who unconsciously wishes to do so is able to find within himself the necessary resources*.

Exaggeration: Study of UFO stories shows that details are often added to increase their strangeness. A noteworthy instance is the Hill abduction case, in which it is frequently asserted that when the couple got home after their interrupted journey, they were astonished to find how long it had taken.

In fact, they did not discover this anomaly until some time later, when it was pointed out to them by investigators from NICAP that their journey seemed to have taken an improbably long time.

Clearly, the story has been 'improved', and if so, we must ask why? Seemingly to conform to the stereotype version of the abduction scenario – to what people want to think happened. In this case the availability of the reliable account enables us to ascertain the true version: but we may wonder in how many other cases the narrative has been (perhaps unconsciously) distorted in order to conform to expectations.

Outright lies: About 1980 I was visited by a man who showed me a remarkable UFO photograph he had taken at Coromandel, New Zealand, in 1978. I subsequently established that it had in fact been taken by Fritz van Nest near Kanab, Utah, on 21 March 1968. In short, my visitor was simply lying. As it happens, I doubted his story even while he was telling it; but if I had never come across the original of his photo, I would to this day be wondering if perhaps his story was true.

Why did he tell a false story? Not for financial gain, certainly, nor can I see any reason why he would seek to impress me. Some obscure personal motivation was evidently at work: it would not surprise me to learn that he had come to believe implicitly that he had indeed taken that photo himself, and would have been as surprised as indignant if I had pointed out the true facts.

Through all these instances there runs one common thread: personal motivation, which misinterprets, distorts, exaggerates, invents. And if we can see personal motivation undermining the value of the evidence in so many cases, should we not suspect that similar motivations may be operating, unnoticed, in *every* claim by *every* witness?

This, surely, would be the attitude adopted by the true sceptic: that no testimony, however sincerely offered, should be taken at face value. Even if the original witness gives an honest and accurate account, it may be distorted by those who investigate or report it.

Scepticism does not mean asserting that *nothing* happened: but that what *seems* to have happened may not be what *really happened*.

Allen Hynek once said that before we believe that extraordinary events have occurred, we have the right to demand extraordinary evidence: and this is, in essence, the sceptic's position. He is not saying: these things *cannot* happen, and so I don't believe they are happening. Rather, he is saying: It is not very likely that these things are happening, and if you want me to believe that they are, you must produce some very convincing evidence.

The evidence for a UFO event, to be convincing, must be free from contamination by personal motivation or cultural expectation, and from exaggeration or distortion, contradiction or ambiguity.

Any explanation for a UFO event, to be convincing, must similarly be free from bias, and must be more likely than any alternative explanation offered by our knowledge either of the physical world or of human behaviour.

When these requirements are met, the sceptic may allow himself to be persuaded; but until then, the only viable approach is that so·neatly expressed by Sir Walter Raleigh: 'The Skeptick doth neither affirm, neither denie any position; but doubteth of it.'

THE CASE FOR SCIENTIFIC STUDY

John Spencer

'If a man will begin with certainties, he shall end in doubts; but if he will be content to begin with doubts, he shall end in certainties.'

When Francis Bacon wrote those words in the sixteenth century in his *Advancement of Learning* he might have had the problems of modern day ufology in mind. There can be little denying that our field is strewn with many who have certainties, from those for whom the Extraterrestrial Hypothesis is an unshakeable fact, to those who maintain that 'UFOs-don't-exist-whatever-the-facts-may-say' and who are equally certain and as prepared to ignore evidence as the 'believers' are to infer it. These certainties are the result not of research which has eliminated other possibilities and left their conclusion proven, but of faith in their beliefs, individual to each, and supported by no, or very little, proven data. Out of their certainties come doubts; doubts in the minds of the witnesses, doubts in the minds of a public wanting answers, doubts in the media as to what really constitutes a UFO phenomenon, with such diversity of opinion. And, most importantly, in the minds of everyone observing ufology, from whatever point of view, doubts that ufologists are objective enough to call themselves researchers and able to give objective opinion, when it seems that they – we – are pronouncing only preconceived notions.

Clearly, then, we must 'be content to begin with doubts' if we are to be ready to accept the neutrality of opinion towards an answer that research offers, and only then can we hope to 'end in certainties'.

These certainties, when they emerge, however, will have value only if we can demonstrate that they are the product of analysis within the constraints of a scientific discipline. This principle is vital for the following reasons:

To be able to place reliability on the results of investigation: Investigation is worldwide but standards vary considerably between individuals, national groups and even to some extent, countries. Most seriously, even if we considered only the top five per cent of investigators we would still find diversity of methods, and therefore of reliability of results, due to personal and preconceived notions. This leads to unscientific, incomparable and unco-ordinated output. If we wish to place reliability on the results of investigations we need a scientifically structured framework within which to work. In almost any field of the sciences, including investigative sciences, the output at the end of the day is not affected by the character of the person performing the work, because of the scientific structure within which the work is performed. In ufology, the work performed in investigating a case can often be dictated by the prejudices of the investigator; a case left halfway through and taken up by a second investigator could take a completely different direction for reasons not dictated by the facts of the case. This is an indication that strict analytical discipline is not being applied.

This is not to suggest that there is no place for intuition; most scientific breakthroughs are the result of inspiration and ufology should not be denied this chance, but the time for intuition to come into play is *after* a proper scientific analysis has been done. All too often, regrettably, investigators begin to use their intuition even before the investigation has started. In these situations the strong influence of the media in promoting the Extraterrestrial Hypothesis often becomes apparent. Despite the fact that ETH, while exciting and interesting, is the least supported major theory by weight of evidence available, investigators will often approach a case on the basis of 'Can I prove it's a space ship or not?' and if not will reject the case as 'failed'.

Worse, and most condemning of all, I can think of two UK investigators (and there will be others) whose conclusions on a case can be predicted, even before they have begun their investigation, because of their proven, extreme, prejudices towards their own chosen 'answers'. Any person seeking an answer to the question 'just tell me what it was I saw' cannot depend on the answer given in these circumstances. So extreme is this situation, in fact, that I can think of no set of circumstances where these investigators would *not* come to their preconceived answers and since they have different belief systems the witness is doomed to different answers from the outset depending on which of them worked on the case.

Clearly, then, one particular sighting could result in several different 'conclusions' because of such diversity of approach (and not because of the facts presented) which makes it difficult to place reliance on case studies.

BUFORA has made some moves to alleviate this situation by instigating a system of accredited investigators of proven worth, but the problem is far from solved.

To introduce into the subject a degree of prediction: It is a tenet of science that a subject once understood should result in prediction of outcome of experiment or observation. For example it was once observed that the sun was sometimes high in the sky, sometimes lower, sometimes not there at all. From this observation a theory was developed that suggested the Earth travelled around the sun and also rotated on its own axis. This theory was open to the test of prediction – it could be calculated that there was a (reasonable!) chance that the sun would rise in the morning. From observation we get a theory or hypothesis, we test it, and we end with a scientifically proven fact. We are not yet at that stage in ufology, indeed we are far from it. Clearly some of the probable answers that will make up the 'solution' are not yet ready to be tested. The psychological and sociological solutions will require input from those sciences to our field. Where UFOs can be, and are, explained by weather and natural phenomena, this should lead us to an understanding of the ways in which they are formed, and give us a chance to predict their occurrence and indeed the rash of reports that will be received. And if UFOs are in fact extraterrestrial then if we understand what they are and what they are doing our predictions will ultimately let us turn the tables.

To give worthwhile answers to those victims of UFOs who so desperately need them: One branch of ufology in which we all play a part, to a greater or lesser degree, is in the field of 'abductions': the perceived attack by aliens against people who are subjected to bewildering, if not horrific, medical 'examination'. There are many who feel that this is not represented by an objective reality in the 'real' world. But it matters not at all to the witnesses whether it is a real event or not. Their experience is real to them, and they need help in coming to terms with it. I can make no better analogy than does Jenny Randles, in 'Living with a close encounter' (See pp 143-54), in which she suggests that abduction is very similar to rape. There is, however, a major difference between victims of

hese two situations; a rape victim has support and
sympathy from the community, the assistance of the
police and aid from the medical profession. An
abduction witness has none of these; the community
will not accept even a perceived reality of the event, the
police have no machinery to deal with an abduction
report, and the medical profession, generally, will not
entertain a reality in the event that needs more than
the attention of psychiatrists. These people, frightened
and moved by their experience, have to come to us!
And what can we do? Whatever we do must be within
scientific disciplines so that the people who come to us
know that the support they are receiving is sound and
truly helpful, that it represents and, hopefully,
includes medical help and that when answers are
offered (often the witness just needs to be told 'what it
was' more than anything else) they can be relied upon.

To liaise with the accepted scientific community in
order to increase the worthwhile output, even
'spin-off' output, from our work and to receive into
our subject worthwhile input from scientists currently afraid to join us because of the stigma
attached: To gain support for victims as outlined
above means having the involvement of more than a
few individual members of the medical profession.
This will not happen if we are perceived by them as
cultists at one extreme or untalented amateurs at the
other. But we are amateurs, although we're still the
best there are, and we appeal for professional help.
Our work will be of use to the medical profession, if
they help to formulate the approaches they think we
should take.

   Most research programmes have 'spin-off' output of
no direct use to the research in question but of use to
other groups. Perhaps the classical case is the varied
spin-off output from the space programme; better
techniques for operating theatre hygiene, even
non-stick cookware. The research conducted into

UFOs may well benefit others if they 'tap into it' but for this we need liaison with these groups. Hopefully, we shall benefit from their involvement, and the overall sum of useful knowledge will be increased.

Our work involves much that is already the province of 'conventional' science, and we need the help of qualified scientists to properly conduct ourselves. Indeed, we are accused of being amateurish in our approach because we do not have scientists with us in our work. It is not for want of trying! Many are afraid that 'getting involved with UFOs' will taint their respectability, but it will not as more and more scientists do involve themselves with us. We can accelerate that acceptance into the scientific community if we act in a manner becoming to that community.

To enable a scientific evaluation of some UFOs to be made which will decrease the 'clutter' in our databases: The answer to some of the less exotic sightings may already lie in the work of other groups conducting scientific research. Our liaison with them would help us to cut away identifiable cases, and leave the 'core' of our own work more clear. This is being done to a great extent, but further recognition from the accepted sciences would increase this liaison.

To prepare an appropriate response to the UFO phenomenon: If the UFO phenomenon is, say, a set of natural phenomena which we can observe, like lightning or thunder, but with the variety of a firework display, then our research amounts to an understanding only of the events. But if the UFO phenomenon includes at least an element of interaction, ie where a human response to the phenomenon will change the phenomenon or elicit further responses from it, then our work must lead us to prepare a suitable and proper response.

In the easiest to describe, but by no means exclusive,

situation, our old favourite the extraterrestrial hypothesis, if we are being subjected to analysis/study/manipulation/invasion by an intelligence from another part of the galaxy, then it is incumbent upon us to react to that. If we are, as the 'ancient astronauts' theory suggests, the children of a superior race then they will no doubt be pleased to know that we are growing to maturity and, like all children, we shall seek to cut our apron strings. If we are being manipulated by these intelligences then our self-will and human dignity will insist that we resist this manipulation. If we are merely being studied by these intelligences then we must demonstrate to them our desire for interaction with them. And if we are to be invaded by these intelligences then our course of action must be extreme; we must understand their motivations and methods so that we may defend ourselves and, if necessary, turn the tables. Human history has clearly indicated, perhaps to our shame, that when two cultures collide there can be no compromise; only one culture will survive. We owe it to ourselves to ensure that that is ours.

We have a long way to go in order both to be a scientific discipline, and to be respected by other scientific disciplines. Moves are being made in these directions. Jacques Vallee has applied sound scientific methods to much of his research and analysis and in this book there are examples of scientific analysis by projects UNICAT and URD, amongst many others. BUFORA's own use of its computerized database is designed to allow scientific analysis, and the restructuring of its own research and investigation methods are to provide a sound basis for this.

But there is much more that must be done; eventually we must be as any other scientific discipline if we are to play our role in the scientific community.

REFERENCES AND BIBLIOGRAPHY

THE COMING OF THE SAUCERS

Le Poer Trench, B (now Lord Clancarty), **Sky People**, Spearman, 1960, and **The Flying Saucer Story**, Spearman, 1966, and other titles.

Adamski, G and *Desmond, L*, **Flying Saucers Have Landed**, Werner Laurie, 1953.

Drake, WR, **Gods or Spacemen?**, Amherst Press, 1964; **Spacemen in the Ancient East**, Spearman, 1968; (and related 'gods or spacemen' books and articles).

Von Daniken, E, **Chariots of the Gods**, Souvenir Press, 1969, and similar titles.

Blumrich, JF, **The Spaceships of Ezekiel**, Corgi, 1974.

Forcet, T, **Strange Signes from Heaven**, etc, 1646, *Spacelink*, Vol 5.

Bonilla, JAY, translated from 'L'Atronomie', *Spacelink*, Vol 5, 1885.

Brooks, PW, **Historic Airships**, Evelyn, 1973.

Doel, GG, 'Did Pennington Build the 1897 USA Airship?' *Spacelink*, Vol 5, Vol 6.

De Wries, L, **Victorian Inventions**, John Murray, 1971.

Fort, C, **The Books of Charles Fort**, Holt, New York, 1941.

Keel, JA, **The Man Who Invented Flying Saucers**, Fortean Times, 1983.

Palmer, R, and *Arnold, K*, **The Coming of the Saucers**, Amherst Press, 1952.

Dan Dare Pilot of the Future, Eagle Comic, commenced 14 April 1950.

Flammonde, P, **UFO Exist!**, Putnam's Sons, New York, 1976.

Sachs, M, **The UFO Encyclopedia**, Corgi, 1981.

Evans, H, and *Spencer, J* (editors), UFOs 1947–1987, Fortean Tomes, 1987.

Catoe, L, **UFOs and Related Subjects**, US Government Printing Office, 1969, Gale Research, Detroit (revised 1978).

'IT SEEMS IMPOSSIBLE, BUT THERE IT IS'

Arnold, K and *Palmer, R*, **The Coming of the Saucers**, Amherst Press, 1952.

Arnold, K, 'How It All Began', in C Fuller (editor), **Proceedings of the First International Congress**, Warner Books, 1980.

Loren G, **Charles Fort, the Fortean Society, and Unidentified Flying Objects**: A Survey of the Unidentified Flying Object Mystery from August 1895 to August 1947, Fremont, California, privately published, 1976.

Herbert, JS, **A Survey of Press Coverage of Unidentified Flying Objects, 1947–1966**, Northwestern University, 1970, edited by Arcturus Book Service, 1982.

Ted B, **Report on the UFO Wave of 1947**, privately published, 1967.

Tacker, Lt Col LJ, **Flying Saucers and the US Air Force**, D Van Nostrand Company Inc, Princeton, 1960.

Keel, J, **The Man Who Invented Flying Saucers**, Fortean Times, 1983.

Arnold, K, 'I *did* see the flying discs!' Fate, Vol 1, 1948; 'Are space visitors here?', Fate, Vol a, 1948; 'Phantom lights in Nevada', Fate, Vol 1, 1948.

Menzel, DH, **Flying Saucers**, Harvard University Press, 1953.

GHOST ROCKETS AND PHANTOM AIRCRAFT

(1) *Umebladet* (daily newspaper), Jan 2, 1934.

(2) Report catalogue, AFU files.

(3) Report to the Secretary of War, April 28, 1934

(4) *Hufvudstadsbladet* (daily newspaper), Jan 5, 1937.

(5) *Hynek, A* and *Vallée, J*, **The Edge of Reality**, Henry Regnery, Chicago, 1975.

(6) *Aftonbladet* (daily newspaper), Nov 3, 1936.

(7) *Social-Demokraten* (daily newspaper), March 17, 1937.

(8) Military war records at the War Archives, Stockholm.

(9) Minutes from a meeting at the Royal Air Administration, July 15, 1946.

(10) A secret draft for a memorandum from Karl-Arvid Norlin to major Frank Cervell, Defence Staff archives.

(11) *Norrbottens-Kuriren* (daily newspaper), May 26, 1984, *AFV Newsletter*, No 27, 1984.

(12) FOA report to the committee, Sept 1946; *Svenska Dagbladet*, July 22, 1946.

(13) A request from the Swedish news agency TT to the newspapers, July 22, 1946.

DISTANT CONTACT: RADAR/VISUAL ENCOUNTER AT BENTWATERS

(1) Personal interview, Oct, 1986.

(2) *Thayer, GD, Optical and Radar Analyses of Field Cases*, Gillmor (editor); **Scientific Study of Unidentified Flying Objects**, Vision Press, London, 1970, (See also: *Thayer, GD*, 'UFO Encounter II', Austronautics & Aeronautics, Sept, 1971; McDonald, JE, 'Science in Default', in Sagan and Page (editors), **UFOs: A Scientific Debate**,

Cornell University Press, Ithaca and London, 1972; *McDonald, JE*, 'UFOs Over Lakenheath', Vol 16, 1970.)

THE LEGEND OF THE CRASHED SAUCERS

Simmons, HM, 'Once Upon a Time in the West', **Magonia**, 20 August, 1985.
Nickell, J, 'The Hangar 18 Tales', **Common Ground**, 9 June, 1984.
Just Cause Newsletter (various).
Klass, P, 'Crash of the Crashed Saucer Claim', **The Skeptical Enquirer**, Vol. 10, 1986.
Moore, W, **Philip Klass and the Roswell Incident**, 1986.
Moore, W, **Crashed Saucers – Evidence in the Search for Proof**, Wm Moore publications, 1985.
Berlitz, C and *Moore, W*, **The Roswell Incident**, Granada, 1985.
Stringfield, L, articles in **FSR**, Vols 25, 28 and 29.

THE DEVELOPMENT OF UFO OCCUPANTS

(1) *Randles, J*, and *Warrington, P*; **UFOs A British Viewpoint**, Britain, 1979.
(2) *Bowen, C*; **The Humanoids**, Britain, 1974.
(3) *Johnson, F*; **The Janos People**, Britain, 1980.
(4) *Keel, J*; **The Mothmen Prophecies**, USA, 1975.
(5) *Adamski, G* and *Leslie, D*; **Flying Saucers Have Landed**, USA, 1953.
(6) *Fuller, JG*; **The Interrupted Journey**, USA, 1966.
(7) *Walton, T*; **The Walton Experience**, USA, 1978.
(8) *Fowler, Raymond*; **The Andreasson Affair**, USA, 1979.
(9) *Strieber, W*; **Communion**, USA, 1987.
(10) *Vallee, J*; **Passport to Magonia**, USA, 1970.
(11) *Wentz, E*; **The Fairy-Faith in Celtic Countries**, Britain, 1911.

INVESTIGATING THE ABDUCTEES

Fuller, JG, **The Interrupted Journey**, USA, 1966.
Fowler, R, **The Andreasson Affair**, and **The Andreasson Affair, Phase Two**, USA, 1979 and 1982.
Hopkins, B, **Missing Time**, USA, 1981; **Intruders**, USA, 1987.

LIVING WITH A CLOSE ENCOUNTER

Henry, A, **The UFO Handbook**, Sphere, 1980.
Randles, J, **UFO Study**, Hale, 1981.
[Both BUFORA and MUFON publish worthwhile manuals containing advice, addresses and hints to investigators.]

TRACES ON UFO LANDINGS

Fuller, P and *Randles, J*, 'The Mystery of the Circles', BUFORA, 1986.

Basterfield, K, **A Source Catalogue of Australasian UFO and Related Reports**, 1978.

Dick, MC, 'Some biological explanations for UFO trace cases and related phenomena', *ACUFOS Journal*, 1980.

Galindez, DA, 'Les empreintes mysterieuses de Canada de Alzogaray', *Phenomenes Spatiaux*, Vol 21, 1969.

Rutkowsky, C, 'The ring phenomenon', *Canadian UFO Report*, 1979.

Hough, M, 'Lightning strikes as the cause of some UFO ground traces', *UFO Research Australia Newsletter*, 1982.

Grassino, GP, 'I solchi di Brescia', *UFO-Rivista Di Informazione Ufologica*, 1986.

Verga, M, TRACAT-Catalogue dei casi ufologicic italiani con tracce al suolo, CISU, Vol 17, 1986.

Scornaux, J, 'Catalogue des traces de pas d'ufonautes', **Lumières Dans La Nuit**, 1986.

Hopkins, P, 'Of hoaxes and hoaxers', *MUFOB*, 1970.

HARNESSING THE COMPUTER

(1) *Hill, PA*, 'Statistical method and transient phenomena', *JTAP*, Vol 1, 1980.

(2) *Bull, M. Gamble, SJ and Digby, RS*, 'The application of low cost computing and data processing to UFO reports and related problems', *JTAP*, Vol 1, 1979.

(3) *Wootten, M*, 'A statistical overview 1980–1982', *JTAP*, Vol 4, 1985.

(4) *Gamble, SJ*, *Digby, RS* and *Phillips, K*, 'Time estimation of simulated UFO events', *JTAP*, Vol 5, 1987.

ADDITIONAL READING

(1) *Evans, C*, **The Mighty Micro**, Gollancz, London, 1980.

(2) For details of the *Computer UFO Newsletter* contact: Maurizio Verga, Via Matteotti 85, 22072 Cermenate (Co.), Italy.

GOVERNMENT COVER-UP AND CONSPIRACY

Greenwood, B and *Fawcett, L*, **Clear Intent**, Prentice-Hall, 1984.

Butler, B, Street, D and *Randles, J*, **Sky Crash**, Daniel, 1984; Grafton (updated) 1986.

Good, T, **Above Top Secret**, Sidgwick & Jackson, 1987.

Randles, J, **The UFO Conspiracy**, Blandford, 1987.

WORKING WITH THE GOVERNMENT

(1)*Chalker, B*, 'UFOs and the RAAF – the Inside Story', *UFO Research Australia Newsletter (UFORAN)*, Vol 3, 1982; *Chalker, B*, 'UFOs – Australia's Secret Documents Revealed', *Omega Science Digest*, Sept–Oct, 1982.

(2) *Killey, K*, and *Lester, G*, **The Devil's Meridian**, 1980.

(3) **Australian Flying Saucer Review**, (UFOIC Edition), No 8, 1965.

(4) 'UFO Tasmania – 1984', TUFOIC, *The Hobart Mercury*, Sept 16, 19 and 22, 1931.

(5) **Australian Saucer Record**, Vol 3, 1957.

(6) RAAF files, personal investigation. See also *Chalker, B*, 'UFOs – Australia's Secret Documents Revealed', *Omega Science Digest*, Sept–Oct, 1982.

(7) *Fischer, R* and *Bristol, L*, 'The Victorian UFO Report, 1954 – A Compilation of Reports from the Victorian Press', *VUFORS*, 1978.

(8) ' "Saucers" Do Exist – and Why', *The Argus Weekender*, (Melbourne), June 26, 1954.

(9) Air Force File Series examined by B Chalker, **Report on Flying Saucers**, December, 1954.

(10) *Chalker, B*, 'The UFO Connection', *Omega Science Digest*, March, 1985.

(11) *Chalker, B*, 'A Stranger Encounter at Bakers Creek Falls', *Australian UFO Newsletter*, Nos 54 and 55.

(12) UFO Research (Queensland) and personal investigations.

(13) VUFORS Investigations; see also *Haines, R*, **Melbourne Episode: Case Study of Missing Pilot**, 1987; *Chalker, B*, 'Valentich – Bass Strait [Australia] Affair', in *Story, R*, **The Encyclopedia of UFOs**, *Killey, K*; and *Lester, G*, **The Devil's Meridian**, 1980; *Chalker, B*, 'Vanished? – The Valentich Affairs Re-examined', *FSR*, Vol 30, 1984.

THE COSMIC PERSPECTIVE

Angelo, JA, Jr, **The Extraterrestrial Encyclopedia: Our Search for Life in Outer Space**, Facts on File, New York, 1985.

Bletchman, RH, 'Setting the UFO agenda,' MUFON 1986 UFO symposium proceedings.

Greenwell, JR, *'Extraterrestrial Hypothesis'*, in *Story, Ronald D*, (editor), **The Encyclopedia of UFOs**, Doubleday.

Grof, S, **Realms of the Human Unconscious**, Viking, 1975.

Hendry, A, **The UFO Handbook**, Doubleday, 1979.

Klass, PJ, **UFOs: The Public Deceived**, Prometheus, 1983.

McCampbell, JM, **Ufology**, Jaymac, 1973.

McCampbell, JM, 'UFO interference with vehicles and self-starting engines', MUFON 1983 UFO symposium proceedings.

McCampbell, J, 'Hum'n'whistle a UFO tune' *MUFON UFO JOURNAL*, No 202, 1985.

McCampbell, J, 'UFO radio interference', *MUFON UFO JOURNAL*, No 227, 1987.

Sheaffer, R, **The UFO Verdict**, Prometheus, 1981.

Stringfield, LH, 'The Fatal Encounter at Ft Dix-McGuire: A Case Study', Status report IV, MUFON 1985 UFO symposium proceedings.

Tough, A, 'What role will extraterrestrials play in humanity's future?',

Journal of the British Interplanetary Society, Vol 39, 1986.
Wright, D, 'Investigator's Jigsaw', *MUFON UFO JOURNAL*, No 209, September, 1985.

EXTRATERRESTRIAL UFOs – WHAT THEY MAY BE

(1) *Behrendt, KW*, 'The UFO Charging System', *AURA (Annals of Ufological Research Advances)*.
(2) *Lorenzen, CE*, **The Great Flying Saucer Hoax**, Fredericks Press, 1962.
(3) *Behrendt, KW, op cit*.
(4) *Milroy, WC* and *Michaelson, SM*, 'Biological Effects of Microwave Radiation', *Health Physics*, Vol 20, 1971.
(5) *Neville, RG, et al*, 'Microwaves', **Kirk-Othmer Encyclopedia of Chemical Technology**.
(6) *McCampbell, JM*, **Ufology**.
(7) *Behrendt, Kenneth W*, 'How UFOs Cause Automotive Failures', **UFOs: Past, Present, and Future**, The Scientific Bureau of Investigation, New York, 1983.
(8) *Behrendt, KW*, 'Compass Needle Deflections by UFOs', *Cambridge UFO Research Group Newsletter*, Cambridge, Ontario, 1984.
(9) *Behrendt, KW, op cit*.
(10) *Ibid*.

GEOPHYSICAL ALTERNATIVES

(1) Many papers have been published on the subject, a large number by Soviet researchers, e.g. *Demin, Vm, et al*, 'The Nature of Mechanoelectric Radiation from Ore Bodies', *Doklady, Academy of Sciences of the USSR, Earth Science Sections*, Vol 260, 1981.
(2) Much has been published on the subject, e.g. *Kerr, RA*, 'Stalking the Next Parkfield Earthquake', *Science*, Vol 223, 1984.
(3) *Buskirk, RE, et al*, 'Unusual Animal Behaviour Before Earthquakes', *Reviews of Geophysics and Space Physics*, Vol 19, 1981.
(4) *Persinger, MA*, 'Earthquake Activity and Antecedent UFO Report Numbers', *Perceptual and Motor Skill*, Vol 50, 1980.
(5) *Bullen, KE*, 'On Strain Energy and Strength in the Earth's Upper Mantle', *Transactions of the American Geophysical Union*, Vol 34, 1953.
(6) *Persinger, MA*, 'Geophysical Variables and Behaviour: III, Prediction of UFO reports by Geomagnetic and Seismic Activity', *Perceptual and Motor Skills*, Vol 53, 1981.
(7) *Persinger, MA*, 'Geophysical Variables and Human Behavior', *Perceptual and Motor Skills', Vol 56, 1983*.
(8) *Hendry, A*, **The UFO Handbook**, Doubleday and Co., New York, 1979.
(9) *Martelli, G* and *Rothwell, P*, 'RAS Discussion Meeting on Electromagnetic Radiation from Earthquakes and Impacts', *Quarterly Journal of the Royal Astronomical Society*, Vol 27, 1986.

(10) Reported by: *Simon, C*, 'Looking Out for Luminous Phenomena', *Science News*, Vol 124, 1983.

(11) *Rakitake, T*, 'Dilitancy Model and Empirical Formulas for Earthquake Area', *Pure and Applied Geophysics*, Vol 113, 1975.

(12) *Brady, BT*, and *Powell, GA*, 'Laboratory Investigations of the Electrodynamics of Rock Failure', *Nature*, Vol 321, 1986.

(13) *Devereux, P et al*, 'Bringing UFOs Down to Earth', *New Scientist*, Vol 99, 1983.

(14) *Wiedeman, CL*, 'Results of the NJ "Spook Light" Study', *Vestigia Newsletter*, Vols 1 and 2.

(15) *Klass, PJ*, 'Plasma Theory May Explain Many UFOs', *Aviation Week and Space Technology*, Vol 85, 1966.

(16) *Charman, WN*, 'Ball Lightning', *Physics Report*, Vol 54, 1979.

SPOOKLIGHTS

Devereux, P, **Earthlights**, Turnstone Press, 1982.

Clarke, D and *Oldroyd, G*, **Spooklights: A British Survey**, Privately published, 1985.

Randles, J, **The Pennine UFO Mystery**, Granada, 1983.

Gaddis, V, **Mysterious Fires and Lights**, 1 Dell, 1967.

Persinger, M and *Lafreniere, G*, **Space-Time Transients and Unusual Events**, Nelson-Hall, 1977.

EARTHLIGHTS

(1) *Lagarde, F, Flying Saucer Review*, Vol 14.

(2) *Persinger, MA* and *Lafreniere, G*, **Space-Time Transients and Unusual Phenomena**, Nelson Hall, 1977.

(3) *Tributsch, H.*, **When the Snakes Awake**, MIT Press, 1982.

(4) *Devereux, P* and *McCartney, P*, **Earth Lights**, Turnstone Press, 1982.

(5) *Derr, JS* and *Persinger, MA*, 'Luminous phenomena and earthquakes in southern Washington', *Experientia* (read as galley proof dated 1986).

(6) *Mattson, D* and *Persinger, MA*, 'Geophysical Variables and Behaviour XXXV', *Perceptual and Motor Skills*, Vol 63, 1986.

(7) *Derr, JS Bulletin of the Seismological Society of America*, Vol 63, 1973.

(8) *Blofeld, J*, **The Wheel of Life**, Rider, 1959.

(9) *Collins, A*, 'Mount Athos', *The Ley Hunter*, Vol 104, 1987.

(10) *Devereux, P, McCartney, P* and *Robins, GV*, 'Bringing UFOs Down to Earth', *New Scientist*, Vol 99, 1983.

(11) *Brady, B* and *Rowell, G, Nature*, Vol 321.

(12) *Derr, JS*, 'Luminous Phenomena and Their Relationship to Rock Fracture', *Nature*, Vol 321, 1986.

(13) *Mereuax, P*, **Carnac -- une porte vers l'inconnu**, Robert Laffont, 1981.

(14) *Harte, J*, **Cuckoo Pounds and Singing Barrows**, Dorset Natural History and Archaeological Society, 1986.

(15) *Persinger, MA* and *Cameron, RA*, 'Are earth faults at fault in some poltergeist-like episodes?, *Journal of the American Society for Psychical Research*, Vol 80, 1986.

(16) *Persinger, MA*, 'Spontaneous telepathic experiences from "Phantasms of the Living" and low global geomagnetic activity', *Journal of the American Society for Psychical Research*, Vol 81, 1987.

(17) *Ruthledge, HD*, **Project Identification**, Prentice Hall, 1981.

(18) *Eitel, EJ*, **Feng-Shui – The Science of Sacred Landscape in Old China**, Synergetic Press edition, 1984.

(19) *Pennick, N*, **The Ancient Science of Geomancy**, Thames & Hudson, 1979.

(20) *Skinner, S*, **The Living Earth Manual of Feng Shui**, RKP, London, 1982.

(21) *Strieber, W*, **Communion**, Century, London, 1987.

IS THERE A UFO STATE OF MIND?

Basterfield, K, **UFOs the Image Hypothesis – Close Encounters of an Australian Kind**, Sydney, 1981.

Bloecher, et al, 'Final Report on the Psychological Testing of UFO "Abductees" ', Fund for UFO Research, 1985.

Hilgard, E, **Divided Consciousness**, New York, 1977.

Holroyd, S, **Briefing for the Landing on Planet Earth**, London, 1977.

Honorton, C, 'ESP and Altered States of Consciousness', in Beloff, J (editor), **New Directions in Parapsychology**, Paul Elek, London, 1974.

Jung, C, **Flying Saucers: A Modern Myth of Things Seen in the Skies**, New York, 1959.

Kolb, L, **Noyes' Modern Clinical Psychiatry**, Philadelphia, 1968.

Lawson, A, 'What Can We Learn from Hypnosis of Imaginary "Abductees"?', *The MUFON UFO Journal*, Nov/Dec, 1977.

Ludwig, A, 'Altered States of Consciousness', Tart, Charles (editor), **Altered States of Consciousness**, New York, 1969.

Mesnard, J, 'Tranquillizing Visitation at Bouahmama', *Flying Saucer Review*, May-June, 1973.

Moravec, M, 'A UFO State of Mind', Proceedings of the Sixth Annual UFO Conference, Australian Centre for UFO Studies, 1981; 'PSIUFO Phenomena: A Study of UFOs and the Paranormal'; ACUFOS 1981; 'The Psychology of Close Encounters', *ACUFOS Journal*, 1982/1983; 'Psychological Reactions to UFO Events', *The MUFON UFO Journal*, 1981; 'Human Reactions Study: A Preliminary Report, presentation at UFOCON 9, Melbourne, Jan 1986.

Reed, G, **The Psychology of Anomalous Experience**, London, 1972.

Sadler, W, **Mental Mischief and Emotional Conflicts**, St. Louis, 1947.

Schwarz, B, 'Berserk: A UFO Encounter', *Flying Saucer Review*, Vol 20; 1, 1974.

Vogel, et al, 'Ego Functions and Dreaming During Sleep Onset', in

Tart, Charles (editor), **Altered States of Consciousness**, New York, 1969.
Hendry, A, **The UFO Handbook**, New York, 1979.
Hynek, JA, **The UFO Experience: A Scientific Inquiry**, London, 1972.

PHYSICAL TRIGGERS/PSYCHIC RESPONSES

Devereux, P, **Earthlights**, Turnstone Press, 1982.
Fideler, D, *Gateways to Mystery*, Fortean Times.
Fowler, RE, **The Andreasson Affair**, Bantam, 1980.
Jung, C, **Flying Saucers: A Modern Myth of Things Seen in the Sky**, New York, 1959.
Lawson, Dr AH, 'The Abduction Experience: A Testable Hypothesis', *Magonia*, No 10, 1982.
Randles, J, **The Pennine UFO Mystery**, Granada, 1983.
Rimmer, J, **The Evidence for Alien Abductions**, Aquarian, 1984.
Von Daniken, E, **Chariots of the Gods**, Corgi, 1971.
Watson, N, 'A Stranger in the City', *MUFOB*, new series 14, 1979.
Watson, N, 'The Shadowland of Ufology', *Magonia*, No 2, 1979 and No 4, 1980.

WHAT ET WOULD MEAN FOR MANKIND – ACKNOWLEDGEMENTS

Over the years, I have talked to hundreds of people about UFOs, their propulsion, interactions with the environment, occupants, purposes, and meaning for society. As they cannot possibly be listed individually, their influences are collectively acknowledged with gratitude. Sincere thanks are extended to the following who in no way are responsible for the final results: Fred Beckman, Thomas M Gates, BA, Richard F Haines, PhD, William D McGuigan, BS, Virgil Staff, BS, Mrs Lavada Staff, Jacques Vallée, MS.

SELECTED BIBLIOGRAPHY

Andrus, WH and *Hall, RH*, (editors), MUFON 1987 International UFO Symposium Proceedings, 1987.
Decker, RM, 'Long-Term Effects of Close Encounters', *MUFON UFO Journal*, No 229, May 1987.
Downing, BH, **The Bible And Flying Saucers**, JP Lippincott, 1968.
Eberhart, GM, **UFOs and the Extraterrestrial Contact Movement: A Bibliography**, Scarecrow, 1986.
Fawcett, L and *Greenwood, BJ*, **Clear Intent**, Prentice-Hall, 1984.
Gallup, G Jr, 'Many Believe There's an ET Out There', *San Francisco Chronicle*, March 12, 1987.
Hopkins, B, **Missing Time**, Richard Marek, 1981; **Intruders**, Random House, 1987.
McCampbell, JM, **Government Policy on UFOs**, in press, 1987.

McCampbell, JM, 'UFO Effects Upon People', *UFOs 1947–1987*, Fortean Tomes, 1987.

Paine, TO, Chairman, **Pioneering the Space Frontier, An Exciting Vision of Our Next Fifty Years in Space**, Bantam, 1986.

Sagan, C and *Thornton P*, **UFO's – A Scientific Debate**, Cornell University Press, 1972.

Sagan, C (editor), **Communication with Extraterrestrial Intelligence**, The MIT Press, 1973.

Schwarz, BE, **UFO Dynamics, Psychiatric & Psychic Aspects of the UFO Syndrome**, Books I and II, Rainbow Books/Betty Wright, 1983.

Simon, A, 'The Zeitgeist of the UFO Phenomenon', in *Haines, RF*, (editor), **UFO Phenomena and the Behavioral Scientist**, Scarecrow, 1979.

Smith, MS, **The UFO Enigma**, Library of Congress, 1976; updated by Havas, GD, 1983.

Strieber, W, **Communion**, Century, London, 1987.

Tough, A, 'What Role Will Extraterrestrials Play in Humanity's Future?', *Journal of the British Interplanetary Society*, Vol 391, 1986.

Vallée, J, **Messengers of Deception**, And/Or Press, 1979.

AUTHOR BIOGRAPHIES

Lionel Beer, FRAS
Joined the London UFO Research Organisation in 1960. In 1962 he coordinated the inaugural convention of BUFORA. From 1977 to 1979 he was chairman of BUFORA and is currently still a director, holding the honorary position of historian.

Pierre Lagrange
Sociologist from University of Paris, currently studying popular responses to the UFO phenomenon.

Nigel Watson
Particular interests in the study of the UFO phenomenon related to the impact of science fiction concepts, to historical sightings of UFO-like phenomena and to the psychological aspects of close encounter and contactee experiences. He is currently compiling a detailed analysis of the British 1912–3 phantom airships scare.

Anders Liljegren
A systems analyst and computer programmer. He is one of the founders of AFU (the Swedish Archives for UFO research) and editor of its newsletter. He has a particular interest in the early years of the phenomenon.

Clas Svahn
A journalist by profession, he specializes in astronomy and space technology in addition to the UFO phenomenon. He is a board member of AFU (the Swedish archives for UFO research) and has investigated several UFO cases since 1974.

Bronislaw Rzepecki
In 1983 he established the Krakow Club of UFO Research and Popularization, in 1984 The Krakowian UFO Research Society, in 1985 The UFO Research Group. He has helped to found more than ten UFO societies in other Polish towns. From 1981 to 1984 he edited Poland's first UFO bulletin, *Peripheral Visions*. In 1986, with Krzysztof Piechota he produced *Catalogue of UFO Observations in*

Poland 1947–1985 and *Bibliography of Polish UFO Publications 1945–1985*.

Kim Møller Hansen

A council member of (Danish) SUFOI since 1980, currently director of the research department and editor of its journal *UFO-Nyt*. Publications include *UFO'er over New Zealand* (1980), *Focus pa UFO'er* (1982), *Travis Walten Sagen* (1983), *Rex Heflin Sagen* (1983), *UFO-Sloring* (UFO-Cover-up) (1985), *Piloter ser UFO'er* (1985), *Spogelsesraketterne; UFO'er over Norden i 1946* (1986), *UFO* (1987).

Paul Norman

Vice-president and investigations officer of Australia's Victorian UFO Research Society. In 1979 joined MUFON as state director for Victoria. He is also an associate member of CUFOS and a member of BUFORA. He has contributed many articles to various publications and now writes a column entitled 'On The UFO Trail' for the VUFORS publication *Australian UFO Bulletin*.

Martin Shough

Co-founder of The Sussex UFO Group affiliated to Contact UK. His specific interests in the UFO phenomenon are the radar/UFO events. He is preparing a catalogue of radar/UFO events from 1947 to the present and has spent more than a year on the detailed study of Bentwaters/Lakenheath radar visual case.

Andy Roberts

Currently a member of the West Yorkshire UFO Research Group, ASSAP (The Association for Scientific Study of Anomalous Phenomena), and BUFORA. He is editor of *UFO Brigantia*, the WYUFORG Journal.

Peter Hough

Since 1975 he has been an investigator for the Manchester UFO Research Association, personally interviewing hundreds of witnesses to the UFO experience as well as other strange phenomena. In 1983 he became the Association's chairman. He has contributed many articles to such journals as *Beyond Science, Fate, Fortean Times, Magonia*, and *The Unknown*. He has also lectured widely and taken part in many radio programmes including a BBC documentary.

Dennis Stacy

Editor of the *MUFON UFO Journal* and a regular contributor to *OMNI's* 'UFO Up-date' column. He is a full-time writer whose articles on UFOs and other subjects have appeared in newspapers and magazines all over the world.

Budd Hopkins

American investigator whose specific sphere of interest in the UFO phenomenon is the abductions' cases. He has investigated over a hundred cases personally and his research and conclusions have been published in, principally, two books **Missing Time** and **Intruders** – The Incredible Visitations at Copley Woods.

Jenny Randles
Joined BUFORA in 1969. In 1973 she was a founder member of the Northern UFO Network and joined MUFORA, the Manchester Association. She is currently *BUFORA's* director of field investigations. Publications include *UFOs, A British Vewpoint* (with Peter Warrington) (1979), **UFO Study** (with Paul Whetnall) (1981), **Alien Contacts** (1982), **The Pennine UFO Mystery** (1983), **UFO Reality – Sky Crash** (with Brenda Butler and Dot Street) (1983), *Science and the UFOs* (1985) with Peter Warrington (1984), **The UFO Conspiracy: the first forty years** (1987). She is also editor of *NUFON News*.

John A Keel
A professional writer since 1946. He is a contributor to numerous journals, science editor for *Funk and Wagnalls Encyclopedia*, a regular columnist of mysteries in *Saga* and sometime editor of the Society for the Investigation of the Unexplained's Journal *Pursuit*. His publications include **Operation Trojan Horse** (1970) (regarded as one of the most notable sources of advanced thinking in the field), **Strange Creatures from Time and Space** (1970), **Our Haunted Planet** (1971), **The Mothmen Prophecies** (1975), **The Eighth Tower** (1976).

Maurizio Verga
Has been involved in UFO research since 1977, taking a particular interest in close encounter and trace cases. In 1985 co-founded the Centro Italiano Study Ufologici and is currently one of its directors. He is editor of the publication *The Computer UFO Newsletter* and author of ITACAT, a survey of Italian close encounters and has compiled a catalogue of sightings with alleged physical traces.

Gerald Mosbleck
One of the few serious ufologists in Germany; an active member of GEP and regular contributor to their journal *Fur UFO-Forsehung*.

John Shaw, LBIPP
A member of the British Institute of Professional Photographers, he runs his own photography business. He is a former director of BUFORA and in 1975 assisted in the setting up of BUFORA's photographic section. He remains a consultant to BUFORA in his professional capacity.

Stephen Gamble
Joined BUFORA in 1972, assisted in the formation of BUFORA's photographic section in 1975, became a member of the research and investigation committee 1975, became physical traces consultant 1976, and became a member of the BUFORA council in 1977. Currently editor of the *Journal of Transient Aerial Phenomenon*, a

specialist BUFORA publication which he helped to found. Became director of Research in 1984 and vice-chairman of BUFORA in 1985. He is currently secretary of the International Committee for UFO Research (ICUR) and is author and co-author of a number of ufological papers and has made a number of presentations to BUFORA meetings and lectures.

J. Danby

James Danby has been a member of the Association since 1974 and has recently taken over the post of membership secretary of BUFORA.

Dr Willy Smith

In 1980 he devoted himself full-time to the study of the UFO phenomenon and at the end of 1983, together with Dr Hynek, he initiated the UNICAT project. He has acquired a wide and intimate knowledge of present day ufology in the US and abroad, travelling and lecturing in many countries, notably Latin America. He is a MUFON state section director. He is a regular contributor to many journals in the USA and Europe on UNICAT and other aspects of UFO research.

Bertil Kuhlemann

Involved in ufology since 1961 he is now chairman of two Stockholm based UFO groups, co-founder and scientific technical adviser to Project URD, co-founder of UFO-Sweden, co-founder and former chairman of the International Committee for UFO Research (ICUR). He is a field investigator and lecturer on UFO related subjects and author of a number of articles including the Project URD documents.

Bill Chalker

He was the first civilian researcher to gain access to the previously classified RAAF UFO files. He takes a special interest in physical trace cases, and co-ordinates the Australian Physical Evidence Study Group. He is a scientific consultant to the Australian Centre of UFO Studies, Australian representative for APRO, New South Wales state representative for MUFON and director of UFO research for New South Wales. He has published many articles and UFO journals including *Flying Saucer Review*, *MUFON UFO Journal*, *APRO Bulletin*, *International UFO Reporter* (for which he is contributing editor) and *UFO Research Australian Newsletter*.

Dr Allen Tough

He is a writer and teacher in Toronto about potential human futures and advanced extraterrestrials. He is the MUFON consultant on future studies. In 1987 he lectured, on a version of the article included in this book, to the 4th International UFO Congress in London.

John Prytz
He is a member of the Australian Centre for UFO Studies and a representative of MUFON. He describes himself as a strong supporter of the extraterrestrial hypothesis and publications include **Ufology and the UFO: an anthology** (1970), *In search of a subject: an Australian SETI programme* (1981), *Information storage and retrieval for ufologists* (1981), *Who's who in Australian ufology* (1982), several ACUFOS volumes and was co-editor of *UFOs over Australia* with Mark Moravec (1985). He is a regular contributor to other journals in Australia and elsewhere.

Kenneth W Behrendt
Became deeply involved in UFO research following the investigation of a friend's abduction encounter. Since 1980 he has contributed many articles to UFO journals attempting to rationalise the reported behaviour of UFOs with known or foreseeable technology. His publications include *UFO propulsions systems, origins and purposes* (1978), *The Physics of the paranormal* (1987) and in 1985 he commenced publication of *The annals of ufological research advances*.

Chris A Rutkowski
First began investigating UFOs in 1975 when he became the Manitoba representative for CUFOS, the Centre for UFO studies. He is a regular contributor to books and journals on the subject of ufology and other fields. He is a member of the Royal Astronomical Society of Canada and has been an editor for a number of publications: including *Folklore*, *International UFO reporter*, *Winnicentrics* and *The Swamp Gas Journal*.

David Clarke
He is an active member of the Sheffield Society for Research and the Paranormal, South Yorks, and North Derbyshire Earth Mysteries Group and ASSAP, the Association for the Scientific Study of Anomalous Phenomenon. He is South Yorkshire area investigator for BUFORA and a contributor to BOLIDE and more regularly to WYUFORG's *UFO Brigantia*. He is also involved in its Project Pennine. His publications include **Spooklights: a British survey** (with G Oldroyd) (1985). He is preparing as co-author, for FUFOR, the *1913 airship scare catalogue*. He is joint editor of *Northern Earth Mysteries* and is also preparing a publication on legends and earth mysteries in South Yorkshire and North Derbyshire. For ASSAP's project Albion he is preparing a publication *Strange Sheffield*.

Paul Devereux
Since 1976 editor of the *Ley Hunter* and author of the *Ley Hunter's Companion* (1979) and **Earth Lights** (1982). He is a regular contributor to many journals such as *New Scientist*, *The Unknown*, *Country Living*, *The Unexplained*, *The Great Outdoors*, *Science Now* etc. In 1977 he was founder and co-ordinator of The Dragon Project, investigating unusual energy effects at certain types of prehistoric

sites. He has lectured to various research and other groups in the UK and abroad and has broadcast widely on radio and television throughout the UK and the United States. He is currently a director for the Centre of Earth Mysteries Studies (UK).

Mark Moravec

Specialises in the psychological and sociological aspects of UFO experiences. A regular contributor to journals such as *The Journal of the Australian Centre for UFO Studies*, the *MUFON UFO Journal*, *The Sceptic*, and *Australian Folklore*. He has also authored or co-edited several publications for the Australian Centre for UFO Studies including *PSIUFO Phenomenon, A study of UFOs in the paranormal* (1981) and *UFOs over Australia: a selection of ACUFOS research findings and debate* (1985). He is currently co-ordinator for the Australian Centre for UFO Studies and editor of its publication *The ACUFOS Bulletin* and *Reports Digest*. Mark also co-ordinates the Percipient Studies Project which aims to research the human factors involved in UFO related experiences by in-depth psychological, sociological and medical studies.

James M McCampbell

He has had a wide ranging career in research and design in the nuclear field and engineering management, including the space environment simulator at NASA Houston, environmental protection for the Alaskan pipeline and work for the Solar Energy Research Institute. He has been MUFON's director of research since 1975. A regular contributor to the *MUFON UFO Journal* and publications elsewhere he is the author of **Ufology, New insights from science and common sense** (1973), widely respected as one of the most constructive contributions to the scientific UFO literature.

Cynthia Hind

MUFON co-ordinator for Africa. She travels widely on behalf of her interest and is a popular speaker at conferences throughout the world. She is a regular contributor to a great many UFO journals and her book **UFOs, African encounters** (1982) is the only English language study of UFOs in Africa.

Kevin McClure

In addition to many articles for various journals he founded and edited his own journal called *Common Ground* devoted to a serious study of anomaly issues. He is co-author, with his wife Su, of **Stars and rumours of stars**, a study of anomalous events associated with the Welsh revival of 1905 and author of **The evidence for visions of the Virgin Mary** (1983).

Hilary Evans

He was a one-time council member of The Society for Psychical Research and a co-founder of ASSAP, the Association for the Scientific Study of Anomalous Phenomena; also compiler of

BOLIDE, the Ball of Light International Data Exchange. He is a council member of BUFORA. He is a regular contributor to many UFO related and other anomaly journals and the author of **Intrusions: society and the paranormal** (1982), **The Evidence for UFOs** (1983), **Visions, apparitions, alien visitors** (1984), **Gods, spirits, cosmic guardians** (1987) and co-editor of and contributing author of *UFOs 1947–1987* (1987).

John Spencer
Member of BUFORA for many years, director of the council of management since 1980, a position still held: specialist publications editor, financial director, and honorary secretary. He is a regular contributor to BUFORA's publications reflecting his particular interest in the field of UFO studies – the interaction of the phenomenon with the human mind. He was joint editor of and contributing author to *UFOs 1947-1987* (1987). He is also treasurer of the International Committee for UFO Research (ICUR) and a research specialist for MUFON.

INDEX